D0081524

Understanding Experience

Understanding Experience: Psychotherapy and Postmodernism is a collection of innovative interdisciplinary essays that explore the way we experience and interact with each other and the world around us. The authors address the postmodern debate in psychotherapy and psychoanalysis through clinical and theoretical discussion and offer a view of the person that is unique and relevant today.

The clinical work of Binswanger, Boss, Fromm, Fromm-Reichmann, Laing, and Lacan is considered alongside the theories of Buber, Heidegger, Husserl, Merleau-Ponty, Sartre and others. Combining clinical data from psychotherapy and psychoanalysis with insights from European philosophy, this book seeks to fill a major gap in the debate over postmodernism and bridges the paradigmatic divide between the behavioural sciences and the human sciences.

It will be of great interest to clinicians and students of psychotherapy and psychoanalysis who wish to come to terms with postmodernism, as well as those interested in the interaction of psychotherapy, philosophy and social theory.

Roger Frie, Ph.D., Psy.D., is Assistant Clinical Professor of Medical Psychology, Columbia University College of Physicians and Surgeons and Staff Psychologist at St. Luke's-Roosevelt Hospital Center. He is the author of *Subjectivity and Intersubjectivity in Modern Philosophy and Psychoanalysis*.

Understanding Experience

Psychotherapy and Postmodernism

Edited by Roger Frie

LONDON AND NEW YORK

First published 2003 by Routledge
27 Church Road, Hove, East Sussex, BN3 2FA
Simultaneously published in the USA and Canada
by Routledge
29 West 35th Street, New York, NY 10001

Routledge is an imprint of the Taylor & Francis Group

© 2003 selection and editorial matter Roger Frie;
individual chapters, the contributors

Typeset in Times by Regent Typesetting, London
Printed and bound in Great Britain by MPG Books Ltd, Bodmin
Paperback cover design by Jim Wilkie

British Library Cataloguing in Publication Data
A catalogue record for this book is available from
the British Library

Library of Congress Cataloging in Publication Data

Understanding experience : psychotherapy and postmodernism /
edited by Roger Frie.
      p. cm.
Includes bibliographical references and index.
    ISBN 1-58391-299-1 – ISBN 1-58391-900-7 (pbk.)
    1. Experience. 2. Psychotherapy–Philosophy. 3. Psychoanalysis
and philosophy. 4. Postmodernism–Psychological aspects. I. Frie,
Roger, 1965-
  B105.E9 U53 2003
  150.19'5–dc21

                                                    2002013357

ISBN 1-58391-900-7 (pbk)
ISBN 1-58391-299-1 (hbk)

Contents

Notes on contributors

Daniel Burston, Ph.D., Ph.D. is an Associate Professor of Psychology at Duquesne University, Pittsburgh, and an associate of the Center for Philosophy of Science at the University of Pittsburgh. He holds doctorates in psychology and in social and political thought from York University, Toronto. His first book, *The Legacy of Erich Fromm*, was translated into Japanese, and articles of his have appeared in translation in German, Spanish and Mandarin. Other books include *The Wing of Madness: The Life and Work of R. D. Laing* and *The Crucible of Experience: R. D. Laing and the Crisis of Psychotherapy*. His books have been reviewed in numerous journals and newspapers, including the *New York Times Book Review*, *New York Review of Books*, *Boston Sunday Globe*, *New Republic*, *Times Literary Supplement*, *Sunday Times*, *Observer*, *Guardian*, *Financial Times*, and *The Economist*.

Betty Cannon, Ph.D. Ph.D. is a psychologist practicing in Boulder, Colorado. She is professor emerita of the Colorado School of Mines, senior adjunct professor at Naropa University, and adjunct professor at Union Graduate School. She is co-founder and co-director of the Boulder Psychotherapy Institute, which offers advanced training for mental health professionals. She is on the editorial board of three international journals, *Sartre Studies International*, *Journal of the Society for Existential Analysis*, and *The Review of Existential Psychology and Psychiatry*. She is the author of a number of book chapters, articles, and an internationally recognized book, *Sartre and Psychoanalysis: An Existentialist Challenge to Clinical Metatheory*, which has been translated into French. She is currently overseeing the entries on "Existential Psychoanalysis" for the *Edinburgh Encyclopaedia of Psychoanalysis*.

Jon Frederickson, M.S.W. is chair of the Advanced Psychotherapy Training Program at the Washington School of Psychiatry and teaches on the faculties of the Clinical Psychotherapy Training Program and Supervision Training Program at the Washington School of Psychiatry. He serves as an adjunct faculty member at Georgetown University and is a consultant to the Clinical Social Work Institute in Washington, DC. He is a social worker in private practice in Washington, DC. A member of the National Academies of Practice, he has published papers in *Psychiatry*, *Psychoanalysis and Contemporary Thought*, *Contemporary Psychoanalysis*, and the *Journal of Clinical Social Work*. He is the author of *Psychodynamic Psychotherapy: Learning to Listen from Multiple Perspectives*, also published by Taylor and Francis.

Roger Frie, Ph.D., Psy.D. is Assistant Clinical Professor of Medical Psychology, Columbia University College of Physicians and Surgeons, Staff Psychologist at St. Luke's-Roosevelt Hospital Center, and a clinic fellow at the William Alanson White Institute of Psychiatry, Psychoanalysis, and Psychology. He received his Ph.D. in phenomenological philosophy and psychology from Trinity College, Cambridge University, and his Psy.D. in clinical psychology from George Washington University. He has taught in the fields of psychology, psychoanalysis, and philosophy at Harvard, New School, and at Northeastern Universities. He has written widely about the interface between psychology, psychoanalysis, and philosophy and his work has appeared in translation in German. He is author of *Subjectivity and Intersubjectivity in Modern Philosophy and Psychoanalysis*.

Maurice Friedman, Ph.D. is Emeritus Professor of Religious Studies, Philosophy, and Comparative Literature at San Diego State University and co-director and founder of the Institute for Dialogical Psychotherapy in San Diego. He is a world-renowned expert on the life and work of Martin Buber, has taught at numerous universities, and has held faculty positions in many training institutes for psychoanalysis and psychotherapy. He is the recipient of three honorary doctorates and has received awards for his distinguished writing career. His books have been translated into many languages. He is author of many articles and twenty-three books including *Martin Buber: The Life of Dialogue*, *Touchstones of Reality*, *Martin Buber's Life and Work* in three volumes, *The Human Way: A Dialogical Approach to Religion and Human Experience*, and *The Healing Dialogue in Psychotherapy*.

Eugene Gendlin, Ph.D. is Emeritus Professor of Psychology at the University of Chicago and the founder of the Focusing Institute, an international center for focusing and for the philosophy of implicit entry. He has been honored three times by the American Psychological Association (APA) for his development of experiential psychotherapy. He was a founder and editor for many years of the APA clinical division journal, *Psychotherapy: Theory Research and Practice*, and has published numerous articles. His book, *Focusing*, has sold over 400,000 copies and is translated into ten languages. He is the author of *Let Your Body Interpret Your Dreams* and *Focusing-Oriented Psychotherapy*. His philosophical books include *Experiencing and the Creation of Meaning*, *Language Beyond Post-Modernism: Saying and Thinking in Gendlin's Philosophy* (edited by David Levin).

Jon Mills, Psy.D., Ph.D. is internship coordinator and clinical supervisor in the Mental Health Program at Lakeridge Health Corporation Oshawa, research associate at the Research Institute at Lakeridge Health, and on core faculty at the Adler School of Professional Psychology, Toronto. He received his Psy.D. in clinical psychology from the Illinois School of Professional Psychology, Chicago, and his Ph.D. in philosophy from Vanderbilt University; he was a Fulbright scholar of philosophy at the University of Toronto and York University. He is editor of the Value Inquiry Book Series in Philosophy and Psychology and a consultant for *Psychoanalytic Psychology*. He is the author of many works in philosophy, psychology, and psychoanalysis including his latest book, *The Unconscious Abyss: Hegel's Anticipation of Psychoanalysis*. He maintains a private practice in Ajax, Ontario.

William J. Richardson, S.J., Ph.D. is Professor of Philosophy at Boston College, and a practicing psychoanalyst. He is a graduate of the William Alanson White Institute of Psychiatry, Psychoanalysis, and Psychology, former director of research of the Austen Riggs Center and has also trained as a Lacanian analyst. He is an internationally recognized expert on the philosophy of Martin Heidegger and author of the acclaimed *Heidegger: Through Phenomenology to Thought* (with preface by Martin Heidegger). He is coauthor (with John P. Muller) of *Lacan and Language: A Reader's Guide to the Ecrits* and *The Purloined Poe: Lacan, Derrida, and Psychoanalytic Reading*. He is also the author of many articles on continental philosophy and psychoanalysis and the recipient of four honorary doctorates in addition to many other awards and distinctions.

M. Guy Thompson, Ph.D. is founder and director, Free Association, Inc., San Francisco, personal and supervising analyst, Psychoanalytic Institute of Northern California, and on the adjunct faculty of the California School of Professional Psychology, Berkeley. He received his Ph.D. in clinical psychology from the Wright Institute, Berkeley, and his psychoanalytic training at the Philadelphia Association, London. He is on the editorial boards of *Psychoanalytic Psychology* and the *Journal of Phenomenological Psychology*, past-president, International Federation for Psychoanalytic Education, and president, Northern California Society for Psychoanalytic Psychology. Among his numerous publications on psychoanalysis, phenomenology, and schizophrenia are the following books: *The Death of Desire: A Study in Psychopathology*, *The Truth about Freud's Technique: The Encounter with the Real*, and *The Ethic of Honesty: The Fundamental Rule of Psychoanalysis*.

Preface

The rise of postmodernism in psychotherapy and psychoanalysis is generally considered new and radical. Yet many of the theories implicit in the postmodern turn were developed much earlier by continental European philosophers and literary theorists. Postmodernism in philosophy and literary theory was initially characterized by the wholesale dispersion and dissolution of the human self. This idea along with many others has since been questioned and revised. But in contemporary psychotherapy and psychoanalysis, the postmodernist dispersion of the self is still in its ascendancy. As is so often the case, disciplinary boundaries between clinical practice and other fields of inquiry stand in the way of a productive and timely exchange of ideas. By combining clinical case material with theoretical discussion, this book seeks to overcome the disciplinary divide and examine the challenges of postmodernism for the contemporary clinician and theorist alike.

I have written this book in order to demonstrate the ongoing interaction that exists between clinical practice and philosophical thinking. Having been academically trained in clinical psychology and continental European philosophy, and having taught in both areas, I am continually struck by the connections between these disciplines. But I am also saddened by the lack of cross-disciplinary dialogue.

In Europe there is still an intellectual tradition of freely combining insights from psychology and philosophy. The authors in this book align themselves with this approach in order to explore and elaborate the nature of human experience. Academic and clinical training, particularly in North America, is often guild-like in its attempt to shut out different ways of thinking or styles of practice. As a teacher, my aim is to help my students think outside standard disciplinary boundaries. As a clinician, I find that my philosophical background helps me to appreciate and endeavor to understand the nature of experience. To my students and my patients, whose experiences of life are so rich, I owe a debt of gratitude.

I would like to thank my colleagues, many of whom are good friends, for contributing their time and effort and making this book possible. Kate Hawes, the senior commissioning editor at Brunner-Routledge, took on and supported this project with enthusiasm. Intellectual reflection is rarely a solitary pursuit. For inspiring conversations, dialogue, and critical readings of my work, I wish to thank Betty Cannon, Cynthia Field, Jon Frederickson, Jon Mills, Jai Ramaswamy, Bruce Reis, and Kirk Schneider. I also owe thanks to the institutions with which I am affiliated. The William Alanson White Institute of Psychiatry, Psychoanalysis, and Psychology has provided an intellectual home where interdisciplinary dialogue is welcomed and supported. Working at St. Luke's-Roosevelt Hospital Center has enabled me to experience a wealth of clinical styles and allows for innovative teaching and discussion.

It is ultimately one's personal experience that makes an intellectual pursuit worthwhile. I wish to thank my parents and my sister, Louise Frie, for their continued support. I am indebted above all to Emily, my best friend and most valuable critic, and to our daughter Elena, whose birth and development over the past two years has been a joyous experience .

Between modernism and postmodernism:

Rethinking psychological agency

Roger Frie

This collection of interdisciplinary chapters seeks to explore the human capacity for experience. The authors address the postmodern debate in contemporary psychotherapy and psychoanalysis through clinical case discussion and theoretical exegesis. They elaborate new perspectives on the embodied self and its role in communicative and therapeutic contexts and reconsider such basic experiences as agency, authenticity, freedom, and choice. In the process, the authors develop a constructive critique of postmodernism and present a view of the person as an active, responsible, embodied being. In the present intellectual climate, so dominated by medical psychology on the one hand and postmodernism on the other, this book provides a way to retrieve the personal and offers an approach for understanding psychological agency in the clinical setting.

Experience is not easily described and always exceeds our attempts to define it in words or concepts. Psychotherapists and psychoanalysts can be very astute practitioners who are attuned to the nature of experience. But they have not usually developed their conceptual thinking about experience. In fact, many clinicians feel that this is a task best left to philosophy. Philosophers, for their part, need to move beyond their reliance on concepts in order to recognize that we can have direct access to our experience. Unfortunately, few people think to link these two disciplines, which are usually seen as separate or opposed.

The authors in this book are a unique group in that they are practicing psychotherapists and psychoanalysts as well as philosophical scholars. Training in the mental health professions, often driven by political and economic forces, has become overly narrow and technical in focus. Most clinicians in the contemporary mental health professions identify themselves within a framework of the natural sciences, which seeks empirical verification for their work. As a result, the fact that every psychology rests on a set of theoretical assumptions about the nature of human experience is generally overlooked. By combining clinical data from psychotherapy and psychoanalysis with insights from European philosophy, this book seeks to bridge the paradigmatic divide between the behavioural sciences and the human sciences.

The aim of this initial chapter is to set out the book's interdisciplinary objectives. The chapter begins with a consideration of the issue of agency as a key problem within the postmodern debate. It then examines the development of postmodernism in clinical theory and practice. The chapter shows the way in which philosophical ideas have been applied in the clinical setting in order to challenge traditional theory and technique. Finally, it introduces the historical and contemporary contexts within which to understand the clinicians, thinkers, and ideas examined in this book.

The challenge of postmodernism

The practice of psychotherapy and psychoanalysis is at a crossroads. Gone are the fixed concepts and universalist assumptions that informed the work of Freud and his followers. Enlightenment themes such as individuality, objectivity, rationality, and truth are being questioned and revised. With the advent of postmodernism, the unity of the individual mind, the notion of an objectively knowable world, and the view of language as the carrier of truth have all been implicitly or explicitly rejected. In place of the ego, the postmodernist speaks of momentary selves to refer to the way in which the self is relationally generated and maintained. In place of objectivity, the postmodernist turns to social constructionism. And in place of language as truth bearing, the postmodernist asserts that meaning in language is inherently unstable and that truth is open to multiple interpretations.

The postmodern turn in psychotherapy and psychoanalysis consists of different voices and outlooks. Yet a central theme is the subordination of the individual person to larger organizing structures that are outside of our awareness and beyond our control. The person is seen as embedded in social, linguistic, and historical contexts and as having no natural or intrinsic organization. As a result, such notions as freedom and choice, which comprise the activities of personal agency, are altogether dismantled. In contrast to the modernist emphasis on the autonomy of the individual mind, postmodernism asserts that the person, or subject, is not only shaped, but also subverted by the contexts in which it exists. More radical versions of postmodernism deny the very existence of a person with the capacity for reflexive thought and self-determining action. In place of the person as an active, responsible being, they herald the so-called death of the subject.

Most psychotherapists and psychoanalysts rightly welcome the postmodern themes of difference and uncertainty as refreshing changes from past adherence to sameness and universality. Postmodernism has demonstrated the degree to which we are all socially and culturally embedded. It has made us aware of the realities of ambivalence and otherness in therapeutic and communicative settings and has freed us from the strictures of a one-person psychology that views the mind in essential isolation from others. The reliance on the analytic neutrality and objectivity that defined classical psychoanalysis has given way to a therapeutic relationship based on mutuality, in which traditional assumptions about authority and reason yield to ambiguity and uncertainty.

The dilemma facing postmodernism, in my view, is not its embrace of difference, multiplicity, or embeddedness, but its denial of the individual person or subject. Psychotherapists and psychoanalysts who endorse the basic tenets of postmodernism seek to overcome the technical and theoretical limitations that characterized classical psychoanalysis. More often than not, however, these same clinicians continue to adhere to a concept of the experiencing individual person, which is precisely what postmodernism rejects. The problem with the postmodern denial of the subject is that the ability to organize experience and pursue a course of action is dependent upon a person for whom that experience takes place. Once the concept of the person is altogether subverted, the notion of personal agency is similarly undermined. And without a psychological agent who develops, changes, and learns, the therapeutic process appears to lose its meaning.

An unqualified embrace of postmodernism thus gives rise to a number of important questions. If there is no person for whom experience takes place, then who can be said to experience anything at all? How do we explain individual change, innovation, or creativity if the person is subverted? And how do we account for the determination of meaning or the ability to choose one course of action over another without a concept of personal agency? When postmodernism collapses the subject into intersubjective, relational, and linguistic contexts, when it rejects the person as agent, it undermines the basis of human experience. In the process, reductionistic versions of postmodernism seem to endorse relativism and skepticism because there is no longer any autonomous ground on which to stand, no one perspective that can reasonably be compared to any other. Nor can there be any theory of truth, since truth, like the subject, is said to exist only in a state of constant and continual flux.

Given the problems intrinsic to the rise of postmodernism, a re-evaluation of the nature of human experience is urgently needed. The contributing authors in this book combine insights from clinical psychology and philosophy to offer new perspectives on the person as an active, embodied being. They critique postmodern reductionism and argue that when the subject is viewed only as a linguistic or social construction, some of the most central aspects of subjective life are overlooked. In contrast to the antisubjectivist attitude of postmodernism, the authors call for a reconsideration of the human subject. Their aim is to formulate a conception of the human being that accounts for our psychological agency and individuality without succumbing to the modernist themes of essentialism, sameness, and universality.

In order to navigate between the obstacles of modernist thought and postmodern reductionism, this book will turn to a relatively neglected but very influential intellectual tradition known as existential-phenomenology. The term refers to a group of European psychoanalysts, psychiatrists, and philosophers whose work bridges existentialism and phenomenology and generally spans the decades between the 1920s and 1960s. Included under the banner of existential-phenomenology are psychoanalysts and psychiatrists such Ludwig Binswanger, Erich Fromm, Frieda Fromm-Reichmann, Medard Boss, and R. D. Laing, who developed their approach in reaction to deterministic and mechanistic theories of human behavior. They drew on the work of philosophers such as Edmund Husserl, Martin Heidegger, Jean-Paul Sartre, Martin Buber, and Maurice Merleau-Ponty, all of whom sought to counter materialistic, positivistic, and Cartesian traditions of thought.

The ideas espoused by these clinicians and thinkers set the groundwork for postmodernism in contemporary psychotherapy and psychoanalysis. European psychoanalysts and psychiatrists in the existential-phenomenological tradition introduced the concept of a socially and historically constituted person; they rejected internalized drives and emphasized the interpersonal and embodied basis of human experience; they questioned the myth of analytic neutrality; and they introduced the notion of a two-person psychology. Yet in contrast to reductionistic versions of postmodernism, they also sought to develop a theory of the psychological agent that was true to our lived, embodied experience and would account for progressive change and understanding. The existential-phenomenological tradition thereby provides an alternative perspective on human experience and psychological agency that avoids the current bifurcation between modernism and postmodernism.

The postmodern turn

The rise of postmodernism has clearly given way to much discussion and debate. For some observers (Gergen 2001) the postmodern notion that meaning is derived less from a single mind than from interdependent relationships implies that theory, research, and practice in psychology must all be revisited from a postmodern perspective. For others (Martin and Sugarman 2000), the stridency with which postmodernism attacks psychological agency is anathema to the very practice of psychology. The ideas underlying the debate over postmodernism may strike some readers unaccustomed to the world of theory as complex and confusing. This overview of the main ideas of the postmodern turn aims to help guide the reader through the debate.

Western culture has traditionally celebrated the individual mind as the locus of reason and knowledge. The foundation for this approach was developed by Rene Descartes, whose famous dictum "I think, therefore I am" championed the human ability to reason and ushered in the age of the Enlightenment. By positing a self-sufficient subject and a separate world of objects, Descartes substantiated the Platonic distinction between a subjective "internal" world of the mind and an objective "external" world outside the mind.

Postmodernism is a direct reaction to this Enlightenment belief that meaning is the creation of an isolated mind. Descartes's belief that the knowledge we have of our own minds is not connected in any essential way to the world around us raises a number of intractable problems. If our minds are really the only thing we can be certain of, then the external world, other human minds, and even the existence of our own bodies must be in doubt. For Descartes, skepticism ultimately led to a proof of God's existence. Today, skepticism is rather less convincing. It is precisely the dilemmas inherent in Descartes's reasoning which form the basis of the postmodern turn.

Postmodern theorists seek to decenter or deconstruct such foundational or objective concepts as truth and knowledge in an attempt to account for the heterogeneity, multiplicity, and difference of our time. Postmodernism operates within diverse disciplines and does not constitute a coherent body of thought. In general, however, its proponents view the self not in isolation, but as a product of history, culture, and language. Postmodernists reject outright any concept of the self or subjectivity that is not understood as discursive or interpreted.

According to poststructuralism, developed in the work of Jacques Derrida, Michel Foucault, and Jacques Lacan during the 1960s and

1970s, we are dependent upon languages that we neither invent nor control. The notion of linguistic structure is replaced by the play of "difference." Meaning is seen as multiple, unstable, and open to various interpretations. In place of the traditional separation between the speaker and spoken language, the human subject is understood to exist within the symbolic order and is constituted by language. For poststructuralism there is essentially no world beyond text.

The ideas developed by Derrida, Foucault, and Lacan are based on the work of earlier thinkers. Thus Derrida draws on Heidegger's philosophy, in which he examines the relation of language and being. Foucault takes his inspiration from Friedrich Nietzsche, who addresses such issues as power and reason. Lacan is often referred to as the "French Freud" since he sought to reinterpret Freudian psychoanalysis from the perspective of structuralism and linguistics. In fact, Freud himself played no small part in the decentering of the individual mind.

Freud sought to do justice to the other of reason, namely the unconscious. His discovery of the unconscious was instrumental in challenging the Enlightenment belief that we are always in control of our own thoughts and actions. By demonstrating the inevitability of distortion in our thinking, Freud presented a more variable picture of the human mind than his Enlightenment predecessors. His conception of the mind combined rationalism with irrationalism.

At the same time Freud retained the concept of objectivity as the cornerstone of classical psychoanalytic treatment. In his view, the analyst is an objective scientist who is able to observe and identify the constituents of the mental processes working within the patient. A crucial aspect of this process rests on the analyst's ability to bracket out distorting prejudices and thereby maintain a neutral stance that allows for objective, scientific observation.

As sociologists of science have shown, every observation has an implicit agenda. Scientists need to have pre-existing theories and suppositions in order to ask the questions which will lead to data; it is the shape of a question that produces the data that will answer it. The scientist is always situated in a specific time and place and his or her scientific theory is itself a product of that culture. When applied to psychoanalytic treatment setting, this suggests that the analyst's subjectivity and clinical perspective will inevitably influence what the analyst knows about his or her patient. The notion of objectivity is thereby placed in question. From a postmodernist perspective, the search for a latent psychic reality beyond analytic interaction – and with it, the belief that the analyst can "know" the content of a patient's unconscious – appears misguided.

The questioning of objectivity in psychoanalysis allows for a range of exciting and innovative possibilities in the treatment setting. Postmodernists rightly reject a one-person for a two-person psychology by turning away from Freud's exclusive focus on the archeology of the psyche in order to explore the interpersonal field between people. On this view, clinical phenomena can be understood only in the interpersonal contexts in which they take form. Patient and psychoanalyst form an irreducible dyad and it is this relationship that becomes the domain of analytic inquiry. Phenomena that have been the traditional focus of psychoanalytic investigation are not understood as products of isolated intrapsychic processes. Rather, they are seen as having been formed in an interpersonal field. The role of psychoanalysis is to reach an understanding of such phenomena as they emerge in the interaction between patient and psychoanalyst.

Bridging theory and practice

Clinicians often feel that philosophy has little to do with what is important to their work. As this overview suggests, however, the postmodern turn in psychotherapy and psychoanalysis is based directly on ideas that hail from European philosophy and literary theory. Since the late 1960s the impact of postmodernism across disciplines has been enormous, and psychology is one of the last fields of research to engage its ideas. More importantly, perhaps, many clinicians involved in the daily vicissitudes of the therapeutic process tend to disregard the fact that theory always and inevitably impacts on their clinical work. No matter what their clinical persuasion, psychotherapists and psychoanalysts are always relying on underlying, often hidden philosophical assumptions about human nature. The purpose of this book is to introduce the existential-phenomenological tradition in such a way that it is possible to address the postmodern debate and to question and challenge the implicit theoretical assumptions we hold.

Most clinicians, whether psychotherapists or psychoanalysts, are neither trained in nor familiar with philosophy. This has not always been true, and quite possibly represents a deficit in our clinical education (Frie and Reis 2001). For example, William James, the founder of psychology in the United States, first achieved recognition and professional stature as a philosopher, and it was in that context that he recognized the merits of philosophy for understanding human behavior. Freud's relationship to philosophy was more tenuous, however. Freud lauded such precursors of existentialism as Nietzsche and Arthur Schopenhauer for their considerable insights into the human mind. Yet he also sought to distance the nascent science of psychoanalysis from what he referred to as the "speculative metaphysics" of philosophy. Freud hoped to ensure that psychoanalysis could claim the "objectivity" of the natural sciences, rather than be seen as a branch of the humanities. In the process, Freud left the unfortunate legacy of an artificial distinction between the disciplines of psychoanalysis and philosophy. The falsity of this distinction is nowhere more apparent than in the debate over postmodernism, a topic that is philosophical in origin and nature.

There is also another factor at work. Analytical philosophy, which is chiefly taught in Great Britain and North America, focuses on technical issues such as logic or truth claims, which are remote from the realities of clinical practice. In Europe, however, the tradition of continental philosophy deals with questions that have greater applicability to clinical work. Philosophers in the continental tradition seek to answer questions with direct practical relevance: how can we achieve insight into the way we live our lives? How can we understand the nature of human love and intimacy? What is the role of the body in my experience and perception of the world around me? How can we account for the multifaceted, often opposing, tendencies of human interaction? And how is the human being situated in a world of shared understandings? All of these questions underlie everyday therapeutic practice.

For many psychotherapists and psychoanalysts, however, one of the greatest impediments to the introduction of philosophy into clinical discourse remains the question of how data are accumulated and assessed. Many clinicians have a stereotyped conception of the philosopher as an isolated scholar who reflects only on his or her own experience in a process of introspection. This view, however, overlooks precisely what postmodernism has taught us: the generation of ideas is always dependent upon difference and otherness. Only by engaging what is other to ourselves is it possible to open up new ways of thinking. And as we shall see, the philosophers considered in this book were directly concerned with the practical application of their ideas, whether through the writing of literature, teaching and research, or the actual practice of psychology.

Over the course of the twentieth century, continental philosophers have also developed tools, such as Edmund Husserl's so-called phenomenological method, to capture their observations of the world around them. Phenomenology, in the broadest sense, refers to the description of phenomena as they appear, and has become a frequently used term in contemporary psychology and psychiatry. Although Husserl never solved the problem of the isolated mind, phenomenology has become a clinical method that seeks to explore the quality of lived experience, giving rise to the field of phenomenological psychology.

Most importantly, perhaps, the existential-phenomenological tradition has engaged the very questions that concern psychotherapists and psychoanalysts confronting the realities of postmodernism today. Existential-phenomenological thought can be read as an endeavor to understand and articulate the meaning of human subjectivity. It asks, in essence, what constitutes subjective experience? Is subjectivity something that is internal and private or is it external and public? Do our subjectivities follow from or precede our interaction with other human beings? Is subjectivity always and inevitably a construction? What role do other people, language, and society play in the development of our subjectivities? It is precisely such issues that underlie the debate over postmodernism. By exploring possible answers to these and other questions, the contributors to this book seek to steer a path between modernism and postmodernism.

The existential-phenomenological tradition

Revisions of classical psychoanalytic treatment, once considered new and radical, are now represented in many perspectives of contemporary psychotherapy and psychoanalysis. What is less well known is the extent to which the ideas implicit in the postmodern turn were developed much earlier in the work of existential-phenomenological clinicians and thinkers. To some extent, the aversion of philosophy among many clinicians explains why there continues to be relatively little knowledge of the contribution made by these European psychoanalysts and psychiatrists. By examining their work in more detail, I will set out the theme of the book as whole and provide a historical and theoretical context in which to understand the arguments of the individual contributors.

Existential-phenomenological clinicians such as Binswanger, Boss, Fromm, Fromm-Reichmann, Laing, and others all fundamentally challenged and revised traditional psychoanalytic theory and technique. They did so not as naïve outsiders, but rather as trained psychoanalysts who founded revisionist institutes and schools of thought. Indeed, the extent to which these clinicians were indebted to and allied with Freud and psychoanalysis is often overlooked. This is most probably because such terms as "existential" and "humanistic" are usually identified in the public eye with the psychotherapy of Irvin Yalom and James Bugenthal, both of whom distance themselves from psychoanalytic thinking. In fact, the close relationship of clinicians such as Binswanger, Boss, Fromm, Fromm-Reichmann, and Laing to psychoanalysis is crucial to the theoretical and clinical efficacy of the existential-phenomenological tradition.

Ludwig Binswanger (1881–1966) first encountered psychoanalysis when he trained as a psychiatrist under Eugen Bleuler at the Burghölzli Psychiatric Hospital in Zurich. He accompanied Carl G. Jung on his initial visit to Freud in 1907 and thereby began a thirty-year friendship and correspondence with Freud that lasted until the latter's death in 1939. By drawing variously on the ideas of Husserl, Heidegger, and Buber, Binswanger developed a new psychiatric and psychoanalytic perspective known as "Daseinsanalysis" and was one of the few serious critics of psychoanalysis with whom Freud maintained collegial relations. Binswanger's younger Swiss colleague, Medard Boss (1903–90), began analysis with Freud in Vienna in 1925, and finished it with Karen Horney in Berlin, where he trained as a psychoanalyst. Boss began his career as a traditional psychoanalyst, but became a Daseinsanalyst after encountering the work of Heidegger and Binswanger. He eventually went on to establish the Daseinsanalytic Institute for Psychotherapy and Psychosomatics in Zurich, whose theoretical foundation is based largely on Heidegger.

Erich Fromm's (1900–80) academic background was in sociology and he trained as a psychoanalyst under Hans Sachs and Theodor Reik in Berlin. He was introduced to psychoanalysis by Frieda Fromm-Reichmann (1889–1957), a psychiatrist who also completed her training with Sachs in Berlin. The two were married in Germany and in 1927 Fromm became a founding analyst of the Frankfurt Psychoanalytic Institute. Later that year, at Max Horkheimer's invitation, Fromm joined the Frankfurt Institute for Social Research, becoming its director for social psychology. During this time, Fromm and Fromm-Reichmann established a relationship with Buber, a connection they maintained throughout their careers. After immigrating to the United States, Fromm and Fromm-Reichmann joined with the interpersonal psychiatrist, Harry Stack Sullivan, and became founders of the William Alanson White Institute of Psychiatry, Psychoanalysis, and Psychology in New York. Fromm-Reichmann was also a central figure at the Chestnut Lodge Hospital, which became famous for its treatment of schizophrenics. Although Fromm and Fromm-Reichmann are not often linked with existential-phenomenology, they were instrumental in communicating and translating the ideas of this tradition. In addition, Fromm was the training analyst of Rollo May, himself an interpersonal psychoanalyst, who first introduced the work of Binswanger to an English-speaking audience and later became a founder of humanistic psychology.

Although R. D. Laing's name is not often identified with mainstream psychoanalysis, he completed his psychoanalytic candidacy at the British Institute of Psychoanalysis during the 1950s. A psychiatrist by training, Laing (1927–89) began to develop his individual perspective early on and was aligned with the so-called Middle Group, between Anna Freud on the one side and Melanie Klein on the other. He was analyzed by Charles Rycroft and supervised by D. W. Winnicott, among others. As his thinking grew more independent, he moved away from the psychoanalytic establishment and in 1965 became a founder of the Philadelphia Association in London, where he taught and began to develop his radical theories and techniques. In elaborating his early approach to the self and other, Laing drew on the ideas of Husserl, Heidegger, Sartre, and Merleau-Ponty and identified his work as phenomenological. The connection to Sartre was particularly important and Laing remains one of the few psychoanalysts to acknowledge a significant debt to the French philosopher.

In discussing the intersection of psychoanalysis and existential-phenomenological thought, it would be remiss not to include the work of Jacques Lacan (1900–81). Because Lacan is generally seen as a representative of poststructuralism, he is not commonly grouped with such clinicians as Binswanger, Fromm, or Laing. While there are many obvious and important differences, there are also noteworthy parallels, which is why his work will be critically assessed in this book. Lacan allied himself early on with Binswanger's phenomenological approach and was similarly critical of Freud's protobiological theory of mind. He turned first to the writings of Hegel, Heidegger, and Sartre, and eventually to structural linguistics in order to rewrite Freud's project from the perspective of language. Lacan's fundamental revisions of classical psychoanalysis resulted in his expulsion from mainstream institutes and led to the subsequent growth of Lacanian language-centered psychoanalysis as distinct from traditional Freudian drive theory. With time, Lacan made fewer and fewer references to existential-phenomenological thought, but his continued attention to such concepts as subjectivity, otherness, and truth bears witness to his early alliance with the work of Heidegger and Sartre.

The proximity of Lacan to the existential-phenomenological tradition is nowhere more apparent than in his trenchant critique of American ego psychology. Lacan believed that the central focus on the ego and its defenses was a return to the very Cartesian thinking that Freud had sought to overcome. Lacan questioned the notion of ego's autonomy because he conceptualized the human subject as embedded in the symbolic realm of language and tradition. The existential-phenomenological tradition similarly rejects the reification of the mind in classical psychoanalysis because it views the subject as inherently embedded in interpersonal contexts. Indeed, the fundamental connection between the self and world challenges the Cartesian distinction between internal and external realms of experience that is carried over into psychoanalysis.

The historical background to the work of clinicians such as Binswanger, Fromm, and Laing thus sheds light on the way in which they combined their psychoanalytic training with new ways of thinking about and engaging the Other. As a group, they helped set the groundwork for the introduction of a two-person psychology. They abandoned Freud's exclusive emphasis on the intrapsychic model of the mind and revised his theory of drives to include the role of social factors on human development and experience. They challenged the notion of analytic neutrality in order to demonstrate the importance of reciprocal interaction between therapist and patient. They emphasized the relevance of the here and now over past experience and rejected the determinism implicit in the psychoanalytic view of symptom formation.

None of these fundamental revisions would have been possible, however, were it not for the ideas developed in the philosophies of Husserl, Heidegger, Sartre, Buber, and Merleau-Ponty, all of which will be examined in this book. Indeed, their work forms a vital part of the foundation upon which the postmodern turn is based. These thinkers fundamentally rejected the traditional Cartesian conception of the human mind as isolated and closed in on itself. In its place, they sought to formulate a conception of the person that is true to our lived experience, paying particular attention to implicit (prereflective) and somatic experience and the ways in which we are embedded in social and linguistic contexts.

The juxtaposition of thinkers as varied as Heidegger, Sartre, Buber, and Merleau-Ponty is also instructive since it illuminates the complex intertwining of social, political and cultural differences that make up the intellectual basis of the existential-phenomenological tradition. Much scholarship, beginning with Rollo May *et al.* (1958), presents existential psychiatry and psychoanalysis as an exclusively Heideggerian enterprise. This is far too simplistic and overlooks the work of other, equally important philosophers and influences. From a social and political perspective, moreover, the work of Heidegger, Sartre, or Buber could hardly be more different.

Whereas Sartre was a public political and intellectual figure, engaged in many left-wing causes throughout his life, and Buber's work had a lasting impact on education and theology, Heidegger's reputation was inalterably tarnished by his political involvement with National Socialism in Germany. Indeed, no discussion that examines the clinical application of Heidegger's ideas is complete without also addressing his political past. The facts speak for themselves. Heidegger was a member of the Nazi Party and Rector of the University of Freiburg for one year (1933–34). Moreover, Heidegger never subsequently repudiated anything he said or did at that time. The debate over Heidegger's political involvement is complex and much has been written about it (cf. Farias 1989; Ott 1993; Wolin 1993). No matter where one might stand on the issue of Heidegger's political past, his thinking remains profound and has affected many academic disciplines. Yet neither can his politics or his actions be ignored. As the contributors seek to demonstrate, Heidegger's philosophy has direct bearing for clinical theory. He strongly influenced the way in which contemporary clinicians and thinkers alike address such issues as subjectivity, otherness, and language. And the work of Heidegger's students, who include Hans-Georg Gadamer and Hans Loewald, continues to have an impact on the wider field of psychoanalysis.

The term "existential" also masks the tremendous variance among the perspectives that comprise this tradition. Whereas Sartre and Heidegger, for example, are both associated with existentialism in the public eye, Heidegger went out of his way to distance himself from the French philosopher's so-called existential-humanism. In his *Letter on Humanism* (1947), which became a cornerstone of French poststructuralism, Heidegger explicitly criticized Sartre for failing to represent the ontological turn in his philosophy. Following the publication of this work, the term "humanism" became an abusive epithet, used to denote the traditional metaphysics of the Cartesian subject. Not surprisingly, the term "existential" has little currency in continental Europe because of these fundamental distinctions. I use the term "existential-phenomenological" in this book because it is both broader and more specific in scope, reflecting the intertwining of two major European intellectual traditions.

Phenomenology, in the most basic sense, is concerned with the question of what it means to experience something. Husserl developed the phenomenological method, but his approach remained indelibly Cartesian. According to Husserl, it is my transcendental ego, the personal core of my consciousness, which ascribes meaning to objects in the world around me, including other people. The existential-phenomenological philosophers that followed Husserl transformed his phenomenological method in new and innovative ways. In order to overcome the notion of the isolated mind inherent Husserl's work, they rejected his concept of the transcendental ego and sought to distance themselves from his subjectivism. Their concern was to demonstrate the way in which phenomenology could provide a descriptive approach to studying human behavior, not from the "inside-out," as is the case in psychoanalytic theory of intrapsychic structures, but from the perspective of lived experience.

Broadly stated, existential-phenomenological philosophy seeks to explore and understand the nature of human experience. Each philosopher develops a different perspective on the issue. Heidegger moves beyond Husserl to argue that conscious experience always develops in a shared linguistic world. Sartre's formulation of implicit awareness provides post-Husserlian understanding of the nature of subjective or "felt" experience. Buber's philosophy of I and Thou develops a perspective on the experience of the Other in a relational, or dialogical context. And Merleau-Ponty elaborates the notion of bodily experience through his formulation of the body-subject, which seeks to overcome the traditional division between mind and body, or intellect and soma. Each of these themes will be elaborated in the course of this book.

Not by chance, many contemporary postmodern clinicians embrace the same perspectives, including experiences that are absent from classical psychoanalysis. Current interest in implicit or unformulated experience has shed new light on dissociative states of mind. The role of bodily or somatic experience has become central to the study of dyadic interaction, and has particularly influenced investigations of gender. Where once there was a focus only on internalized objects and object choices, psychotherapists and psychoanalysts now conceptualize human development in terms of interactions between embodied subjects, not objects.

The existential-phenomenological tradition is clearly relevant to many contemporary issues in psychotherapy and psychoanalysis. The notion of two interacting embodied subjects, for example, is central to recent feminist and postmodern perspectives in psychoanalysis. Beginning with the work of the existentialist writer Simone de Beauvoir, Sartre's long-time partner, feminist theorists have sought recognition of the Other, not as a female object but as an equal subject. Psychoanalysts such as Nancy Chodorow and Jessica Benjamin have developed this theme within the context of object relations and intersubjective psychoanalysis. Others, such as the French postmodern psychoanalysts, Luce Irigaray and Julia Kristeva, have shown how the notions of gender and sexuality are essentially social and linguistic constructions that rest on hidden and not so hidden assumptions about power and authority. As a result of feminist psychoanalysis, we see the way in which gender and authority always and inevitably impact on the clinical setting.

Although this study does not directly address feminism and its role in the postmodern debate, many of the thinkers and clinicians considered in this book contributed to the development of postmodern feminism. Lacan's rereading of Freud from the perspective of language has allowed for the development of a feminist perspective in psychoanalysis freed from the strictures of Freud's biological determinism. Buber's conception of the I–Thou relation has been instrumental in helping conceptualize the notion of equality within relationship. Sartre's discussion of the dialectic of power in terms of sadism and masochism, and his attempt to grant autonomous status to the Other are similarly relevant to the feminist discussion. And indeed, in a larger sense, the entire project of relational psychoanalysis is based on the recognition of the irreducibility of the Other.

Individuality and agency

Although the parallels between the existential-phenomenological tradition and the postmodern turn in psychotherapy and psychoanalysis are many, there are also crucial differences. In contrast to postmodernism, the existential-phenomenological perspective argues that such notions as individuality, autonomy, freedom, and agency all require revision, but remain vitally important nonetheless. Existential-phenomenological clinicians and thinkers emphasize the inevitable subjectivity of knowledge, but they also continue to insist that the individual person can be known. Their perspective on the person problematizes any simple conception of the mind as unified or absolute and rejects the myth of individuality as self-contained. Yet they emphasize the notion of authenticity and retain a conception of personal agency in order to account for our ability to choose one course of action over another.

It is precisely the conception of an experiencing person that makes it possible to navigate between modernist essentialism and postmodern reductionism. Heidegger's philosophy, for example, introduced the decentering of the self and laid the foundation for much postmodern thinking. Yet Heidegger never did away entirely with the person, or subject, coining the terms "Dasein" and "being-in-the-world" to refer to the instrument and process by which our conscious experience comes into being. Sartre formulates a conception of the human subject that anticipates Lacan's "split subject" and undermines the postmodern attack on the unity of the mind (Frie 1999). His idea of "prereflective" or implicit consciousness keeps the experiencing individual at the heart of therapeutic consideration, while making room for understanding divisions in consciousness that are an object of psychoanalytic investigation. In his emphasis on "the Other," Buber made clear that the self can never be understood in isolation. When the Other, or Thou, is recognized as an irreducible part of the relationship, understanding is never one-sided and takes place in a process of mutuality. The philosophy of dialogue ultimately also shows us not only how relationships determine the individual self, but the way in which individuals also determine the relationships they are in. For Buber, the self discovers and realizes its uniqueness in dialogue with the Other.

From an existential-phenomenological perspective, the self is indelibly connected to others and the world around it. Yet, despite its fundamental embeddedness, the self also retains the ability to act on its agency. Some readers may question this characterization of the existential-phenomenological tradition. By embracing the themes of agency, autonomy and authenticity, the existential-phenomenological tradition is often thought to limit the impact of our personal histories, unconscious motivations, and most importantly, our embeddedness in contexts beyond our control and outside of our awareness. Was it not Sartre, after all, who argued that we alone determine our fate when we embrace our freedom and make choices? Did not Heidegger insist that we must confront our potential for authenticity? According to this stereotype, which is unfortunately all too common, existential philosophies and psychologies assert that we are always the ultimate agents of our own experience. To avoid such misunderstandings, it is important to stress at the outset that the concept of agency developed here is not a reification of the omnipotent Cartesian subject which single-handedly creates its own experience. Indeed, to think that we could ever be omnipotently self-determining creatures is sheer hubris and not endorsed by any of the philosophies or psychologies considered in this book.

The problem with stereotypes is that they usually result in simple clichés and artificial distinctions. Indeed, from a reductionistic postmodern perspective there are only two versions of the self: the Cartesian conception of the self as an essential, non-relational entity, and the postmodern notion of the self as a social construct, embedded in relational, linguistic, and cultural contexts. In the process, an entire tradition of thinking about the self and subjectivity in terms of implicit, embodied experience, ranging from early German Romantic philosophy through phenomenology and modern neuroscience (Critchley and Dews 1996; Frie 1997; Gendlin [1962] 1997; Damasio 1999), is essentially ignored. As a result of this bifurcation, moreover, such concepts as the "individual" and "agency" are usually labeled as examples of Cartesian isolated mind thinking. This type of reaction is unfortunate since it forestalls any meaningful discussion about the role and importance of agency in the clinical setting.

The notion of the person as the agent of change is central to clinical practice. Yet ironically the concept of agency remains largely unformulated or is altogether rejected in much recent discussion. The absence of a concept of personal agency in psychoanalysis is not new. Freud saw personal choice as causally determined by mental phenomena. His theory of drives and his reification of the mind into impersonal constructs left little room for a concept of personal action. An exception to this trend is Roy Schafer's (1976) rejection of Freud's mechanistic model of mind in favor of an "action language" that emphasizes individual agency. But Schafer's work appears to have had a limited impact on a broader elaboration of individual agency.

On the other end of the psychoanalytic spectrum, opposite Freud, is the work of Harry Stack Sullivan, whose ideas provide a foundation for interpersonal and relational psychoanalysis. Drawing on the sociology of G. H. Mead, Sullivan argues that the self is always relationally generated and maintained. In an article entitled "The illusion of personal individuality," Sullivan maintains that the content of consciousness is socially derived and gives rise to an illusory sense of self. He concludes that: "no such thing as the durable, unique, individual personality is ever clearly justified. For all I know, every human being has as many personalities as he has interpersonal relations" (Sullivan [1950] 1964: 221). Sullivan defines the human being as the total of his or her relations with others and makes possible the development of a theory of "multiple selves." He recommends that clinicians give up their attempt to define a unique individual self and try instead to grasp what is going on at any particular time in the interpersonal field. Sullivan, as such, has no interest in the problem of agency, and in similar fashion the contemporary theory of multiple self-states makes it difficult to address the issue of agency with any clarity.

It is precisely the denial of an enduring individual self that is central to the postmodern project. With the rise of postmodernism, the turn away from such concepts as individuality and agency appears complete. The postmodern critique of individuality is based on the myth of the self-contained, unitary individual and rejection of the notion that it is possible to study individuals and their actions separately from their social context. Neither of these positions is endorsed by the existential-phenomenological approach. Instead, clinicians and thinkers in this tradition emphasize an alternative conception of the personal agent as existing in relational, linguistic, and cultural contexts.

Without a conception of personal agency, moreover, it is difficult to see how psychotherapists and psychoanalysts can avoid the dilemmas inherent in postmodernism. When the person is reduced to the interpersonal field and the "I" is equated with the self-state of each social relationship, the subject is entirely decentered. When psychotherapy and psychoanalysis rely on traditional theories of motivation, or define the self as a social construct, agency is undermined. Yet, if we are so thoroughly determined from without, what happens to individuality, choice, and autonomy, all of which comprise the activities of agency? If the individual is merely a fiction, how do we explain individual change? Without a concept of personal agency, how do we account for the ability to choose one course of action over another?

Once the concept of the experiencing person is reduced to a self-determining system, personal agency appears to give way to psychological compulsion. The authors in this book will argue that individuals develop in relational contexts but retain the ability to affect these contexts. In other words, although we are fundamentally relational beings and dependent upon our relationships and the contexts in which we exist, we are never wholly determined by them. We determine our worlds just as our worlds determine who we are. Agency remains a vital part of this dialectical process of becoming that defines us as human beings. We are always more than our contexts. There is inevitably a surfeit of meaning that cannot be reduced to the contexts or constructs we use to explain individual experience.

What is important, then, is not only the way in which individual persons experience their environments, but also the extent to which they influence them. It is the latter that has been neglected by much postmodernism because any theory of agency, or autonomy of action, is seen as a reification of the Cartesian self and denial of our contextual embeddedness. In their emphasis on the social aspects of the self, proponents of postmodernism appear to lose sight of the way in which individuals use increased self-understanding to engage the world in new ways and bring about significant change in their lives.

In the clinical setting, therapeutic change can take place in a variety of ways. Many of the authors in this book will argue that the assumption of agency is a vital part of the therapeutic process. In order for patients to create change, they need to be agents of their actions. Agency is rarely a matter of simple choice, however, just as therapeutic action is never a linear process. Patients desire change, but they are unable to bring it about on their own. From an interpersonal perspective, we can observe the way in which patients are often mired in familiar patterns of relating to the world that they feel helpless to alter. In order for change to occur, patients must become aware that they are relying on a view of the world that is determined by a compilation of past and present experience. By recognizing that their patterns of relating are simply maintaining the status quo, patients can begin to understand their need for choice and self-determination.

The underlying difficulty is how to change patterns of relating. These patterns are familiar and although they may be a cause of fundamental discomfort and unhappiness, they can also appear safe because they enable us to avoid anxiety. Change requires both a desire and a will to open up new possibilities of being. It is the response from the Other within the therapeutic dyad that makes possible the realization of agency in a tangible way. Once we come to understand ourselves as agents of our world, it becomes possible for us to imagine making different choices, and begin relating to others and acting in our worlds in new and different ways. As such, the assumption and experience of agency always takes place within a relational context.

Self-experience

In discussing the problem of individuality and agency in the therapeutic process, this book seeks to expand the postmodern debate about self. No matter how constructed and contextualized the person is, we retain an ability to reflect on our experience, make decisions, and act on our agency. The postmodern embrace of social constructionism has essentially silenced discussion of this aspect of self-experience because it confuses individual subjectivity with a materialistic, essentialist notion of the self. Indeed, for most postmodernists such terms as individuality and agency are inherently linked with Cartesianism and it will no doubt be a challenge for these readers to develop a different perspective on the issue.

The existential-phenomenological tradition rejects outright the solipsistic, mind's eye view of the world that defined the Cartesian subject. In developing their view of subjectivity, the authors argue that self-experience is always grounded in the body, world, and language. Their emphasis on the body, world, and language suggests that the nature of individuality is not only dependent upon, but also enhanced by history, culture, and community. Even direct bodily experience, which some of the authors argue forms the ground for our individual subjectivities, does not occur in a vacuum because the body is inherently interactive. We are indelibly connected to the world through our bodies.

Nor when the authors address the question of authenticity do they suggest that either the patient or therapist can "know" definitively what course of action is best at all times or what its consequences will be. The fact that meaning is often ineffable and knowledge is fraught with uncertainty puts to rest the myth of the absolute knowledge upon which postmodernism bases its critique. In contrast to reductive versions of postmodernism, however, the authors argue that there is a necessary role for freedom, choice, and agency in the understanding and practice of therapeutic action. And an unqualified embrace of postmodernism overlooks this necessity.

The self develops in, and is dependent upon, human interaction. But the self also maintains a sense of cohesion and identity from within. As therapeutic process demonstrates, it is our ability to reflect and act on our self-perceptions that is crucial to organizing our experience. The importance of agency for determining individual experience is captured by Otto Rank in his conception of will:

> By will, I do not mean will-to-power as conceived by Nietzsche and Adler or "wish" in the Freudian sense, though it might include both these aspects. I mean rather an autonomous organizing force in the individual that does not represent any particular biological impulse or social drive but constitutes the creative expression of the total personality and distinguishes one individual from another
>
> (Rank 1941: 50)

Rank's perspective on how our individual wills are expressed in and through our agency characterizes an Enlightenment view of the world, but it also suggests that agency remains important to the therapeutic process.

In spite of our sociocultural embeddedness, there is room for choice and agency. As Erich Fromm (1941, 1947) so often pointed out, individuals retain the ability to act on their understanding and effect change within themselves and the world around them. Fromm was attuned to the social, political, and economic factors at work in daily life. In contrast to many of his fellow psychoanalysts, he asserted that it was not possible, or even advisable, to bracket these factors out of the clinical setting. Rather, he sought to help his patients live more authentically, and strove to engage his fellow citizens in the social and political events around them.

The danger is that by subverting the subject and rejecting the notion of agency, postmodernism ultimately endorses a relativistic worldview that undermines our ability to choose a set of social, political and ethical values. If everything exists only in relation to something else, if everything is merely socially constructed or linguistically determined, then there is no longer any ground on which autonomous thinking and speaking can take place, thus giving rise to a new form of determinism.

By mapping out a space between modernism and postmodernism, this book argues that it is possible for the psychotherapist, psychoanalyst, and philosopher alike to avoid the relativistic pitfalls of postmodernism and account for the role of agency. Contemporary psychotherapy and psychoanalysis needs to recognize and acknowledge the way in which the individual is able to make choices and facilitate change despite the larger forces at work in determining life experience.

Chapter outline

This book addresses both psychotherapy and psychoanalysis in the belief that traditional, static definitions of what constitutes a course of therapy or analysis have become considerably more fluid. Beginning with Freud, psychotherapy and psychoanalysis were seen at odds with one another, indicating entirely separate spheres of theory and technique. However, with the rise of interpersonal, relational, and intersubjective approaches in psychoanalysis, earlier distinctions have given way to the possibility of integrating different theories and techniques. This dispersion points towards a broadening of psychoanalysis. It suggests that psychoanalysis is not a monolithic entity, and cannot be owned or appropriated by an exclusive set of ideas and beliefs. As such, the authors are concerned with elaborating the links between psychoanalysis, broadly conceived, and the work of existential, phenomenological, and structuralist traditions of thought.

The chapters are written by psychotherapists and psychoanalysts, who are also philosophical scholars engaged in the current debate on postmodernism. As a group, the authors bring considerable clinical and theoretical knowledge to bear. The chapters address the issues raised by postmodernism and seek to demonstrate the relevance of existential-phenomenological ideas for clinical practice. They are organized around individual thinkers, clinicians and themes. The initial chapters take as their starting point the philosophies of Sartre, Buber, Heidegger, and Merleau-Ponty and elaborate clinical theories that draw on their ideas. The later chapters address the clinical work of Binswanger, Lacan, Fromm, and Laing. The theories of Boss and Fromm-Reichmann are addressed to varying degrees throughout. Some readers will note that other important thinkers and clinicians could well have been included: the philosophy of Emmanuel Levinas, for example, or the clinical work of Sandor Ferenczi, Eugen Minkowski, Otto Rank, and Erwin Strauss is ripe for consideration in the present context. Clearly a book is defined as much by its limitations in scope and size as by its attempts break new ground.

This book does not present a single perspective and readers will find many distinctions between the authors and chapters. There are, for example, differences of opinion concerning the constitution of the self, the role of language, and the impact of larger forces in determining experience. Nor do the authors agree on a single theory of technique: some favor interaction and reciprocity, while others emphasize the value of analytic neutrality. The lack of commonality does not indicate a lack of cohesive agenda however. All the authors are fundamentally concerned with finding a place in contemporary theory and practice for such concepts as agency, authenticity, freedom, choice, and truth. And it is precisely the attempt to grapple with these concepts, rather than reject them, which distinguishes the perspectives developed in this book from reductionistic versions of postmodernism.

In the first chapter on "Sartre's contribution to psychoanalysis," Betty Cannon explores the contributions that a shift from Freudian to Sartrean metatheory can make to contemporary psychoanalysis. Despite Sartre's deeply ambivalent relationship to traditional psychoanalysis, he nevertheless considered psychoanalysis the only possible mode of understanding the insertion of the individual subject into history. Cannon argues that in existential psychoanalysis the fictional nature of the ego as subject must be revealed and the analysand's current ego deconstructed. In contrast to postmodernism, however, human consciousness as the source of experience retains its centrality. A Sartrean perspective allows for a divided consciousness, yet eschews the postmodern deconstruction of subjectivity. Cannon addresses the difference that this view on the ego and consciousness can make to clinical theory and practice. She examines the human desire for an illusory "solid" sense of self as well as the importance of anxiety raised by the realization that we are free to make choices that can impact our lives. Case illustrations are used to demonstrate the relevance of a Sartrean perspective in clinical practice, especially for the analytic relationship.

The second chapter on "Martin Buber and dialogical psychotherapy" examines the contemporary clinical relevance of Buber's philosophy of dialogue. Drawing on his personal relationship with Buber, Maurice Friedman introduces dialogical psychotherapy as an extension of Buber's philosophy of dialogue and elaborates the nature of human relating. He provides a full account of dialogical psychotherapy by examining its key elements, paying particular attention to the way in which Buber elaborates a concept of the unique person within the context of a relational interaction. The therapeutic significance of Friedman's dialogical approach is demonstrated in a detailed case example. Friedman also argues that the influence of Buber's theory of dialogue in contemporary psychotherapy and psychoanalysis has gone largely unnoticed. To this end, he provides a historical and contemporary overview of Buber's impact on recent psychotherapy and psychoanalysis and examines the growing movement of dialogical psychotherapy.

The third chapter on "Truth and freedom in psychoanalysis" explores the relation of Heidegger's philosophy to psychoanalysis and examines the work of Medard Boss and Jacques Lacan. Focusing in particular on Lacan and Heidegger, William J. Richardson's objective is to help us understand and conceptualize the place of truth and freedom in a clinical setting. The author demonstrates the way in which the problem of truth and freedom remains significant from a Lacanian perspective, even though Lacan turned away from his early interest in existential-phenomenology to embrace the formalism of structural linguistics. Richardson elucidates Lacan's position by exploring Heidegger's notion of freedom as the letting-be-manifest of truth. This conception is correlated to the role that language plays in the clinical process. The ways in which clinicians and philosophers alike can interpret truth and freedom in order to understand the nature of therapeutic action and change is elaborated through the use of clinical case material.

The fourth chapter on "Beyond postmodernism: from concepts through experiencing" builds on the notion of lived experience developed by Merleau-Ponty and the existential-phenomenological tradition. Eugene Gendlin takes Merleau-Ponty's conception of embodiment as a starting point for his own elaboration of embodied experience. Gendlin explores the nature of bodily experiencing in the clinical setting and seeks to unravel the complex relationship between concepts and experience. According to Gendlin, the postmodern fascination with social construction is mistaken when it suggests that the human being is only the product of sociocultural and historical contexts because it overlooks our direct access to experiencing. He argues that the human being is inherently interactional and has the potential to experience continuity. Gendlin elaborates his practice of "focusing" as a process of developing our "felt-sense" and thus demonstrates the relevance of embodied experience for clinical work.

The fifth chapter, "A phenomenology of becoming: reflections on authenticity," addresses the problem of authenticity from both an existential-phenomenological and a psychodynamic perspective. Jon Mills argues for a conceptualization and treatment of the self that challenges postmodern critiques of authenticity and agency, and elaborates a phenomenology of becoming. He examines the early philosophy of Heidegger to focus on Dasein's quest for authenticity and draw connections with Sartre's notion of self-deception. A bridge between existential-phenomenological philosophy and psychoanalysis is built by exploring the relevance of Winnicott's theory of the false self and its implications for the therapeutic encounter. Mills provides a detailed case study in which the notion of authenticity is examined in a clinical setting. In tracing the dialectic of the lived experience as vacillating between authentic and inauthentic modes of creativity and self-discovery, he shows how selfhood and the process of therapy is a becoming of one's possibilities.

The sixth chapter on "Language and subjectivity: from Binswanger through Lacan" addresses the impact of language on human development and experience in contemporary psychoanalysis and philosophy. Roger Frie argues that the work of Jacques Lacan has spurred an increased interest in the role of language in clinical and theoretical pursuits, but that the rise of postmodernism has also led to an overvaluation of the linguistic dimension. When language is used to define the human subject, nonverbal, embodied experience is often left unaccounted for. Frie turns to the work of Ludwig Binswanger, and his elaboration of nonverbal experience in therapeutic and communicative contexts. Connections are drawn between Binswanger and the existential-phenomenological theories of Heidegger, Buber, and Merleau-Ponty. Drawing on their work, Frie argues that it is possible to achieve a conception of personal agency and interpersonal interaction that accounts both for the centrality of language *and* for the significance of the nonverbal dimension. Case material is examined in order to demonstrate the clinical implications of Binswanger's perspective on language and therapeutic interaction.

The seventh chapter on "Psychoanalysis and subjectivity in the work of Erich Fromm" explores the contribution of Fromm's work to contemporary psychoanalysis and philosophy. Daniel Burston argues that Fromm's conception of the human subject is particularly relevant in light of the rise of reductionistic versions of postmodernism that argue for the dissolution of the self. He demonstrates the way in which Fromm was an early and articulate critic of the positivist underpinnings of the Freudian metapsychology. Fromm's emphasis on the primacy of the striving for human relatedness and the ethical dimension in psychoanalysis anticipated many more recent trends in object relations theory, self-psychology, and relational psychoanalysis. Fromm never addressed such contemporary philosophical trends as poststructuralism or deconstructionism explicitly. Yet Burston shows that Fromm's views on the origins and nature of human subjectivity, and the role of economic, cultural and linguistic factors in the (de)formation of the human subject are significant, because of the ways in which they challenge postmodernism.

The eighth chapter explores "The primacy of experience in R. D. Laing's approach to psychoanalysis." M. Guy Thompson questions the place of human experience in postmodern psychoanalysis. Drawing on his personal relationship with Laing, he examines the role of experience in Laing's treatment philosophy and conception of psychoanalysis. The chapter explores Laing's complicated and enigmatic relationship with psychoanalysis with a view to emphasizing those features of his perspective that comply with the interpersonal and relational schools of analysis. The author's aim is to emphasize Laing's debt not only to existentialism and phenomenology but especially to skepticism, which he argues is also the basis of the postmodern critique of contemporary culture. In the process, Thompson suggests that Laing's treatment philosophy allows for an elaboration of authenticity, which is excluded by the postmodernist dispersion of the self.

The final chapter addresses "The eclipse of the person in psychoanalysis." Jon Frederickson critically examines recent postmodern trends in psychoanalysis that challenge the existence of personhood and agency. He begins by outlining some of the problems inherent in the concept of the postmodern self that is decentered by language, culture, and society. In particular, reductionistic tenets of postmodernism in psychoanalysis are called into question. Frederickson argues that the physical presence of the Other, as a living, evolving person, can never be reduced to a linguistic phrase, analysis, or theory. There is always some surplus of meaning that transcends the words we use to describe the Other. He calls for a return to the project of self-knowledge in psychoanalysis and introduces an alternative concept of the person as active and embodied. He draws on the work of the Russian personalist philosophers, who emphasize the importance of the body, action, and agency as the ground of our knowledge. Clinical case material is presented to illustrate the nature of agency in therapeutic action and the achievement of self-knowledge.

References

Critchley, S. and Dews, P. (eds.) (1996) *Deconstructive Subjectivities*. Albany, NY: State University of New York Press.

Damasio, A. (1999) *The Feeling of What Happens: Body and Emotion in the Making of Consciousness*. New York: Harcourt Brace.

Farias, V. (1989) *Heidegger and Nazism*. Philadelphia, PA: Temple University Press.

Frie, R. (1997) *Subjectivity and Intersubjectivity in Modern Philosophy and Psychoanalysis: A Study of Sartre, Binswanger, Lacan, and Habermas*. Lanham, MD: Rowman and Littlefield.

—— (1999) "Subjectivity revisited: Sartre, Lacan, and early German Romanticism," *Journal of Phenomenological Psychology* 30: 1–13.

Frie, R. and Reis, B. (2001) "Understanding intersubjectivity: psychoanalytic formulations and their philosophical underpinnings," *Contemporary Psychoanalysis* 37: 297-327.

Fromm, E. ([1941] 1965) *Escape from Freedom*. New York: Avon.

—— (1947) *Man for Himself: An Inquiry into Psychology and Ethics*. Greenwich, CT: Fawcett Premier.

Gendlin, E. ([1962] 1997) *Experiencing and the Creation of Meaning*. Evanston, IL: Northwestern University Press.

Gergen, K. (2001) "Psychological science in a postmodern context," *American Psychologist* 56: 803–13.

Heidegger, M. ([1947] 1977) *Letter on Humanism*, in *Basic Writings*, ed. D. F. Krell. London: Routledge.

Martin, J. and Sugarman, J. (2000) "Between the modern and the postmodern: the possibility of self and progressive understanding in psychology," *American Psychologist* 55: 397-406.

May, R., Angel, E. and Ellenberger, H. (eds.) (1958) *Existence: A New Dimension in Psychiatry and Psychology*. New York: Basic Books.

Ott, H. (1993) *Martin Heidegger: A Political Life*. New York: Basic Books.

Rank, O. (1941) *Beyond Psychology*. New York: Dover.

Schafer, R. (1976) *A New Language for Psychoanalysis*. New Haven, CT: Yale University Press.

Sullivan, H. S. ([1950] 1964) "The illusion of personal individuality," in *The Fusion of Psychiatry and Social Science*. New York: W. W. Norton.

Wolin, R. (ed.) (1993) *The Heidegger Controversy*. Cambridge, MA: MIT Press.

Chapter 1

Sartre's contribution to psychoanalysis

Betty Cannon

The work of the French philosopher Jean-Paul Sartre has impacted many fields, but is not often linked to psychoanalysis. This chapter considers the relevance of Sartre's work for contemporary psychoanalytic theory and practice. I argue that adopting a Sartrean perspective can clarify a major theoretical difficulty in ego psychology, object relations theory, and self psychology: the problem of reconciling the discovery of new relational needs in earliest infancy and childhood with Freudian drive theory. I also believe a Sartrean perspective can help us reconceptualize the goal of psychoanalysis and the relationship between analyst and analysand, leading to more effective ways to facilitate significant change in therapy. In a certain sense, existential theory lies between traditional psychology, with its view of a substantive psyche, and postmodern views, which deconstruct and hence discard subjectivity altogether. Sartre's idea of "prereflective consciousness" or implicit awareness keeps the experiencing subject at the heart of our considerations, while making room for understanding those divisions in consciousness which are the object of psychoanalytic investigations.

Linking existential philosophy with psychoanalysis, while not new, is hardly a dominant trend in English-speaking countries. In North America, for example, existential philosophy is more often considered to inform humanistic psychology with its emphasis on the here and now as opposed to classical psychoanalysis with its emphasis on the childhood origins of adult behavior. The term "existential/humanistic psychology" is often used to described the "third wave" in clinical practice, the first two being psychoanalysis and behaviorism. Hence the notion of an "existential psychoanalysis" may seem somewhat strange to readers unfamiliar with European traditions of thought.

Existential psychoanalysis is nonetheless a strong tradition. Indeed, Freud himself may have sensed the connection when he expressed a reluctance to read the existentialist philosopher Friedrich Nietzsche for fear his own ideas may have been preempted there (Freud [1914] 1953–74: 15–16). The European tradition of existential psychoanalysis spans the work of psychiatrists such as Ludwig Binswanger, Medard Boss, and Viktor Frankl, and draws on philosophical ideas from Edmund Husserl and Martin Heidegger through Martin Buber (see for example Binswanger 1963; Boss 1957, 1963; Frankl [1959] 1985; Husserl [1913] 1967; Heidegger [1927] 1962; Buber [1923] 1970).

There are, in addition, many psychoanalysts who do not readily identify themselves as existential, yet cite the influence of existential and phenomenological philosophy on their work. They include Erich Fromm and Frieda Fromm-Reichmann, who were friends and colleagues of Buber, and Hans Loewald and Stanley Leavy, who both acknowledge the influence of Heidegger. Roy Schafer (1976), who trained with Loewald and Leavy, introduces a new, action-oriented language for psychoanalysis, which moves strongly in the direction of existential-phenomenological thought. Rollo May, who trained at the William Alanson White Institute as an interpersonal psychoanalyst, first introduced European "existential analysis" to the English-speaking world with his influential work (coedited with Ernest Angel and Henri Ellenberger), *Existence: A New Dimension in Psychiatry and Psychology* (*May et al.* 1958).

The reader may notice that what is missing in this account of the development of existential psychoanalysis is the significant influence of Sartre. Since Sartre is usually considered to be among the most important existential philosophers, it is surprising that the only prominent European psychoanalyst to acknowledge a significant debt to him is R. D. Laing ([1959] 1979, [1961] 1976), whose roots lie in the British object relations school. This is curious in light of the fact that a major section of Sartre's early philosophical masterpiece, *Being and Nothingness* ([1943] 1956), is entitled "Existential psychoanalysis." Indeed Sartre employed the methodology of existential psychoanalysis in his psychobiographies. Sartre also found himself deeply in agreement with Freud's insistence on the phenomena of disguise and repression. He merely disagreed with the mechanistic metapsychology that Freud used to explain them. Furthermore, in his later philosophy, Sartre came to insist that only psychoanalysis can account for the insertion of the individual into history. The intention of his later philosophy, as described in *Search for a Method* ([1960a] 1968), is to wed psychoanalysis to Marxism under the auspices of existentialism. His psychobiography of Flaubert is the offspring of that union.

Why then has there been this failure to mine the work of Sartre for psychoanalytic insights? I suspect part of the reason may lie in Sartre's adamant insistence on rejecting the Freudian unconscious. Perhaps Sartre's stance as a radical and activist also may have influenced this oversight, since American psychoanalysis in the guise of ego psychology appears curiously apolitical. Perhaps the more likely reason lies in what Sartre's friend and former student, J.-B. Pontalis, called Sartre's "thirty-year-long [forty-year-long by the time of Sartre's death in 1980] relationship with psychoanalysis, an ambiguous mixture of *equally* deep attraction and repulsion" (Pontalis in Sartre [1972] 1979: 220, emphasis in original). Sartre was as capable of criticizing psychoanalysis as of using its premises to understand human reality.

Pontalis was interested in reinterpreting the work of Sartre in the light of his relationship with psychoanalysis. In this chapter, I am interested in the possible impact that Sartre might have on psychoanalysis. I begin by examining Sartre's ambivalent relationship with classical psychoanalysis and then explore the potential impact that a shift to a Sartrean view of human reality might have on psychoanalysis. I consider a theoretical crisis in contemporary ego psychology, object relations theory, and self psychology and contend that moving to a Sartrean perspective would solve the theoretical difficulties and further elucidate psychoanalytic developmental theory. Finally, I assess the impact of a Sartrean perspective on clinical practice, focusing in particular on the analytic relationship.

Sartre's ambivalent relationship with psychoanalysis

Sartre's debt to Freud is evident in a variety of his writings. To begin, the chapter on "Existential psychoanalysis" in *Being and Nothingness* could not have existed without the prior existence of Freudian psychoanalysis. It is both a critique and a tribute to Freudian psychoanalysis. Similarly Sartre's psychobiographies of Genet ([1952] 1963), Baudelaire ([1946] 1950), and Flaubert ([1971] 1981, 1987) are demonstrations of the technique of existential psychoanalysis, and all owe to classical psychoanalysis the meticulous examination of their subjects' childhoods as a way to understanding adult behavior. Sartre's autobiographical sketch of his own childhood, *The Words* ([1963] 1964), is an essay in existential self-analysis. While all of these incorporate existentialist principles, they clearly demonstrate Freud's significance for Sartre.

Furthermore there is a posthumous publication deriving from what is perhaps the strangest chapter in the history of Sartre's relationship to psychoanalysis: his acceptance of an offer by producer John Huston to write a screenplay on Freud's life. Sartre's attraction to psychoanalysis is apparent in *The Freud Scenario*, written in 1958-59 and published under the editorship of Pontalis in 1984. Here Sartre presents a sympathetic Freud making a quite exciting discovery of the unconscious. To prepare himself to write it, he reread *Studies in Hysteria* and *The Interpretation of Dreams* and read Freud's *Autobiography*, the Freud–Fleiss correspondence, and the first volume of Ernest Jones's biography of Freud, which had just been translated into French. He had Michelle Vian laboriously translate aloud, line by line, the other Jones volumes. In *Search for a Method*, written shortly afterward in 1960, Sartre insisted that only psychoanalysis can provide the entrance into the world of childhood that is a necessary cornerstone for any viable social science theory. One can further see the influence of Freud on Sartre's account of Flaubert's hysterico-epilepsy in the first volume of *The Family Idiot* ([1971] 1981), written during the following decade.

The other side of Sartre's relationship to psychoanalysis, his criticism, ranges from his famous critique of the unconscious in *Being and Nothingness*, to his later discussion of the analyst/analysand relationship in an article from *Les Temps modernes* (1969), republished in *Situations VIII and IX (Between Existentialism and Marxism*, [1972] 1979). "The man with a tape recorder" is a transcript of a tape recording made by a patient of a session with his analyst, presumably his last session. Sartre defends the man's right to bring the tape recorder into the session and his own right to publish the interaction as representing "the irruption of the *subject* into the consulting room, or rather the overthrow of the univocal relationship linking the subject [analyst] to the object [patient]" (Sartre [1972] 1979: 200, emphasis in original). The tape recorder turns the tables on the analyst because there is now a "third" in the consulting room – a witness to the dyadic interaction that makes the analyst also an object, depriving him of his position as all-knowing observer. The analyst, of course, objects. Sartre says that the ensuing dialogue points to a critique not only of this particular doctor–patient relationship but also of the psychoanalytic relationship itself in situations where it does not include the aspect of reciprocity.

Let us be clear about what Sartre is critiquing. He is *not objecting* to the phenomenal reality lying behind what therapists and analysts alike see as the significant discoveries of Freud: transference, resistance, the defenses, the impact of childhood on adult life. Sartre explains his objections, which he maintains from his early philosophical work through *Search for a Method, Critique of Dialectical Reason*, and the Flaubert biography, in an interview:

I remain shocked by what was inevitable in Freud – the biological and physiological language. . . . Right up to the time of Fliess, as you know, he wrote physiological studies designed to provide an equivalent of the cathexes and equilibria he had found in psychoanalysis. The result is that the manner in which he describes the psychoanalytic object suffers from a kind of mechanistic cramp. This is not always true, for there are moments when he transcends this. But in general this language produces a *mythology* of the unconscious which I cannot accept. I am completely in agreement with the *facts* of disguise and repression, as facts. But the *words* "repression," "censorship," or "drive" – words which express one moment a sort of finalism and the next moment a sort of mechanism, these I reject.

(Sartre [1972] 1979: 37, emphases in original)

Whether we retain or reject the words, I think it is important to take Sartre's critique seriously, since the "mechanistic cramp" to which he objects still affects many schools of psychoanalysis today.

While a majority of psychoanalysts probably no longer take seriously Freud's metabiological and hydraulic metaphors, many are still encumbered by a view of the psyche as a "thing" that obeys laws of cause and effect similar to those affecting objects in the physical world. It is from this perspective that a particular analysis may become a "tragedy of impossible reciprocity," as Sartre called the psychoanalytic dialogue discussed above (Sartre [1972] 1979: 202). The consequent reification of the psyche is the source of many therapeutic mistakes in an approach that otherwise has much to contribute to alleviating human misery. And this is true of contemporary ego psychology, object relations theory, and self psychology, which otherwise have valuable new insights, as well as classical analysis. In fact, I think we can easily recast many of the discoveries of contemporary psychoanalysis in Sartrean terms and thereby increase our understanding and therapeutic competence. Before doing so, however, we will first need to look at Sartre's fundamental view of human reality as contrasted with Freud's.

Nothingness at the heart of being: Sartre's view of human reality

Sartre's objections to the "mechanistic cramp" in Freud's metapsychology are more thorough going than his well-known rejection of the Freudian unconscious. Indeed his rejection of the unconscious is based on a philosophical premise that separates his perspective from that of all versions of psychology as a positivistic science. Human reality, Sartre tells us, is a perspective on Being rather than an absorption in Being. It is the source of that nothingness or *no-thingness* by which Being is revealed. Or, as Sartre rather poetically says in *Being and Nothingness*, "Nothingness lies coiled in the heart of being – like a worm" (Sartre [1943] 1956: 56). Human reality is the source of this nothingness.

The phenomenology of philosopher Edmund Husserl is the source of Sartre's objections to Freud's reification of the psyche. For Sartre, there is no possibility of subdividing the psyche into consciousness, preconscious, and unconscious or ego, superego, and id. This is so because, from a phenomenological perspective, there is no independently existing psyche confronting an independently existing real world. Because consciousness is always intentional consciousness, that is, because it is always *consciousness of* this or that object, there is no division between consciousness and its objects in the usual sense. Consciousness discovers itself out there in the world, not in interiority. What passes for interiority is the attempt to take an objective perspective, the perspective of the Other, on the self. This results in the creation of that "quasi-object," as Sartre calls it, the ego. It should not be mistaken for the "subject" or agent, which Sartre describes as "irrupting into the consulting room" in the remarks quoted above.

Sartre does not speak of the psyche but of consciousness because he does not see consciousness as a thing in the usual sense. Indeed, as Sartre says, consciousness is *no thing*. It is the "nothingness," the perspective on being, the negation which is the foundation of all determination. Sometimes, in giving a lecture, I use the podium from which I speak as an example. Because I am *not* this podium, I can have a vantage point on it. This *no-thingness* is also the source of my freedom; indeed it is my freedom. Because I am not the podium, I can take a vantage point on the podium; for instance, I can use it as an example in the lecture. If I were a small child, I might climb on top of it and pretend to fly or crawl under it and pretend it is a house. Or if I were a demagogue, I might pound it to make a point. Similarly, a mountain is a very different object for a mountain climber, a geologist, or a person out for a pleasant drive. My intention, my way of grasping an object, determines my experience of that object. I discover my "self" in this interaction.

This is why the past looks determined – at least to the point in therapy where we re-experience it in its immediacy. Then hopefully it comes alive with all the objects through which I find myself making some original choice of a way of being in the world. The past looks determined because I do not find there a past self in the usual sense, but instead the objects which I constituted in this way or that as a part of my project or way of *pro-jecting* myself toward a particular future. For example, I might find a particular father whose rantings and ravings I lived as an admonition to silence, a silence that I find myself continuing to the present day despite the change in circumstances. Or perhaps it is more correct to say that I do not recognize the change in circumstances: I live my present circumstances as though my silence prevents the catastrophe of someone yelling at me. This is what they are for me until self/world hopefully changes in the course of analysis or in some other way. I am not dealing here with a mechanical "transference" of the past onto the present, but a way of grasping self/world that has its roots in my past and through which I am in the process of bringing into being a particular kind of future.

The situation, however, is more complicated than this because we do all develop forms of that quasi-object, the ego. We develop a vantage point on the self as well as the world, and we mistake that vantage point for the agent who creates it. All the confusion which exists in current psychoanalytic terminology about self, ego, and the like could perhaps be clarified by understanding that there is no "self" or "ego" in the usual sense of a fixed entity which is the author of my actions or reality orientation. When we go to the source of our actions, all we find is the "nothingness," the intentional consciousness that relates to the world in this way or that, or else we find the world related to. This basic world-relatedness is experienced through "prereflective consciousness" or intentional implicit or gut-level awareness. It is not even verbal, since language according to Sartre is "for others." Prereflective consciousness is, however, a seat of awareness that divides Sartre's perspective from those of postmodern thinkers who would deconstruct the subject and reveal its totally fictional nature.

The ego, from this perspective, is a construct of "reflective consciousness." It has a structure, but it is a structure which I give it and by which I develop and sustain a sense of "who I am" rather than the real structure of a solid object – although in a certain sense it is I who create any object's structure by discovering and classifying it in this way or that (remember the mountain climber and the geologist with the mountain). The ego as subject is therefore unreal, and it must be de-structured and its fictional nature revealed in any thorough analysis. It is also contaminated by the voices of the original others which I mimic in an attempt to grasp this elusive object, my self.

For Sartre, then, there are three categories of Being: Being-in-itself or the phenomenal world which can never be known objectively as it is and which always overflows my attempts to grasp and categorize it;

Being-for-itself or human reality which is a future directed perspective on Being with roots in the phenomenal world and my particular past; and Being-for-others, which is my awareness of the Other's awareness of me. Human consciousness, Being-for-itself, is divided into two categories: reflective and prereflective. These are not two parts of the psyche, since consciousness has no component parts, but rather two moments of relating to the world: a nonreflective and a reflective moment. When consciousness turns and makes an object of itself, prereflective consciousness turns reflective. Sartre's third category, Being-for-others, is not a necessary corollary of the other two, but rather a discovery. Through an experience which Sartre designates as the *Look*, I discover the Other as another subject who sees and names me. This becomes, as we shall see, extremely important to my reflective view of self and the cornerstone of an existential perspective on human development.

As for Sartre's rejection of the Freudian unconscious, it is predicated on the above description of Being. From a Sartrean perspective, we may explore the past as the "background depth of all my thoughts and feelings." But we must never see the past as determinative or aspects of my past as having been repressed into the unconscious. Instead, in exploring the past, we are exploring early choices and "prereflective experience" – or as Sartre would much later call this, the thickness of *le vecu* or lived experience. A phenomenological perspective would obviously disallow the existence of an unconscious realm *in* the psyche, simply because consciousness as *no-thing* has no inside. It is world-related. What is at stake is not a lack of consciousness (prereflective consciousness) but a lack of knowledge (reflective consciousness). Sartre says,

> [Spontaneous consciousness] is penetrated by a great light without being able to express what this light is illuminating. We are not dealing with an unsolved riddle as the Freudians believe; all is there, luminous. . . . But this "mystery in broad daylight" is due to the fact that this possession is deprived of the means which would ordinarily permit *analysis* and *conceptualization*. It grasps everything, all at once, without shading, without relief, without connections of gradeur [*sic*] – not that these shades, these values, these reliefs exist somewhere and are hidden from it, but rather because they must be established by another human attitude and because they can exist only *by means of* and *for* knowledge.
>
> (Sartre [1943] 1956: 570–1, emphases in original)

The task of psychoanalysis, from this perspective, would not be to make the unconscious conscious but to make the unknown known.

In his early philosophy, Sartre claims that I may through a process he calls "pure" or "purifying reflection" or the simple presence of the consciousness reflecting to the consciousness reflected on become directly aware of my prereflective experience. Pure reflection may be somewhat like the observing ego in psychoanalysis or the Buddhist idea of the "witness." It differs from "impure" or "accessory reflection" in that pure reflection reveals the freedom or nothingness at the heart of one's fundamental project whereas impure reflection reveals a concretized self or ego.

Later Sartre came to see that all of my experience will never yield itself up to reflective conceptualization and to relate this to psychoanalytic investigation. He develops the notion of "lived experience" [le vecu], which "is always simultaneously present to itself and absent from itself" (Sartre [1972] 1979: 42). Sartre says that le vecu "is neither the precautions of the preconscious, nor the unconscious, nor consciousness, but the terrain in which the individual is perpetually overflowed by himself and his riches and consciousness plays the trick of determining itself by forgetfulness" (Sartre [1972] 1979: 39). He maintains in this sense that a neurosis is a psychic fact that can neither be named nor known. It is "a specific wound, a defective structure which is a certain way of living a childhood" (Sartre [1972] 1979: 42) and its adult transmutations. Because the stress of a neurosis is simultaneously intentional and unknown to the subject, it cannot sustain itself when it enters the domain of knowledge, as in analytic treatment. This is as close as Sartre ever came to a rapprochement with the Freudian unconscious.

Yet because le vecu is intentionally and consciously lived but not known, I can on principle come to know the meaning in terms of my life project of many of the concrete gut level choices that I have not yet subjected to reflective characterization. I can, for instance, learn the significance of a particular bodily stance or gesture that contradicts my usual idea of myself. Or I can learn the significance of a symptom that seems to me an alien affliction rather than something which I myself do, as, for example, when I as an analysand feel persecuted by my own obsessive thoughts or my depression. It is understanding this significance and glimpsing other possibilities in life (which one must, of course, abandon one's old way of creating self/world to grasp) which lead to cure or the alleviation of misery.

Sartre therefore believes that the proper attitude for the existential analyst is not intellectual understanding, but comprehension: an attitude that seeks to grasp the other's project as a free determination within a particular situation. He would not deny the circumstances of a person's life, but he would wish to understand that person as an agent living those circumstances in this way or that. Otherwise, to view one's client, say, as only a diagnosis or as the plaything of hereditary and environmental forces or unconscious wishes is to miss the point. This is not to say that Sartre's philosophy is a pull yourself up by your own bootstraps philosophy. Freedom, from a phenomenological perspective, is always freedom within a particular situation and that situation has its impact. It is just that it is a *situation*, not an environment: that is, it is composed of a unity of what the world brings and how I live and conceive what the world brings.

The task of psychoanalysis, from an existential perspective, is to untangle the dense lack of understanding of one's choices (past and present) and to allow for a shift in one's "project of being" in the world. In other words, we must abandon the view of human beings as determined which is so prevalent not simply in classical psychoanalysis but in all forms of positivist psychology. Instead we must attempt to grasp an analysand's *situation* as it is lived and experienced in order to help the analysand recover his or her full humanity. We need not at the same time jettison the brilliant clinical insights of Freud or abandon the attempt to understand the impact of an analysand's past on current choices and behaviors.

What then does all this have to do with contemporary psychoanalysis? I believe it may allow us to understand and reframe a current difficulty in psychoanalytic theory as well as to draw some important implications for clinical practice.

A current crisis in psychoanalytic thinking

Jay Greenberg and Steven A. Mitchell, in their book *Object Relations in Psychoanalytic Theory* (1983), have pointed out that the premier problem in modern psychoanalysis is reconciling Freudian drive theory with the discovery of new relational needs. Of course, the interpersonal psychoanalysts, including Harry Stack Sullivan, Clara Thompson, and Frieda Fromm-Reichmann, had long insisted on the importance of the analyst–analysand relationship to analytic cure and on the relational needs of childhood. But the American ego psychologists, British and American object relations theorists, and American self psychologists take this understanding a step further. They present us with a whole intrapsychic world peopled by "internal objects" which are the residue of those earliest relationships. In doing so, they are more influenced by Freud's statement that the task of future analysts is to investigate the development of the ego from the earliest stages of infancy and childhood than they are by his drive-oriented metapsychology. They have often attempted to complete this mission by working with children and deeply disturbed persons, psychotics or people with character disorders, who were previously considered poor candidates for analysis. And they have taught us a great deal about what goes wrong in those earliest stages of development. But they have also discovered relational needs much at variance with Freudian drive theory – needs which can perhaps be better explained by Sartre's account of relations with the Other as subject than by Freud's theory of the other as libidinal object.

What is the profound discovery made by these theorists about the development of the ego? It is that "object relations," that is relations with others, shape the development of the ego. Theorists adopting this perspective include Melanie Klein (1975), W. R. D. Fairbairn (1954), D. W. Winnicott (1965a, 1965b, 1971), Harry Guntrip (1973), R. D. Laing (1959, 1961), Edith Jacobsen (1964), Heinz Kohut (1978), Otto Kernberg (1975), James Masterson (1981), and many others. And what is it about relations with others that is so crucial to development? Whether one calls this "reflected appraisals," as Sullivan (1953) did from his interpersonal perspective, or "mirroring," as modern ego psychologists, object relations theorists, and self psychologists tend to do, what is important is how the original others see and name the child. Where mirroring is highly distorted, manipulative, or lacking, pathology tends to develop. The child develops a "false self," as Winnicott (1965a, 1965b, 1971) says, an "as if personality" as Helene Deutsch ([1942] 1965) called it, or fails to develop a "real self," as James Masterson (1985) likes to say. Sometimes the result is a split self and split view of others, or split object relations unit, which Masterson says is the case with borderline personality disorders. Or one develops a grandiose self that demands adoring mirroring from others lest the empty, devalued self emerge, as happens with narcissists. As with Freud, the phenomena described are undoubtedly there. What we are going to object to is the mechanistic explanation, which may impact treatment.

First of all, there is the term "object relations." It derives, of course, from Freud's idea of the "libidinal object." The question is: are we talking here about either libido or the other as object? If the child needs mirroring from the mother and later the father to develop a coherent sense of self, is it not rather the child who is the object and the others who are perceived as subjects who see and name the child? In other words, are we not talking about a sense of self as object which develops normally beneath the accepting gaze of loving parents or abnormally beneath the unloving gaze of hostile, self-involved or indifferent parents? We are not, of course, talking about treating the child as an object like a table or chair. Merely meeting physical needs does not produce normal development, as Rene Spitz's (1965) films of infants in orphanages who died or became analytically depressed despite adequate physical care so poignantly demonstrate. Rather, we are talking about giving a child an adequate sense of self, a sense of "This is the person I am. What I experience inside matches in some way with the information I am given from the outside. I am OK." Libido is not an issue here. This is not a matter of drive hunger. It is a matter of identity hunger.

From the perspective of drive theory, this makes little sense. For example, Mahler's account of early infantile development does not accord well with the idea of the mother as libidinal object (Mahler *et al.* 1975). Mahler tells us that the practically newborn infant develops a smiling response sooner and is otherwise more developmentally precocious if the mother gazes at the infant as the infant nurses rather than props a bottle beside the infant or turns her attention elsewhere. She points out that similar needs for mirroring obtain throughout the "pre-Oedipal" subphases. The infant and young child discover both body self and psychological self through interactions with others. If the original others fail to accept and more or less accurately mirror the child's experience, if they are too intrusive or too distant, then according to Winnicott, Mahler, and others the child will develop a false self which is more interested in compliance and pleasing others than in self-expression and autonomy.

From a Sartrean perspective, the experience being described here has nothing at all to do with "object relations" in the Freudian sense. It has to do with my discovery of the Other as another subject and my attempt to appropriate this discovery into a project of discovering who or what I am. The discovery of the subjectivity of the Other is made through an experience which Sartre calls the "Look." Unlike Freud, who believed that, like the assumption of consciousness in animals, "the assumption of a consciousness in [others] rests upon an inference and cannot share the immediate certainty which we have of our own consciousness" (Freud [1915] 1953–74: 169), Sartre believed that we have an experience of "apodictic certainty" of the presence of the Other as subject. We do not infer or hypothesize it, we know it through a shudder in our being.

Sartre gives as an example of the Look a man looking through a keyhole, totally absorbed in the scene inside a room. Suddenly he hears footsteps. The shift in consciousness that occurs, from sovereign subject to shameful object, makes one simultaneously experience the other as subject and oneself as object. Obviously, this does not necessarily have to be a physical look, since a blind person can also experience the Look; it can also be a touch or a word which gives me that same shudder. The object that this person is encountering is none other than myself, and it is a self which I shall never know in the same way that the other knows it. It is here that the search for a solid sense of self begins in earnest. It is a desire that can never be fulfilled. I can never know myself in the same way that the other knows me or that I know objects in the world. I am both too close and too distant from the self I would know.

Nonetheless, the ego psychologists and object relations theorists are in a certain sense correct: the reflections of the original others are important to my psychological health or illness. It is important for me to develop an adequate ego, so long as we understand that we are talking about the ego as an object not as a subject and that to some extent – not totally, as Jacques Lacan would have us believe – the ego is an illusion. Certainly, as Lacan followed Sartre in reiterating, with respect to the ego, "I is another" (Sartre [1937] 1957: 97; Lacan [1966] 1977: 23, [1978] 1988: 7), in the sense that the "I" identified in my discourse when I speak of my-self as a person with such and such qualities is other than the speaker. The nothingness that separates the subject of the discourse from the object of the discourse is unsurpassable.

Yet we all continue to act as if the subject speaking and the "I" spoken of were identical. Sartre explains in a passage from the first volume of his biography of Flaubert why this illusion of identity, which he calls a "true lie," is necessary to human development. There Sartre discusses the way in which Flaubert's mother treated him as a mere object in earliest in-fancy, without the maternal love and the kind of loving touch which invokes the infant to experience himself as a valued object and hence to go forth to try out his subjecthood. The love of the parents guarantees the valorized child's value and mission – a mission which "becomes a sovereign choice, permitted and evoked in the subjective person by the presence of self-worth" (Sartre [1971] 1981: 135). Without this mandate to live, which Sartre acknowledges is more often than not missing in children's interactions with their parents, a child will be left afloat in a meaningless universe where physical laws perhaps point to a sense of a future but where one's own existence appears senseless or wrong. Time, for such children, becomes "a slack succession of present moments that slip back into the past" (Sartre [1971] 1981: 134), leaving them unable to cross the "barrier of the moment" (Sartre [1971] 1981: 133) to create a meaningful existence. In this way, unvalorized children, such as Sartre imagines was the case with Flaubert, are discouraged from experiencing themselves as agents. Because the past holds no empathic nourishment, the future holds no promise.

A reader familiar only with the early work of Sartre may be wondering at this point whether this sense of a meaningless universe, upon which the individual must impose meaning, is not exactly what Sartre himself has declared to be the case. Is this not the familiar existential *angst* over the absurdity of human existence? And from this perspective, is the valorized child's sense of mission not an expression of bad faith because it rests on the a priori mandate of the parents? Is the "teleological urgency" (Sartre [1971] 1981: 133) of the loved child not based on an illusion? Sartre replies that the mandate to live is, in fact, a necessary deception that makes possible a later encounter with the truth of existence. The sense-less existence which the unloved child discovers in himself or herself, echoed in the borderline client's complaints of emptiness and lack of pur-pose or direction in life, is a lying truth, whereas the meaningfulness which the loved child has conferred on him or her is a true lie.

Sartre therefore believes that the "ethical-ontological" truth that one must create one's own value "must be revealed slowly" at the "end of a long vagabond delusion" (Sartre [1971] 1981: 136). To reveal it earlier through lack of valorization is to subject the child to the delusion not simply of being unjustified but of being "unjustifiable" – that is, unable to make a meaningful life – which is "a hundred times farther from his real condition" than the lying truth which convinces the loved child that he or she is justified in advance (Sartre [1971] 1981: 136). The lie of the parental mandate leads to the truth of discovering one's existence as a temporal being who creates meaning. Thus we come to understand the borderline client's complaints of meaninglessness and emptiness as a lack of ego development in the Sartrean rather than the Freudian sense.

From a Sartrean perspective, then, there are no internalized objects in the sense of components of a reified psyche. Nor is there an ego that con-tains these internalized objects in the usual sense. Yet there is the impact of the *Looks*, touches and words of the original others on the developing self – and the way in which their way of regarding one becomes part of one's way of reflectively characterizing the self. The ultimate explan-ation for this incorporation of the voices of others into one's mode of reflecting on the self is ontological: it lies in the desire of the for-itself, as Sartre says, to be a freedom which is its own foundation: Being-in-itself-for-itself. It is an impossible desire. As Sartre says, "Impure reflection is an abortive effort on the part of the for-itself *to be another* while *remain-ing itself*" (Sartre [1943] 1956: 226, emphases in original). I can never co-incide with the self I am in the process of bringing into being or with the other who sees and names me. The attempt to do so is a project in "bad faith" or lying to myself about the nature of reality. The ego remains al-ways an object and never a subject. I am never going to *be somebody*, in popular phraseology, as a tree is a tree. I cannot escape my freedom, my *no-thingness*.

Implications for clinical practice

What does this Sartrean shift in perspective suggest would be the goal of analytic treatment and the role of the analyst? Must we build ego in the analysand with a defective ego, as many contemporary psychoanalysts suggest? In a certain sense, this is correct, if by it we mean that the analysand who has never received adequate mirroring must receive something similar to this from the analyst, as Kohut (1978) thinks. However, there is more to the situation than this. As Masterson (1981) points out, the acting out borderline patient needs more than mirroring; he or she needs confrontation about the self-destructive behavior. Also, even the narcissist will not get better simply by receiving empathic mirroring. Indeed if what is mirrored is the grandiose self, rather than the narcissistic wound, such mirroring may perpetuate the narcissist's illness.

In addition, even the most severely character disordered analysand has developed an ego of sorts. To be sure, it is a fragile and unstable ego based on an identity derived from the proposition that "I am bad, wrong, unimportant, or falsely important in order to hide my defectiveness." Yet for all of us, with whatever varying degree of psychopathology we manifest, the reactions of others and even their lack of reactions are incorporated into our developing sense of self. Hence the ego must not only be built in therapy but dismantled at the same time. Even the most deeply disturbed individual must come face to face with the existential truth that the ego as subject is an illusion in the course of a thorough analysis. Otherwise one simply substitutes one "false self on a compliance basis" for another. In the course of this dismantling, an uneasy truth inevitably dawns on the analysand: there is no solid self. The dismantling of the ego therefore involves deep anxiety, even in less severely disturbed analysands. It is even more difficult for those who are more severely disturbed, though in some sense they are more familiar with it because of the terrible "disintegration anxiety" (Erik Erikson's (1959) term) they have so often experienced as a result of not having developed a viable and stable sense of self.

An example is a woman whose therapy I describe in the last chapter of *Sartre and Psychoanalysis* (Cannon 1991). This woman, whom I call Martha, probably fits Masterson's description of the "closet narcissist," the analysand who presents as unassuming but who has the same issues with mirroring that the overt narcissist does. The difference is that the overt narcissist seeks to have his or her grandiosity mirrored by others in order to avoid feelings of emptiness and loss of self, while the closet narcissist seeks to mirror some grandiose other and thereby derive a sense of self. When Martha first came to see me, she was experiencing severe disintegration anxiety because of the breakup of a love relationship. Without her lover to mirror, she felt she had lost all sense of self. After several years of therapy, she began to know in a very deep way the family origins of her decision to "be the perfect mirror." She also started to develop other kinds of relationships, ones where she allowed more reciprocity and attention to her own needs. As this happened, she became once again very anxious. She experienced heart palpitations and a sense of having no ground beneath her feet. She felt she was standing over an abyss. Self and world both felt very nebulous. "Who will I *be* if I stop being the perfect mirror?" she wailed in one session.

As time went on, Martha discovered that she did not die in the course of letting go her old sense of self/world, which, defective and unsatisfactory though it was, was the only self/world she had ever known. The old ego did, in a sense, die, since she was no longer attached to it and therefore no longer willing to sustain it. And although the support of having me as a witness to her newly developing way of being in the world was certainly important, it did not hide the fact that she did not have a "self" in the sense of a fixed entity. In this sense, the therapy did not build ego structure in the psyche, though it did allow her to take a new and different look at herself. As Martha put all this toward the end of therapy: "I find it scary to realize how fluid I am, but I guess that's what being alive is all about." I could not help thinking of Sartre's idea of the lightness and anxiety associated with the "spirit of play," which is the spirit in which we encounter our freedom.

None of this, I think, is recognized quite so well in classical or even contemporary psychoanalysis. I think it is important, particularly since anxiety over the confrontation with one's freedom, one's *no-thingness,* could be mistaken for the other kind of anxiety which Freud rightly associated with the "return of the repressed." It is not helpful at this point in therapy to return to analysis of the past, though the analysand would be ever so happy to do so. Rather, what must be kept in focus is the deep uncanny feeling of discovering that neither self nor world are what one had previously taken them to be, indeed of discovering that one has no self in the usual sense. The analysand at this point in therapy will at times most likely appear to "regress," with old difficulties reappearing with a vengeance, as tends to happen each time one makes a significant change that threatens the old sense of self. If the analyst misses the point and fails to recognize the existential anxiety that motivates the regression, this can set the therapy back considerably if not provide a permanent stumbling block. If significant change is to take place, what must be understood and worked with is the fact that the client is anxious about the loss of a solid sense of self, however miserable, rather than about facing any particular unpleasant or painful truth about oneself or one's life.

Sartre calls the moment of significant change in which one takes a different vantage point on being in the world the "psychological instant." It is a moment of "double nothingness" (Sartre [1943] 1956: 466) because I find that I am no longer what I was, and that I am no longer in the process of becoming what I was about to become. I take a different perspective on both past and future. It is as though I am suspended over an abyss, grasping in order to let go and letting go in order to grasp a new way of being in the world. Of course, it is not an instant or a moment in any static sense, since time is a continuous flow. Also, the process usually takes place over time, with many starts and stops, though there are some instances of sudden shifts that affect a lifetime. They are usually referred to as conversions, whether of a religious or a secular nature. The important point is that significant change is frightening because it is not simply the case that one trades one static self for another, better static self in an unchanging world. Rather, because consciousness is always intentional, that is, always world-connected, self and world both change together. I find myself acting differently and apprehending a different world. People can be quite articulate about this. They often speak of feeling like they are suspended over a void, of feeling like the ground beneath their feet is giving way, of not knowing themselves any more, and, in the beginning, of feeling confused and unable to remember a session.

An example is a woman in group therapy who protected herself by being suspicious of the motives of others. She said to another group member,

> I was wishing you would call me and when you did I found myself wondering what it was you wanted from me. When I hung up the phone, I started to cry because I realized you were just reaching out to me. I guess it's hard for me to accept that because things might start to be really different then. I mean I might start to be really different.

She meant both.

Consider also the situation of a man with whom I worked who had been depressed and socially isolated since early childhood. As he began to discover a sense of humor in himself and a capacity for connection in the course of therapy, he started to feel intolerable anxiety. As he put this experience, "At least I know this lousy, withdrawn self. I've always been him. But this new person frightens me to death. I feel paralyzed. I can't go back and I can't go forward." I asked him to substitute "won't" for "can't": I won't go back and I won't go forward. This man's anxiety was obviously not about the return of the repressed at this point in therapy, though we had done much exploration of his unhappy childhood and the feelings he could not allow himself to experience there. It was about moving forth into a future in which self and world both felt alien.

When I as an analysand allow myself to comprehend the significance of a symptom or painful way of being in the world, I will feel threatened on two counts. The significance of my symptom will threaten the equi-librium I have precariously established in order to go on living an early intolerable situation – which I experience as being recapitulated in the present. This is the return of the repressed in Freudian terms. But giving up the symptom will also threaten to destabilize my sense of self in another way: I will no longer be who I have been, and the world will no longer be what it has been. Hence understanding the significance of my symptom makes me doubly anxious. I am anxious about the return of the repressed because it destabilizes me, and I am anxious about the destruc-tion of my previous sense of self/world because it announces to me that I have no solid self. The two, of course, are obviously linked, which is part of what makes significant change so difficult.

Yet it is the very source of existential anxiety, the fact that I am not a solid self, which is the condition that makes deep level change possible. The man I mentioned above with serious depression, who was a scientist by profession, often invoked a rather twisted version of the scientific method as proof that his future life would always be miserable: "I'm a scientist," he would say, "and as a scientist I know that the past predicts the future." This, of course, is exactly what existentialism denies is the case in human affairs. It took an experience as a member of a therapy group to provoke this man to change his worldview. In the group, he for the first time experienced himself as belonging somewhere and people as responding to him in what he clearly could not deny was a positive fashion. The group appreciated his intelligence, his sensitivity to other members, and his capacity for capturing experience in metaphor. Group members alternately sympathized and felt angry with his negativity and expressed both with directness and care. After a time, he sank into a deeper depression. He dismissed the experience in the group as being "in here" whereas "out there in the real world" things were and would always be as they had been. He reported that he often felt good at the end of group, but could not hold onto the feeling for more than thirty minutes before his negative thinking totally obliterated the experience. He was not even sure he wanted to hold onto the good feelings, since he regarded them as false.

Finally, he announced that he was leaving the group, quitting his job, and, he implied, leaving the world through suicide. The group and I were quite concerned. He did agree to come to the next several group meetings and not to harm himself for a specified amount of time. Finally, one night, listening to another group member grieve the loss of a friend by suicide and having group members extend themselves to him one more time, he began to make a miraculous turn around. "Now I understand what love is," he said, "and I want it." A group member gave him a stone to help him remember the good feeling in the group, and he used it to link his experience in the group with his experience outside. He went on, with some ups and downs, to transform his life. He began to spend time with people, to develop friendships and interests, and to go on long hikes by himself where before he had sat alone in his apartment watching television. He also began to mourn the many years he had spent in black depression. In one of his images, he saw himself as liberating a small boy from a cave filled with stalagmites and stalactites that were frozen tears. His life was not perfect at this point, but for the first time, as he put it, he began to feel himself "a part of the human race."

Obviously, what is going on in this situation is something other than analysis that aims only to make the unconscious conscious or to work through personal historical material. It is true that we deceive ourselves and others without knowing that we do so. It is true that the place where our worldview was first formed is our personal past and that this most often must be explored if significant change is to take place. It is also true that analysis at its best helps us to get at our own truth and hence at more authentic living. What is going on in this man's case, in addition to all this, is exploring his attachment to the old self and his existential anxiety about changing – a subject on which he was very articulate when he said that he might rather die than face the anxiety of changing.

Such is the goal of analysis from an existentialist perspective: to facilitate a situation in which the analysand goes beyond merely reconstructing the past and uncovering repressed material to discover that the ego itself is an illusion. In doing so, the analysand will simultaneously be faced with the possibility of a radical reorientation of his or her way of being in the world.

The analytic relationship

What then is the analyst's role in this voyage of discovery? Is it analytic neutrality or some other attitude? What techniques will the Sartrean analyst use? Obviously, from what I have said so far, the analyst is a certain kind of witness. The analyst's Look is important to the analysand's healing. It heals the previously distorting looks of the original others by allowing the analysand to comprehend himself or herself in a different way. Of course, the analyst will not be able to provide perfect understanding. Indeed a part of therapy, as Kohut (1978) so well recognized, involves the recognition that no one, including the analyst, can provide perfect mirroring. The analyst can only be a "good enough" analyst in a way that is perhaps similar to that in which Winnicott's "good enough mother" provides more or less what the child needs. It is also true that the therapist's Look can be a source of further alienation from the self if it does not promote the "explosion of the agent," to use Sartre's term, not only into the analytic setting, but also into the analysand's life.

How do we effect this? Sartre suggests that without reciprocity analytic cure is impossible. After all, the man with the tape recorder gets revenge; he does not, presumably, get well. Does Sartre mean that the analyst should treat the analysand as an equal, that they should be compatriots in the analysis? In a certain sense, he does. Sartre believes that the analysand's cure has to take place in a "joint undertaking in which each person takes his chances and assumes his responsibilities" (Sartre [1972] 1979: 201). He admires Laing and Basaglia, who are "seeking to establish a bond of reciprocity between themselves and those they are treating" (Sartre [1972] 1979: 204). And he dislikes interpretations that "come" to the analysand "anonymously, like stone tablets," rather than being "proposed to him in the course of a long common adventure" (Sartre [1972] 1979: 201). Certainly he has insisted, from *Being and Nothingness* onward, that existential psychoanalysis claims the "final intuition of the subject" rather than the pronouncements of the analyst as "decisive" (Sartre [1943] 1956: 733).

Yet Sartre also understands that the analysand is a "damaged, derailed subject" (Sartre [1972] 1979: 201) attempting to recover himself. If we take Sartre's own developmental principles, we can further elaborate on the analyst's role. First of all, at the beginning of analysis, only a modicum of "reciprocity" may be possible because the analysand's project of being with others precludes it to a greater or lesser extent, and this is usually the more true the more deeply disturbed the analysand. Second, the analysand is seeking the analyst as a new kind of Look to neutralize the original Looks that led to the analysand's difficulties in the first place. There is no strict equality in such a relationship. Yet at the same time, psychoanalysis traditionally insists on the importance of the therapeutic alliance; it is in the context of this alliance that the transference can be analyzed. Such an alliance suggests mutuality. To this extent, Sartre would agree with the premises of traditional psychoanalysis.

What more does Sartre require of the existential psychoanalyst? One thing more is required of both analyst and analysand at moments of significant change in therapy. They must embrace their own and the other's freedom. Perhaps this is also the end point of normal development, the point where the developing child or adolescent or young adult lets go of the "true lie" of his or her a priori value as conferred by the loving parents and understands that value is created rather than given – that oneself and others are never what they are but are always becoming. The self never is; it is always in the making.

Perhaps what Sartre means by reciprocity in the psychoanalytic session can better be grasped by an example. A good illustration occurs in a videotape in which R. D. Laing interviews a homeless paranoid schizophrenic woman at the Milton Erikson Foundation's Evolution of Psychotherapy Conference in Phoenix in 1980. The circumstances are certainly a challenge to reciprocity, since the interview takes place before video cameras in a room beyond which a live audience of about a thousand people is watching. The woman begins by noting fairly soon that she knows that Laing can read her mind. Unlike the psychiatrists and social workers from the homeless shelter where the woman is being treated, who display their expertise and distance in the panel discussion following the interview, Laing allows himself to enter the woman's phenomenal world and talk with her as one human being to another about the "conspiracy" she perceives around her of which she supposes (if it exists) he is a part. Occasionally, he reveals a piece of personal information when this might be helpful to her, as when he says, in response to her saying she needs to ask her parents whether she can send them Christmas gifts that he couldn't imagine needing to *ask* his parents that. But mostly he is simply present with her in a very human way, gently nudging the conversation toward her deepest concerns.

Laing and his patient discuss philosophical questions such as how God or universal consciousness can allow evil. By the time they are finished talking, the woman is not only making contact with Laing but also asks to go with him to meet the audience. She is by this time quite coherent, answering questions and joking with Laing, the audience, and panel members. During the interview, Laing had taken her discussion of a conspiracy and turned it toward the possible benign conspiracy that the conference might be. Laing again discusses the "divine conspiracy" which has brought the audience together and its hellish counterpart. And she jokingly tells the audience, "I don't know for sure about a conspiracy. *This guy* says there's one." Her transformation, in fact, is so complete that her psychiatrist on the panel feels the need to assure the audience that she is atypical of the poor psychotic souls usually dealt with at the shelter whom no one can love.

As audience members question and sometimes quarrel with Laing about his "technique" in working with this woman, she continues to interact with him and them in a very human, seemingly normal way. Finally the family therapist Salvadore Minuchin attempts to explain the conundrum to the audience: what they have seen is not the effects of technique (though he notes that Laing *is* very skillful at "joining" her), but the effects of "love" – in the words of the philosopher Martin Buber ([1923] 1970), an I–Thou encounter between Laing and this woman. The contrast between Laing's attitude and that of the other panelists and some audience members could not be more striking. He is willing to enter this woman's world and to dialogue with her about her experienced reality, and the results are remarkable. He is willing at times to put himself at risk, noting similarities and differences between her world and his. While one may doubt that Laing has fully "cured" this woman in a single session, there is no doubt about the healing nature of the human encounter seen on the tape.

I believe this is similar to what Sartre means by "reciprocity" in the psychoanalytic session. Reciprocity is not abdication of responsibility in the sense of being chums with one's analysands. Rather it is the willingness to enter their worlds and to risk oneself through genuine dialogue. It also must include the willingness to be a different kind of witness than the original others – not to step into the parents' shoes and take their place in the process of failed mirroring in the child's early development, but to provide the kind of Look that allows the analysand to look at his or her life anew and to begin to live in a radically different way. It means promoting and accepting the "irruption of the subject into the consulting room." Because Laing is willing to allow this paranoid schizophrenic woman a voice and to listen to what she says as the utterances of a human being like himself, she takes on the task of speaking to an audience of a thousand people in a way that she has perhaps never spoken to anyone in her life.

Reciprocity begets reciprocity. It is born not of a belief in the determined nature of human beings, but of a recognition of my own and the other's freedom, no matter how damaged and unfree I or the other feel. It involves a deconstruction of the ego, but not a deconstruction of subjective consciousness. Of course, it also includes compassion in the face of suffering, past and present. Analytic neutrality is good if what we mean is not imposing ourselves on the analysand and creating a space for the unfoldment of his or her process. But it is not good if it means the kind of distance into which the utterances of the analysand fall like "petrified thoughts" and the interpretations of the analyst come like "stone tablets." Where, after all, am I as a derailed subject going to learn reciprocity if I do not experience it in the therapeutic encounter?

Conclusion

Throughout this chapter, I have suggested that a Sartrean perspective could free the contemporary psychoanalyst from tendencies to reify the psyche which may get in the way of effective clinical practice. If we recognize, as Sartre does, that consciousness is always world consciousness, we will understand that our therapeutic task is to encounter the individual analysand in the process of world making and to call attention to this process in such a way that significant change can take place. In doing so, we will be less likely to objectify the analysand and more likely to recognize when an analysand is approaching one of those moments of significant change which make the whole analysis worthwhile. We will work with existential anxiety as well as neurotic anxiety and be able to distinguish between the two. We will look at the future as meaning as well as the past as ground to an analysand's project. We will understand why it was so important that the young child receive accurate and empathic mirroring from the original others as subjects (not objects) and why it is so important to receive something like this from the analyst as the analysand remakes his or her project of being. We will understand that analysis is a joint project in which two subjects encounter each other in the subject–object alternation. And we will value the free determination that the analysand chooses to make of this new situation and the risks that we ourselves must take in this authentic encounter.

References

Binswanger, L. (1963) *Being in the World*, ed. and trans. J. Needleman, with critical commentary. New York and London: Basic Books.

Boss, M. (1957) *The Analysis of Dreams*. London: Ryder.

—— (1963) *Psychoanalysis and Daseinsanalysis*, trans. L. B. Lefebre. New York: Basic Books.

Buber, M. ([1923] 1970) *I and Thou*, trans. W. Kaufmann. New York: Charles Scribner's Sons.

Cannon, B. (1991) *Sartre and Psychoanalysis: An Existentialist Challenge to Clinical Metatheory*, Lawrence, KS: University Press of Kansas.

Deutsch, H. ([1942] 1965) "Some forms of emotional disturbances and their relationship to schizophrenia," *Psychoanalytic Quarterly* 11: 301–21, reprinted in *Neurosis and Character Types*. New York: International Universities Press.

Erikson, E. (1959) *Identity and the Life Cycle*. New York: International Universities Press.

Fairbairn, W. R. D. ([1954] 1984) *Psychoanalytic Studies of the Personality*. London: Routledge & Kegan Paul.

Frankl, V. K. ([1959] 1985) *Man's Search for Meaning: An Introduction to Logotherapy*. New York: Pocket Books.

Freud, S. ([1914–15] 1953–74) "On the history of the psychoanalytic movement" and "The unconscious," in *The Standard Edition of the Complete Psychological Works of Sigmund Freud*, vol. 14, ed. and trans. J. Strachey. London: Hogarth Press.

Greenberg, J. R. and Mitchell, S. A. (1983) *Object Relations in Psychoanalytic Theory*. Cambridge, MA and London: Harvard University Press.

Guntrip, H. ([1969] 1985) *Schizoid Phenomena, Object-Relations and the Self*. New York: International Universities Press.

—— (1973) *Psychoanalytic Theory, Therapy, and the Self*. New York: Basic Books.

Heidegger, M. ([1927] 1962) *Being and Time*, trans. J. Macquarrie and E. Robinson. London: SCM Press.

Husserl, E. ([1913] 1967) *Ideas*, trans. W. R. Boyce Gibson. New York and London: Collier Books.

Jacobsen, E. ([1964] 1986) *The Self and the Object World*. Madison, CT: International Universities Press.

Kernberg, O. F. ([1975] 1985) *Borderline Conditions and Pathological Narcissism*. New York: Jason Aronson.

Klein, M. (1975) *Envy and Gratitude and Other Works, 1943–1963*. New York: Delacorte Press.

Kohut, H. (1978) *The Search for the Self: Selected Writings of Heinz Kohut: 1950–1978*, 2 vols, ed. P. H. Ornstein. New York: International Universities Press.

Lacan, J. ([1966] 1977) *Ecrits*, trans. A. Sheridan. New York: W. W. Norton.

—— ([1978] 1988) *The Seminar of Jacques Lacan: Book II – The Ego in Freud's Theory and in the Technique of Psychoanalysis, 1954-55*, trans. S. Tomaselli, with notes by J. Forrester, and ed. J-A. Miller. New York: W. W. Norton.

Laing, R. D. ([1959] 1979) *The Divided Self*. New York: Penguin.

—— ([1961] 1976) *Self and Others*. New York and London: Penguin.

Laing, R. D. and Cooper, D. G. ([1964] 1971) *Reason and Violence*. New York: Vintage Books.

—— (1980) "Existential psychotherapy." Videotape. Phoenix, AZ: Evolution of Psychotherapy Conference (presented by the Milton Erikson Foundation).

Mahler, M. S., Pine, F., and Bergman, A. (1975) *The Psychological Birth of the Human Infant*. New York: Basic Books.

Masterson, J. (1981) *The Narcissistic and Borderline Disorders: An Integrated Developmental Approach*. New York: Brunner/Mazel.

—— (1985) *The Real Self: A Developmental, Self, and Object Relations Approach*. New York: Brunner/Mazel.

May, R., Angel, E. and Ellenberger, H. (eds.) (1958) *Existence: A New Dimension in Psychiatry and Psychology*. New York: Basic Books.

Sartre, J-P. ([1937] 1957) *The Transcendence of the Ego* [La Transcendance de l'ego], trans. R. Kirkpatrick and F. Williams. New York: Farrar, Straus and Giroux.

—— ([1943] 1956) *Being and Nothingness: An Essay on Phenomenological Ontology* [L'Etre et le neant: essai d'ontologie phenomenologique], trans. H. E. Barnes. New York: Philosophical Library.

—— ([1946] 1950) *Baudelaire*, trans. M. Turnell. New York: New Directions.

—— ([1952] 1963) *Saint Genet: Actor and Martyr* [Saint Genet, comedien et martyr], trans. B. Frechtman. New York: George Braziller.

—— ([1960a] 1968) *Search for a Method* [Questions de methode], trans. H. E. Barnes. New York: Vintage Books.

—— ([1960b] 1982) *Critique of Dialectical Reason* [Critique de la raison dialectique], ed. J. Ree and trans. A. Sheridan-Smith. London: Verso/New Left Books.

—— (1963) *The Words* [Les Mots], trans. B. Frechtman. New York: George Braziller.

—— ([1971] 1981, 1987) *The Family Idiot* [L'Idiot de la famille], 2 vols, trans. C. Cosman. Chicago: University of Chicago Press.

—— ([1972] 1979) *Between Existentialism and Marxism* [Situations VIII and IX], trans. J. Mathews. New York: Morrow Quill.

—— (1986) *Quintin Hoare*. Chicago: University of Chicago Press.

Schafer, R. (1976) *A New Language for Psychoanalysis*. New Haven, CT: Yale University Press.

Spitz, R. (1965) *The First Year of Life*. New York: International Universities Press.

Sullivan, H. S. (1953) *The Interpersonal Theory of Psychiatry*. New York: W. W. Norton.

Winnicott, D. W. (1965a) *The Family and Individual Development*. London: Tavistock.

—— (1965b) *The Maturational Process and the Facilitating Environment*. New York: International Universities Press.

—— ([1971] 1985) *Playing and Reality*. London: Tavistock.

Chapter 2

Martin Buber and dialogical psychotherapy

Maurice Friedman

The philosopher Martin Buber is known worldwide for his classic work *I and Thou*. His "philosophy of dialogue" has had a tremendous impact on philosophy in general, and on the philosophy of religion, education, aesthetics, and social thought in particular. What is less known is that Buber's philosophy of dialogue has also had a striking influence on the theory and practice of psychotherapy and even on psychoanalysis. This chapter has two objectives. The first is to show the clinical relevance of Buber's philosophy of dialogue and to present the elements of dialogical psychotherapy as I have formulated them, based, for the most part, on Buber's thought. I show that Buber's philosophy of dialogue enables us to see the way in which relationships determine uniqueness in individuals, but also the way in which unique individuals determine the relationships they are in. As such, Buber's philosophy, and my own "dialogue of touchstones," falls between the essentialist approach of modernism and the social constructivist approach of post-modernism. I then provide a case example to demonstrate the clinical perspective of dialogical psychotherapy. The second objective of this chapter is to provide a historical and contemporary outline of the dialogical psychotherapy movement. I draw a contrast between "therapists of dialogue" who use some of the elements of dialogical psychotherapy in their theory and practice without making "healing through meeting" central, and the "dialogical psychotherapists" who, directly influenced by Buber's philosophy of dialogue, make healing through meeting central to their theory and practice. Finally, I examine certain interpersonal and relational psychoanalysts who, under the direct or indirect influence of Buber, integrate the notion of healing through meeting into their clinical work.

The life of dialogue

Dialogical psychotherapy is based in most cases on Martin Buber's philosophy of dialogue and his philosophical anthropology – the study of the wholeness and uniqueness of the human being. In his classic work *I and Thou* Buber (1958) distinguishes between the "I–Thou" relationship that is direct, mutual, present, and open, and the "I–It," or subject–object, relation in which one relates to the other only indirectly and non-mutually, knowing and using the other. What is essential is not what goes on within the minds of the partners in a relationship but what happens *between* them. For this reason, Buber is unalterably opposed to that psychologism that wishes to remove the reality of relationship into the separate psyches of the participants. "The inmost growth of the self does not take place, as people like to suppose today," writes Buber, "through our relationship to ourselves, but through being made present by the other and knowing that we are made present by him" (Buber 1988: 61).

Being made present as a person is the heart of what Buber calls confirmation. Confirmation is interhuman, but it is not simply social or interpersonal. Unless one is confirmed in one's uniqueness as the person one can become, one is only seemingly confirmed. The confirmation of the other must include an actual experiencing of the other side of the relationship so that one can imagine quite concretely what another is feeling, thinking, and knowing. This "inclusion," or imagining the real, does not abolish the basic distance between oneself and the other. It is rather a bold swinging over into the life of the person one confronts, through which alone I can make that person present in his or her wholeness, unity, and uniqueness.

This experiencing of the other side is essential to the distinction that Buber makes between "dialogue," in which I open myself to the otherness of the person I meet, and "monologue," in which, even when I converse with the person at length, I allow him or her to exist only as a content of my experience. Wherever one lets the other exist only as part of oneself, "dialogue becomes a fiction, the mysterious intercourse between two human worlds only a game, and in the rejection of the real life confronting him the essence of all reality begins to disintegrate" (Buber 1985: 24).

Buber's I–Thou philosophy is concerned with the difference between mere existence and authentic existence, between being human at all and being more fully human, between remaining fragmented and bringing the conflicting parts of oneself into an active unity, between partial and fuller relationships with others. No one ever becomes a "whole person." But one may move in the direction of greater wholeness through greater awareness and fuller response in each new situation.

It is an illusion to think that genuine relationship can be achieved when two people or groups of people are focused on getting their needs met, even if in the interest of self-discovery, personal wholeness or spiritual growth. A genuine relationship must cultivate the total ground of existence. This means I cannot simply lay claim to you or your abilities because it suits my interests. Even if I believe we share an interest that requires you to do something for me, I cannot make real the life of dialogue between us by claiming your attention, time or resources in the name of intimacy or community.

In relationship together, it is important that we set one another at a distance and view each other as independent. This enables us to enter into relationship as *individual* selves with those like ourselves. The very essence and meaning of the self is this interrelatedness. I am called into being by you and you by me. When you embrace me as the unique person that I am and when you confront me in your own uniqueness, we confirm each other, not as role models for each other, but as the unique persons we are called to become. By bridging the distance between us and repeatedly entering into relationship with each other, we cultivate the sphere of the between and strengthen the "we" that Buber describes.

We are used to thinking in terms of polarities – the individual versus community, or inner versus outer. But to see only the polar extremes obscures a great deal of human reality. The primary human reality is the life of dialogue that takes place *in* family and *in* community. To view the individual or the community outside the context of the life of dialogue is like trying to draw a map of the world with only the north and south poles as references. For the life of dialogue the self versus the world is an abstract notion. The self in the world is the basic reality we all share. While we exist in many and often different modes, sometimes pitted against the world and sometimes part of it, the life of dialogue calls each of us to respond to the unique moment and circumstance in which we find ourselves. To this extent, the life of dialogue stands on the narrow ridge between a complete withdrawal from the world and a complete surrender to it.

Inner and outer are constructions arising from a human wholeness that precedes them both and gives rise to them. Only the possibility of direct contact between whole human beings gives rise to the sphere of the between. Divisions between inner and outer are useful for a certain ordering of our lives, such as the distinction between what we see, what we dream, what we envision, and what we hallucinate. Yet a true event in our lives is neither inner nor outer but takes up and claims the whole of us. When I give a lecture there is no way I can divide the event into inner feelings and outer impressions. My response to the audience comes from the whole of who I am as I stand in their presence and experience, both psychically and physically, the event.

Only if we can get beyond this deep-seated construct of inner and outer can we understand the sense in which the life of dialogue can alone be fully realized in the sphere of the between. I meet you from my ground and you meet me from yours, and our lives interpenetrate as person meeting person in the life of dialogue. Our very sense of ourselves comes only in our meeting with others as they confirm us in the life of dialogue. It is through this confirmation that we can grow to the strength of Socrates, who said, "I respect you, Athenians. But I will obey the god and not you." Socrates made his contribution when he expressed his responsibility to his fellow Athenians – precisely in opposing them. But if Socrates had not had seventy years of confirmation in the life of dialogue with his family of origin, his own wife and children, and the Athenians with whom he met in daily discussion, he would not have been able to stand his ground.

The uniqueness that one partner experiences in genuine dialogue with another is hidden from the individual who comes merely as objective observer, scientifically curious analyst, or prying manipulator. We cannot and will not allow another to "see into our soul" if we sense a prying, unsafe or indifferent presence. That is why a friend can understand another friend's troubles in a way that the trained psychologist with thematic apperception tests cannot, even though the psychologist may provide a more accurate "objective" and clinical description of the friend's problem. For example, after being presented with the results of an assessment, a patient remarked to the psychologist that undertook the testing: "But *you* don't know me at all!" The psychologist replied: "I know all I need to know about you. I have seen the results of your MMPI [Minnesota Multiphasic Personality Inventory]." If we sense that someone is trying to find out "what makes us tick," we may shut off precisely those parts of us that make us unique persons.

By dialogical psychotherapy, then, we mean a therapy that is centered on the *meeting* between the therapist and his or her client or among family members as the central healing mode, whatever analysis, role-playing, or other therapeutic techniques or activities may also enter in. If the psychoanalyst is seen as an indispensable midwife in bringing up material from the unconscious to the conscious, this is not yet "healing through meeting." Only when it is recognized that everything that takes place within therapy – free association, dreams, silence, pain, anguish – takes place within the context of the vital relationship between therapist and patient do we have what may properly be called dialogical psychotherapy. Healing through meeting is a two-sided event that is not susceptible to techniques in the sense of willing and manipulating in order to bring about a certain result. What is crucial is not the skill of the therapist but, rather, what takes place between the therapist and the client and between the client and other people – what Aleene Friedman calls "The Healing Partnership" (A. M. Friedman 1992).

To become aware of a person, Buber points out, means to perceive his or her wholeness as a person defined by spirit: to perceive the dynamic center that stamps on all utterances, actions, and attitudes the recognizable sign of uniqueness. Such an awareness is impossible if, and as long as, the other is for me the detached object of my observation, for that person will not thus yield his or her wholeness and its center. It is possible only when he or she becomes present for me as a partner in dialogue.

From my reading, most postmodern writers seem to think that one must either see the self as an essential, non-relational entity or as a social construct, the product of social interaction with no uniqueness of its own. This is an unnecessary and untrue either/or distinction that fails to recognize that in the life of dialogue the self discovers and realizes its uniqueness precisely in the dialogue with the other, the Thou. Because of the analytical, reductive, and deriving look that prevails today, writes Buber, the mystery between man and man is in danger of being radically destroyed. "The personal life, the ever-near mystery, once the source of the stillest enthusiasms, is leveled down" (Buber 1988: 70f.).

If we recognize, instead, that there are two quite different meanings of the social – one that of the I–Thou relationship and the other that of the I–It relation, we shall not fall into this reductive either/or. The self becomes a self in its direct and unmediated dialogue with the Thou. Only in this dialogue, as I have said, does the self discover its uniqueness just through such dialogue with the Thou. The social environment, on the other hand, exercises its dominant influence on the self only in the indirect I–It relation, and this "social self" is not unique, except when it is taken up into the I–Thou relationship.

The elements of dialogical psychotherapy

In my book *The Healing Dialogue in Psychotherapy* (M. S. Friedman 1985), I first introduced the elements of dialogical psychotherapy that I will elaborate here. The first is *the "between"* or the *"interhuman,"* namely the recognition of an ontological dimension in the meeting between persons, or the "interhuman," that is usually overlooked because of our tendency to divide our existences into inner and outer, subjective and objective. The second is the recognition of *the dialogical* – "All real living is meeting" (Buber 1958) – as the essential element of human existence in which we relate to others in their uniqueness and otherness and not just as a content of our experience. From this standpoint the psychological is only the accompaniment of the dialogical and not, as so many psychologists tend to see it, the touchstone of reality in itself. The third element is the recognition that underlying the I–Thou, as also the I–It relations, is that twofold movement of *setting at a distance* and *entering into relation* that Buber makes the foundation of his philosophical anthropology (M. S. Friedman in Buber 1988: ch. 1; Buber 1988: ch. 2). We have discussed these three elements above in the section on "The Life of Dialogue."

These elements lead in turn to the fourth element – the recognition that the basic element of healing, when it is a question not of some repair work but restoring the atrophied personal center, is *healing through meeting*. One of the most important issues the approach of healing through meeting addresses is the extent to which healing proceeds from a specific healer and the extent to which healing takes place in the "between" – in the relationship between therapist and client or among the members of a therapy group or a family. When it is the latter, is there a special role, nonetheless, for the therapist as facilitator, midwife, enabler, or partner in a "dialogue of touchstones"? To what extent does healing through meeting imply that meeting must also be the *goal* as well as the means to that goal? And to what extent are we talking about a two-sided event that is not susceptible to techniques in the sense of willing and manipulating in order to bring about a certain therapeutic result? Another important problem that healing through meeting encounters is that of the limits of the responsibility of the helper. To what extent should therapists feel themselves a success if the patient is healed and a failure if he or she is not? Finally, in healing through meeting therapy should not proceed from the investigation of individual psychological complications but rather from the whole person and the relation between persons. The patient must be summoned to bring his or her inner being to unity so that he or she may respond to the address of the being or beings that face one.

The fifth element of dialogical psychotherapy is *the unconscious* seen, as Buber (1990a: 65-71) saw it, as the wholeness of the person before the differentiation and elaboration into psychic and physical, inner and outer. Freud and after him Jung made the simple logical error of assuming that the unconscious is psychic since they denied that it was physical. They did not, Buber holds, see this third alternative and with it the possibility of bursting the bounds of psychologism by recognizing that the division of inner and outer that applies to the psyche and the physical need not apply to the unconscious. Here, in contrast, there might be direct meeting and communication between one unconscious and another.

The unconscious is a state out of which the physical and the psychical have not yet evolved and in which the two cannot be distinguished from each other. The unconscious is our being itself in its wholeness. Out of it the physical and the psychic evolve again and again and at every moment. The unconscious is not a phenomenon. It is what modern psychology holds it to be – a dynamic fact that makes itself felt by its effects, effects that the psychologist can explore. But this exploration, as it takes place in psychiatry, is not of the unconscious itself but rather of the phenomena that have been dissociated from it. We cannot say anything about the unconscious in itself. It is never given to us. The radical mistake that Freud made was to think that he could posit a region of the mind as unconscious and at the same time deal with it as if its "contents" were simply repressed conscious material that could be brought back without any essential change into the conscious.

Dissociation is the process in which the unconscious "lump" manifests itself in inner and outer perceptions. This dissociation, in fact, may be the origin of our whole sense of inner and outer. Our conscious life is a dualistic one as we know it; our objective life is not dualistic, but we do not know this life. We can, to some extent, be conscious of the coming together of our forces, our acting unity, but we cannot perceive our unity as an object. The unconscious has its own existence: we do not have a deep freeze that keeps fragments. The patient with the supervision, help, and even initiative of the therapist can accomplish the radical change that comes with dissociation (Buber 1990a: 166). Patients, in any case, bring up something that they sense is wanted of them, something that is the product of their relationship with the therapist.

Since the material that the patient brings forth in therapy is made and produced rather than simply brought up from the unconscious, the responsibility of the therapist is greater than has been supposed. The deciding reality, Buber declares, is the therapist, not the methods. At times when the unique person of the patient stands before the unique person of the doctor, the doctor might properly throw away as much typology as he or she can and accept the unforeseeable happening that goes on between therapist and patient. The usual therapists impose themselves on their patients without being aware of it. What is necessary

is the conscious liberation of the patient from this unconscious impos-
ition of the therapist – leaving patients really to themselves and seeing
what comes out of it. "It is much easier to impose oneself on the patient
than it is to use the whole force of one's soul to leave the patient to himself and not to touch him. *The real master responds to uniqueness*"
(Buber 1990a: 168, emphasis in original).

It is Hans Trüb who has best spelled out the implications of this
approach to the unconscious for healing through meeting. Repression,
instead of being a basic aspect of human nature or an inescapable manifestation of civilization and its discontents, becomes the early denial of
meeting, and its overcoming means the reestablishment of meeting, the
breakthrough to dialogue. As Trüb states:

> *The unconscious touched by us has and takes its origin from that*
> *absolute "no" of the rejected meeting behind whose mighty barrier*
> *a person's psychic necessity for true meeting with the world secretly*
> *dams itself up, falls back upon itself, and thus,* as it were, *coagulates*
> *into the "unconscious."* ... What is meant by the unconscious is pre-
> cisely the personal element that is lost in the course of development
> ... that escapes consciousness.
>
> (Trüb 1952: 95, 98f., 103f. in M. S. Friedman 1991: 504)

In the relatively whole person, the unconscious would have a direct impact, not only on the conscious life, but also on others, precisely because
it represents the wholeness of the person. In the relatively divided person,
on the contrary, the unconscious itself has suffered a cleavage so that not
only are there repressed materials that cannot come up into consciousness, but also what does come up does not represent the wholeness of the
person but only one of the fragments. As the unconscious of the relatively
whole person is the very ground of meeting and an integral part of the interhuman, the unconscious of the relatively divided person is the product
of the absence or denial of meeting. From this we can infer that the overcoming of the split between the repressed unconscious and the conscious
of the divided person depends on healing through meeting. This includes
such confirmation as the therapist can summon from the relationship with
the client to counterbalance the "absolute no" of the meeting rejected or
withheld in childhood.

This approach to the unconscious applies to *dreams* too, which from
this standpoint are never just the raw material of the unconscious but,
upon being remembered, have already entered into the dialogue between
therapist and client and between the client and others. The result of this

approach is the possibility of having dialogues with our dreams themselves, as with any other person or thing that comes to meet us. Dreams have a certain continuity and connection of their own, but we cannot understand this connection or compare it to that of the waking world. The dreamer, so long as he or she is dreaming, has no share in the common world and nothing, therefore, to which we can have access. Dreams are the residue of our waking dialogues. Not only is there no real meeting with otherness in our dreams, but even the traces of otherness are greatly diminished. We cannot speak of dream relations as if they were identical with relations to person in waking life. What we can say is that having set the dream over against us, thus isolated, shaped, elaborated, and given form as an independent reality, we enter into dialogue with it. From now on it becomes one of the realities that address us in the world, just as surely and as concretely as any so-called external happening (Friedman 1985: ch 14).

One cannot interpret the dreams of one patient by the same methods as one interprets the dreams of another. The therapist must be ready to be surprised. From this type of "obedient listening," a new type of therapist may evolve – a person of greater responsibility and even greater gifts, since it is not so easy to master new attitudes without ready-made categories (Buber 1990a: 167f.).

Existential guilt, the sixth element of dialogical psychotherapy, is not basically inner or neurotic but an event of the "between." Existential guilt is guilt that you have taken on yourself as a person in a personal situation. Freud's guilt is repressed into the unconscious; you do not know it. But existential guilt you do know. Only it is possible that you no longer identify yourself with the person who committed the injury. It is just here, in the real guilt of the person who has not responded to the legitimate claim and address of the world, that the possibility of transformation and healing lies. Guilt does not reside in the person, says Buber. Rather, one stands, in the most realistic sense, in the guilt that envelops one. Similarly, the repression of guilt and the neuroses that result from this repression are not merely psychological phenomena, but real events between persons.

Existential guilt also arises, writes Buber (1988: ch. 6) from injuring the common order of existence, the foundation of which we know – at some level – to be the foundation of our own and of all human existence. Each of us understands – in terms of our family, our friendships, the people we work with, our social groups of whatever kind – what it means to injure the social realities in which we share.

Buber puts forward three steps that can be taken toward overcoming existential guilt. The first is illuminating this guilt: "I who am so different am nonetheless the person who did this." Second, we have to persevere in that illumination – not as an anguished self-torment but as a strong, broad light. If we were guilty only in relation to ourselves, the process might stop there. But we are always also guilty in relation to others. Therefore, we must take the third step of repairing the injured order of existence – restoring the broken dialogue through an active devotion to the world. If *we* have injured it, only we can restore it. We may not be able to do so with the person we injured; yet there are a thousand places where we can restore the injured order of existence (Buber 1988).

The seventh element, *inclusion* or *"imagining the real,"* must be distinguished from that empathy that goes to the other side of the relationship and leaves out one's own side and that identification that remains on one's own side and cannot go over to the other. Therapy too rests upon the I–Thou relationship of openness, mutuality, presence, and directness. Imagining what you are perceiving, thinking, feeling, and willing is how I include you in genuine dialogue. I can be empathetic or intuitive in our relationship, but unless I swing boldly and wholeheartedly in your direction I will not make you fully present to me. Any lesser action on my part will result in my including you in part – keeping you at a distance by way of distraction or disinterest. If you have ever been the object of someone's undivided attention, then you have experienced inclusion in genuine dialogue.

It would be misleading to think that inclusion means that I should be so taken with you that I lose my own sense of being grounded in the relationship. Buber's inclusion is not synonymous with being symbiotically joined. Inclusion is "imagining the real" which means to experience the other side of the relationship while not losing your own ground in the process. It is in the process of being fully present in relationship to you that I initiate genuine dialogue. When I see you in your unique and separate way of responding to a situation that is common to us both, I am practicing inclusion.

Inclusion, or "imagining the real," does not mean at any point that one gives up the ground of one's own concreteness, ceases to see through one's own eyes, or loses one's own "touchstones of reality." In this respect it is the complete opposite of empathy in the strict and narrower sense of the term. Empathy attempts to get over to the other while leaving oneself; identification tries to tune in to the other through focusing on oneself. Neither can grasp the uniqueness of the other person, the uniqueness of oneself, and the uniqueness of the relationship. Neither empathy nor identification can really confirm another person, since true confirmation means precisely that I confirm you in your uniqueness as a really other person. Only inclusion, or imagining the real, can confirm another; for only inclusion really grasps the other in his or her otherness and brings that other into relationship to oneself.

We find ourselves as persons through going out to meet the other, through responding to the address of the other. But we do not lose our center, our personal core, in an amorphous meeting with the other. If we see through the eyes of the other and experience the other side, we do not cease to experience the relationship from our own side. We do not understand the other's anger because of our anger; for the other may be angry in an entirely different way from us. But we *can* glimpse something of the other's side of the relationship. This is because real persons do not remain shut in themselves or use their relations with others merely as a means to their own self-realization.

The I–Thou relationship in dialogical psychotherapy can never be fully mutual. There is mutual contact, mutual trust, and mutual concern with a common problem but *not* mutual inclusion. The therapist can and must be on the patient's side too and, in a bipolar relationship, imagine quite concretely what the patient is thinking, feeling, and willing. But the therapist cannot expect or demand that the patient practice such inclusion with him or her. Yet there *is* mutuality, including the therapist sharing personally with the client when that seems helpful. For this reason, the eighth element of dialogical psychotherapy is called the *problematic of mutuality*.

The amount of mutuality possible and desirable in therapy depends not only upon the stage of the relationship, but also upon the unique relationship between this particular therapist and client and upon the style and strength of the therapist. Many therapists testify to bringing their feelings into the therapeutic encounter to a greater or less degree, and many testify to themselves being healed through that encounter or at the very least growing in creativity and wisdom. None of this changes the basic fact that the dialogical therapist's expression of emotion ought always to be made in the service of the therapy and never in the service of the healing of the therapist or of mere self-indulgence on the part of the therapist.

As we have pointed out in the discussion on the unconscious, there is undoubtedly a meeting of the unconscious of the therapist and that of the patient. What the patient picks up in this way may become the subject of the therapy, as the Jungian analyst Marvin Spiegelman and the relational therapists stress. The healing relationship must always be understood in terms of the quite concrete situation and life-reality of those participating in it. It is not always necessary or even helpful to label the client by such terms as "schizophrenic," "neurotic," "obsessive-compulsive," "border-line" or any of the other categories of diagnostic manuals. But it *is* necessary to recognize that in the healing partnership one person feels a need or lack that leads him or her to come to the other for help and that the other is a therapist or counselor who is ready to enter a relationship in order to help. This excludes neither Erich Fromm's nor Harold Searle's conviction that the therapist him- or herself is healed in some measure through the relationship between the therapist and the patient nor Carl Rogers' feeling of the equal worth and value of the client. But it does exclude accepting the therapist's *feeling* of mutuality as equivalent to the actual existence of full mutuality in the situation between therapist and patient.

Having stressed this limitation, we must also stress the fact that healing through meeting *does* imply mutuality between therapist and patient, that the therapist is called on to be present as a person as well as a smoothly functioning professional, that the therapist is vulnerable and must take risks, that he or she is not only professionally *accountable*, but also personally *responsible*. Professionally oriented therapists tend to regard those of their patients who commit suicide as their personal failures and those who get better as their personal successes, as if the patient's actions were simply the effect of which the therapist is the cause. Healing through meeting, in contrast, accepts the reality of the *between* and recognizes that it is not entirely to the therapist's credit if the therapy goes well, or to his or her discredit if it does not.

Only the bipolar relationship in which the therapist is simultaneously at his or her own side and at the same time at the patient's side can produce the ninth element – *confirmation*. If confirmation is central to human and interhuman existence, then it follows that disconfirmation, especially in the early stages of life, must be a major factor in psychopathology. Instead of finding the genesis of neurosis and psychosis in frustrated gratification of drives, à la Freud, we shall find it more basically and more frequently in disconfirming situations in the family that impair the child's basic trust.

In the time of the strongest transference, said Martin Buber, patients need, in their unconscious, to give themselves up into the hands of the therapist so that contact may occur. The therapist's openness and willingness to receive whatever comes is necessary in order that the patient may trust existentially. Existential trust of one whole person to another is necessary if the healing of the very roots of the patient's being is to take place. Without such trust, even masters of method cannot effect existential healing. Accepting and confirming a person *as he* or *she is* is only the first step. The therapist is also concerned with the potentialities of this person and can directly influence their development. Healing does not mean bringing up the old, but rather shaping the new. It is not confirming the negative but rather counterbalancing with the positive. For this reason a part of the confirmation the therapist brings to the patient may be wrestling *with* the patient, *for* the patient, and *against* the patient (Buber 1990a: 169–73).

Caring often means a contending with the patient within the dialogue with him. Hans Trüb (M. S. Friedman 1991: 498f.) helps us understand the meaning of confirmation in therapy through his conception of the two stages. In the first stage the person who comes before the therapist is the person who has been unconfirmed, disconfirmed by the world, a person who needs a confidant, a big brother or sister, someone who really hears and who "imagines the real" while listening. The second stage is made necessary because a part of the patient's sickness is that because of this nonconfirmation, the person has withdrawn from active dialogue with family, friends, and community. At some point, therefore, without putting aside the first stage, the therapist must enter a second stage in which he or she helps the client resume the interrupted dialogue with the community. The therapist represents and bears the community values that he or she embodies. Without this second stage – not replacing, but combined with the first stage – there can be no real healing.

The tenth and last element of dialogical psychotherapy – my own and not Buber's – is the *dialogue of touchstones*. This element takes up into itself both inclusion and confirmation. Through his or her greater experience in inclusion and imagining the real, the therapist enables the patient to go beyond the terrible either/or of remaining true to one's unique "touchstones of reality" (M. S. Friedman 1972) at the cost of being cut off from the community or of entering into relation with the community at the cost of denying one's touchstones. The therapist must help the patient bring his or her touchstones of reality into dialogue with really other persons, beginning with the therapist him- or herself. Touchstones of reality and the dialogue of touchstones offer an alternative to the either/ors of objective versus subjective, absolute versus relative, mind versus body, and the rejection of the "schizophrenic" versus the romantic glorification of him or her.

From the standpoint of the dialogue of touchstones much of what we call "mental illness" can be seen as something that has happened to distort, objectify, or make merely cultural our touchstones of reality. Touchstones and the dialogue of touchstones begin in, and are renewed by, immediacy. Sickness is what prevents the return to immediacy.

From this standpoint mental and emotional "health" is not "adjustment," becoming rational or emotional, but rather coming to a firmer grasp of one's own touchstones of reality in dialogue with the touchstones of others. In this sense the dialogue of touchstones may be the goal of therapy as well as the means. This goal helps the therapist avoid three equally bad alternatives – adjusting the client to the culture, imposing his or her own values on the client, or accepting whatever the patient says and does as healthy and romantically celebrating it.

The terrible dilemma of the "sick" person is having to choose between giving up his or her touchstones in order to communicate or giving up communication in order to retain one's unique touchstones. Such a person needs the help of someone who can glimpse and share the unique reality that has come from this person's life experience and help this person find a way of bringing it into the common order of existence so that he or she too may raise what has been experienced as "I" into the communal reality of "We." Such persons need the help of a therapist who can imagine the real and practice inclusion in order to help them enter into a dialogue of touchstones.

The case of Dawn

An illustration of dialogical psychotherapy is my work with Dawn, a 40-year-old Caucasian woman, who came to see me for four years in individual and couples therapy. Dawn complained that Bob, her husband of ten years, never talked to her but spent his hours at home watching television and that he did not do his share of taking care of the children or of babysitting when she went to graduate school. She told me of a time when she broke the television set in a fit of anger and Bob simply replaced it. Dawn's response to this troubled, tense family atmosphere was symptoms of depression: lack of interest and enjoyment in sex, disturbance of concentration and sleep, low energy, and periods of sadness. The flat affect with which she told me how her children were having night terrors indicated clearly the depth of her depression and its impact upon the family.

What struck me most about Dawn was the enormous contrast between her evident intellectual superiority and her inner sense of her self. Dawn's need to compare herself with others seems to stem from a basic distrust in her relationships with others. Only this can account for the veritable split between Dawn as an active, well-functioning person on the outside and as the inferior person that she saw herself as being.

I saw as the *basic* goal of our therapy helping Dawn enter into dialogue and a relationship of trust. My therapeutic interventions included exploring her family of origin and pointing out patterns, such as Dawn and her siblings as "delegated" children (a term of Helm Stierlin's (1974)), encouraging expression of feelings, especially anger, getting her to write down dreams, bringing a divorce mediator to group therapy, sending Dawn to a psychiatrist for medication, discussing school plans, suggesting support groups, sending Dawn for psychological testing, and discussing how her daughter's adolescent acting out had brought back problems with her sister, mother, and husband.

Analysis of the past was never the main focus of our therapeutic dialogue, but was done only for the sake of re-presenting the past and inviting ever deeper layers of her walled-off self to enter into a relationship of trust. The goal of Dawn's therapy was neither the preservation of her relationship with Bob nor establishing her in a new, long-term relationship after Bob's departure. Nor was it any specific matter, such as overcoming Dawn's anxiety and depression, getting Dawn to be able to write papers, or healing her inner split. What was essential, rather, was the relationship of trust that developed between us over the four years in which we entered and re-entered together into dialogical therapy. My behavior of support, facilitation, confrontation, silence, questioning, reinforcement, interpretation, and modeling was always grounded in a relational stance.

My approach to Dawn's therapy was at times insight oriented, at times process oriented, and at other times support oriented. But it always evolved from the relationship and returned back to my relationship with her. This was true even when I tried traditional Gestalt therapy techniques, such as asking Dawn to play different roles in her family or move from chair to chair addressing herself from the standpoint of some member of her family that she had just spoken to.

I did not simply impose these actions on Dawn but explored with her when it was helpful. The same is true of my interpretations. I did not offer them as authoritative pronouncements but rather asked her whether they rang a bell and modified them in dialogue with her. Thus the choice of therapeutic goals and objectives was a shared responsibility between Dawn and me, unlike many psychodynamic or behavior therapists who see it as their task to set goals *and* unlike process-oriented therapists who see it as the task of the client. Inclusion, or "imagining the real," was also very necessary *from my side* if the habitual mistrust on which Dawn's life and actions were established was to be healed to the point where she could enter a relationship of trust with me and later with others.

What was most impressive in our therapy together is the remarkable change that I witnessed in Dawn during the years of therapy and the more than six years since it concluded. (We have stayed in touch sufficiently that I have been in a position to judge this.) This was precisely her movement from virtual isolation to being a person-in-relationship, a person ready and open for give-and-take with others. Over the years I witnessed in Dawn a gradual but unmistakable warming, opening, flowering, and maturing.

Because I approached Dawn's therapy from the standpoint of the healing dialogue, it seems both fitting and meaningful to me to conclude this account of Dawn's case with Dawn's own evaluation of our relationship in her own words, which I suggested she write when I decided to use our therapy as a case study.

> When I think about our past therapeutic relationship, the process stands out in my memory rather than the content. Up until the time I met Maurice, I had always "picked out" a male authority figure – usually a teacher or psychologist – and put him on a pedestal – obsessed about him a lot – not usually in a romantic or sexual way, although there was an erotic element. I just wanted him to like me and approve of me and to think I was smart and interesting. A real relationship, though, was terrifying to me – I kept my distance and rarely ever talked to them – the greater the attraction, the greater the fear.
>
> When I first met Maurice, I could feel myself wanting to fall into this same pattern with him. However, I could never quite feel intimidated by him – although I think I really wanted to. He was too human for that. I never felt that I had to be interesting or smart, good, bad, happy or sad – it just wasn't something I had to be concerned with. If the therapist can be human and fallible, that gives me permission to be human and fallible too. This was an entirely new experience for me. I soon found that I was involving myself in relationships with other "male authority figures" with much less fear and anxiety than I had felt in the past. I also became aware that I no longer wanted the kind of superior–inferior, vertical type of relationship that I used to seek out. I think this change is, by far, the most valuable result of my therapy relationship with Maurice.
>
> In my relationship with my husband, Maurice helped me to understand that it wasn't Bob or me that was necessarily inadequate – it was our relationship. In my relationship with Maurice, I began to realize that I wanted a "relationship," that relationship was important and life sustaining and that Bob and I both deserved to be involved with those with whom we could have a "relationship." Seeking to get

my "neurotic needs" met leads to "death." Relationship, with all its imperfections, is "life" – I know that very well now, and my first teacher in this area was Maurice. But because he doesn't "need" to be my teacher – I am now able to be my own teacher. Because he doesn't "need" me to follow in his path, I am free to find my own.

The dialogical psychotherapy movement

Dialogical psychotherapy is not a distinct school of therapy but a movement that has had its representatives and pioneers in many major schools of psychotherapy, most of whom have been directly influenced by Buber. It is important, however, to distinguish between "therapists of dialogue," who have moved toward healing through meeting, whether or not they were influenced by Buber, and "dialogical psychotherapists," who have made healing through meeting central rather than ancillary and whose work is directly influenced by Buber. Included in the dialogical psychotherapy movement, but not examined here, are "contextual therapists" (Ivan Boszormenyi-Nagy) who make healing through meeting central in the interactions of intergenerational family members (M. S. Friedman 1989).

I define therapists of dialogue as those whose writings have illuminated one or more of the elements of dialogical psychotherapy – even though many of them would not see themselves in such terms. Therapists of dialogue are a diverse group that range from Carl Jung to psychodynamic and existential-phenomenological clinicians. Thus, for example, Jung goes far beyond Freud in the direction of recognizing the otherness and uniqueness of the patient and the therapist. Jung insists that analysis is always a dialogue between two human beings (Jung 1954). Ludwig Binswanger similarly sees the self as coming to be in the I–Thou relationship of "communal love" and "we-ness," in contrast to Heidegger's authentic existence for oneself (Binswanger 1963). Harry Guntrip describes his own theory of "object relations" as close to but not yet reaching Buber's I–Thou relationship (Guntrip 1969). Carl Rogers sees change in the client as coming about through relationship. He uses Buber's term "I and Thou" to characterize the therapeutic relationship and manifests a deep concern for confirming the client (Rogers 1961). R. D. Laing draws heavily on Buber's "inclusion" and "confirmation" and understands schizophrenia in terms of separateness and relatedness (Laing 1965, 1971). And Rollo May understands healing through meeting as the channeling of impersonal force into personal dialogue through intentionality, responsibility, and decision (May 1969).

In contrast to therapists of dialogue, dialogical psychotherapists draw directly on Buber. The work of Hans Trüb, whom I introduced earlier, focuses above all on the life of dialogue. Initially trained as a Jungian analyst, Trüb tells of how the closed circle of the self was again and again forced outward toward relationship through those times when, despite his will, he found himself confronting his patient not as an analyst but as human being to human being. From these experiences, he came to understand the full meaning of the analyst's responsibility. The analyst takes responsibility for lost and forgotten things, and with the aid of his or her psychology, helps to bring them to light. But the analyst knows in the depths of his or her self that the secret meaning of those things that have been brought to consciousness first reveals itself *in the outgoing to the other* (Trüb in M. S. Friedman 1991: 497–505; 1985: 30–6, 148, 166–8).

In his introduction to Hans Trüb's posthumous book *Heilung aus der Begegnung* ("Healing through Meeting") Buber wrote:

> This way of frightened pause, of unfrightened reflection, of personal involvement, of rejection of security, of unreserved stepping into relationship, of the bursting of psychologism, this way of vision and risk is that which Hans Trüb trod. . . . .Surely there will not be wanting therapists like him – awake and daring, hazarding the economics of the vocation, not sparing and not withholding themselves, risking themselves – therapists who will find his path and extend it further.
>
> (Buber 1990b: 97)

There are indeed therapists who have followed Hans Trüb's path, even if they did not know of Trüb's work.

A significant extension of the life of dialogue and of dialogical psychotherapy is the theory of "will and willfulness" developed under Buber's influence by the Sullivanian psychoanalyst Leslie H. Farber. Farber sees genuine will as an expression of real dialogue, arbitrary willfulness as a product of the absence of dialogue. The proper setting of wholeness is dialogue. When this setting eludes us, "we turn wildly to will, ready to grasp at any illusion of wholeness (however mindless or grotesque) the will conjures up for our reassurance" (Farber 1966: 111). Willfulness then is nothing other than the attempt of will to make up for the absence of dialogue by handling both sides of the no longer mutual situation. (M. S. Friedman 1985: 80–7; 1992a: 78–82)

A third writer who must be mentioned here is Richard Hycner, author of *Between Person and Person: Toward a Dialogical Psychotherapy* (Hycner 1991). He argues that the "unfettered elementalness of human meeting demands that the therapist *first* be a person available to others as a human being, and *secondarily* be a professional trained in the appropriate methods of practicing psychotherapy" (emphasis in original). What keeps the therapy fully alive, responding moment by moment to the ongoing changes, is present-centeredness. Psychopathology is an aborted dialogue – the residue of an attempted dialogue that was not responded to, a desperate calling to the world to respond and to recognize the face of human need behind the face of human hurt. By the same token, the healing of the psychopathological means an entrance into dialogue with others, truly meeting them, "*not* 'projection to projection,' but person to person." To Hycner (1991: 135) "resistance is inextricably a phenomenon of the 'between.'" The greatest challenge the therapist faces is that of establishing a dialogue with this person and his or her resistance (see M. S. Friedman 1992a: ch. 5; Hycner with Jacobs 1995).

In his book *The Healing Between: A Clinical Guide to Dialogical Psychotherapy* William G. Heard (1993) adds to my elements of dialogical psychotherapy the element of personal direction, an important part of Buber's philosophy of dialogue. The client's direction, according to Heard, does not arise within the client as the result of introspective self-realization, but unfolds between the client and the therapist without any predetermined notion or course. Only through this dialogue between client and therapist does it fulfill the client's uniqueness (Heard 1993: 66–8). Expanding on Buber's concept of existential guilt, Heard asserts that neurotic guilt feelings are what others load on us: "Ontically speaking, the client is not guilty, but he experiences guilt feelings as if he were." Through therapy the client "can alleviate his guilt feelings without impairing his existence." Existential guilt cannot be alleviated this way; we must take it on ourselves (Heard 1993: 132f.).

Another important dialogical psychotherapist is Mordecai Rotenberg, Professor of Social Work at the Hebrew University of Jerusalem. Taking off from the Lurian kabbalistic notion of *tzimtzum*, the divine withdrawal that precedes creation, Rotenberg sees *human* contraction as requiring

> that in order to reach the other, one should make his assertive strength less felt, but instead of withdrawing it and deserting the other, leave his strength present in the background to let the other feel his latent presence in order to give him space to grow and to enable him to enter into a relationship with him.
>
> (Rotenberg 1983: 74).

This is very close to that "confirmation" that is central to Buber's philosophical anthropology, but in this case Rotenberg applies it to the relationship between couples.

Rotenberg employs Buber's term "inclusion" and like Buber stresses that inclusion is not empathy but rather a process in which one's personality, without leaving its own ground, extends to include a piece of the "other." Like Buber and myself, Rotenberg distinguishes between the dialogue that goes on between persons and the dialectic that goes on in the head of the individual thinker or in the mind of debaters. Dialectic psychotherapy wants to replace the pleasure principle by the reality principle, writes Rotenberg, whereas dialogical psychotherapy seeks a dynamic balancing tension between these supposedly conflicting forces. Dialectic progress uses up its energy in the mutually conflicting process of patricide (killing the Oedipal parent) and self-blame ("the psychoanalytic trial bench"), whereas in dialogical progress the "I" may emulate and even surpass the "Thou" without having to destroy him or her.

In close affinity to my concept of "the dialogue of touchstones of reality" Rotenberg propounds an egalitarian "dia-logo therapy" "in which the therapist is committed to learn his patient's language rather than impose his own doctrinaire interpretation" (Rotenberg 1991: 10). The rational "reader-therapist" must converse with an "author-patient" who might speak the irrational-mystic language of schizophrenia, obviating the otherwise inevitable manipulative superiority of the therapist. This leads to a mutual growth via the dialogue of touchstones: "Growth and therapy are possible through the coexistence of a multiplicity of interpretations of life" (Rotenberg 1991: 4, 22).

Relational psychoanalysts

If we define a dialogical psychotherapist as one who sees healing through meeting as central rather than ancillary, then we must also count as dialogical psychotherapists certain psychoanalysts who identify themselves as "relational" or "interpersonal." In his book *A Meeting of Minds* (1996) Lewis Aron has given us a comprehensive historical and contemporary overview of the relational approach to psychoanalysis beginning with Sándor Ferenczi and Otto Rank. "Among all 20th century philosophers," writes Aron, "Martin Buber elaborated a philosophy of dialogue that most closely resonates with the relational psychoanalytic approach and its emphasis on mutuality" (Aron 1996: 154). Not surprisingly, a quotation that Aron cites from I. J. Philipson is in itself an ideal summary of "healing through meeting":

The relational model therapist . . . is a participant in the therapeutic encounter far more than an observer. She not only acknowledges her own countertransference as a normative component of therapy but she utilizes it as a means of deciphering what her client is experiencing. Rather than emphasizing interpretation, she privileges the therapeutic relationship as curative rather than hierarchical in nature.

(Philipson 1993: 115, quoted in Aron 1996: 21)

Aron similarly views interpretation not as something that conveys information about the mind of the patient but as a bipersonal and reciprocal communication process, a mutual meaning-making process. "Meaning is generated relationally and interpersonally . . . Analytic objectivity is dialectical and dialogical. . . . Meaning is arrived at through a meeting of minds" (Aron 1996: 263). Aron holds that analysis takes place between the patient and analyst as they analyze each other. Much of this analysis takes place implicitly or unconsciously, of course, and the relative contributions of the two participants are in the nature of things not equal (Aron 1996: 127). Aron summarizes his approach as follows:

Unless patients can feel that they have reached their analysts, moved them, healed them, known them in some profound way, they themselves may not be able to benefit from their analyses. From this perspective, psychoanalysis is a profound emotional encounter, an interpersonal engagement, an intersubjective dialogue, a relational integration, a meeting of minds.

(Aron 1996: 136)

The balance of mutuality and the unique experience of the self that takes place in relational analysis may promote the patient's capacity for dynamic autonomy. Important to note in this connection is Aron's declaration that "relational theory does not embrace the radical and cynical postmodern rejection of the subject; rather it draws on an affirmative postmodern sensibility and maintains both that relationships determine individuals and that individuals determine relationships" (Aron 1996: 158). Buber's philosophy of dialogue, as Steven Kepnes points out, and my own philosophy of the "dialogue of touchstones" fall at this same midway point between the essential self of modernism and the deconstructed, non-unique, socially constructed self of postmodernism (Kepnes 1992; M. S. Friedman 1995).

A further resemblance between dialogical psychotherapy and relational analysis is found in the approach to resistance. Aron, Otto Rank, and P. M. Bromberg view resistance in a way quite close to that of Richard Hycner, cited above:

> The human personality, in order to grow, needs to encounter another personality as a separate center of subjective reality, so that its own subjectivity can oppose, be opposed, confirm, and be confirmed in an intersubjective context. "Resistance-as-obstacle" functions inherently as a necessary guardian of self-continuity during this process and, in that sense, as obstacle, as opposition, an intrinsic aspect of the growth dialectic that makes clinical psychoanalysis possible.
>
> (Bromberg 1995: 176, quoted in Aron 1996: 187)

Another psychoanalyst who is very close to Buber's philosophy of dialogue and to dialogical psychotherapy is the interpersonalist Darlene Ehrenberg. She offers us a metaphor of "the intimate edge" not as a given, but as an interactive creation, unique to the moment and to the sensibilities of the specific participants in relation to each other. For her, a "real relationship" between analyst and patient is not a facilitating condition but the actual medium of the analytic work and the new experience that is generated within it. Through the intimate edge one becomes more "intimate" with one's own experience through the growing relationship with the other, and then more intimate with the other as one become more attuned to oneself. Thus the "intimate edge" is, for Ehrenberg, the "growing edge" of the therapeutic relationship. Aiming at reciprocity and expanded awareness through authentic relation, risking the unknown are all ways of extending the reach of psychoanalytic interaction (Ehrenberg 1992: 34f., 41, 48).

Although she does not acknowledge any direct influence of Buber, the well-known feminist psychoanalyst Jessica Benjamin can also be subsumed under dialogical psychotherapy through her concern with the healing relationship between therapist and client. Benjamin's emphasis on "recognition" as the concept that unifies intersubjective theories of self development is very close to Buber's concept of confirmation. "Recognition . . . includes not only the other's confirming response, but also how we find ourselves in that response" (Benjamin 1988: 21). In particular, Benjamin feels that no psychological theory has adequately articulated the mother's independent existence:

> The need for *mutual* recognition, the necessity of recognizing as well as being recognized by the other – this is what so many theories of the self have missed. The idea of mutual recognition is crucial to the

intersubjective view. It implies that we actually have a need to recognize the other as a separate person who is like us yet distinct. This means that the child has a need to see the mother, too, as an independent subject, not simply as the "external world" or an adjunct of his ego.

(Benjamin 1988: 23)

The paradox of recognition, through which the need for acknowledgment can turn us back to dependence on the other, can bring about a struggle for control. At the same time it reaches its own limit, for if we assume complete control over the other and destroy her identity we shall have negated ourselves as well; for then there is no one to recognize us (Benjamin 1988: 39). In her conclusion Benjamin gives us a succinct expression of the logic of paradox that comes with sustaining the tension between contradictory forces.

Perhaps the most fateful paradox is the one posed by our simultaneous need for recognition and independence: that the other subject is outside our control and yet we need him. To embrace this paradox is the first step toward unraveling the bonds of love. This means not to undo our ties to others but rather to disentangle them; to make of them not shackles but circuits of recognition

(Benjamin 1988: 221; see also Benjamin 1998).

Conclusion

In 1950 when I was staying at the Jewish Theological Seminary in New York City as a guest of my friend Abraham Joshua Heschel, I ran into Carl Friedrichs, who had taught me a course in government when I was an undergraduate at Harvard. I told Professor Friedrichs that I had recently received a Ph.D. from the University of Chicago with a doctoral dissertation on Martin Buber. Knowing of Buber from his own studies in Germany, he responded, "Buber is a seminal thinker." In the half century since then this has proved to be true in many fields. In this chapter I have shown Buber's influence not only on those whom I classify as dialogical psychotherapists, but also on many of those whom I call therapists of dialogue and relational psychoanalysts. I have also set forth, in greater fullness here than anywhere previously, the elements of dialogical psychotherapy, to which I add that unique "personal direction" discovered in the dialogue between therapist and client to which William Heard points in *The Healing Between* (1993).

In this chapter I have sought to describe the remarkably fruitful interaction and interweaving of the theory of therapists from many different schools. In so doing I have kept in focus a number of key concepts from Buber's own approach to the life of dialogue and to psychotherapy. These include: "all real living is meeting;" the psychological as the byproduct and accompaniment of dialogue; the centrality of confirmation, inclusion and imagining the real as the road to confirmation, not to be confused with empathy; the normative limitation of mutuality in psychotherapy; the unconscious as the wholeness of the person before it is dissociated into the physical and the psychic; plus my own metaphor of the dialogue of touchstones of reality. Dialogical psychotherapy, in short, has grown into a movement that deserves the attention of psychologists, psychotherapists, and psychoanalysts of every kind.

References

Aron, L. A. (1996) *A Meeting of Minds: Mutuality in Psychoanalysis*. Hillsdale, NJ: Analytic Press.

Benjamin, J. (1988) *The Bonds of Love: Psychoanalysis, Feminism, and the Problem of Domination*. New York: Pantheon.

—— (1998) *Shadow of the Other: Intersubjectivity and Gender in Psychoanalysis*. New York and London: Routledge.

Binswanger, L. (1963) *Being in the World: Selected Papers of Ludwig Binswanger*, ed. and trans. J. Needleman. New York: Basic Books.

Bromberg, P. M. (1995) "Resistance, object-usage, and human relatedness," *Contemporary Psychoanalysis* 31: 173–91.

Buber, M. (1958) *I and Thou*, 2nd rev. edn. with postscript by author added, trans. R. G. Smith. New York: Charles Scribner's Sons.

—— (1985) *Between Man and Man*, introd. M. S. Friedman, trans. R. G. Smith. New York: Charles Scribner's Sons.

—— (1988) *The Knowledge of Man: A Philosophy of the Interhuman*, ed. with an introductory essay by M. S. Friedman, trans. M. S. Friedman and R. G. Smith. Atlantic Highlands, NJ: Humanities Press International (now distributed as a Humanity Book by Prometheus Books, Amherst, NY).

—— (1990a) *A Believing Humanism: My Testament*, trans. with explanatory notes and comments by M. S. Friedman. Atlantic Highlands, NJ: Humanities Press International (now distributed as a Humanity Book by Prometheus Books, Amherst, NY).

—— (1990b) *Pointing the Way: Collected Essays*, ed. and trans. by M. S. Friedman. Atlantic Highlands, NJ: Humanities Press International (now distributed as a Humanity Book by Prometheus Books, Amherst, NY).

Ehrenberg, D. B. (1992) *The Intimate Edge: Extending the Reach of Psychoanalytic Interaction*. New York: W. W. Norton.

Farber, L. H. (1966) *The Ways of the Will: Essays toward a Psychology and Psychopathology of the Will*. New York: Basic Books.

Friedman, A. M. (1992) *Treating Chronic Pain: The Healing Partnership*. New York: Insight Books (Plenum).

Friedman, M. S. (1972) *Touchstones of Reality: Existential Trust and the Community of Peace*. New York: E. P. Dutton.

—— (1985) *The Healing Dialogue in Psychotherapy*. New York: Jason Aronson (paperback edn 1994, Northvale, NJ: Jason Aronson).

—— (1989) "Martin Buber and Ivan Boszormenyi-Nagy: the role of dialogue in contextual therapy," *Psychotherapy* 26: 402–9.

—— (1991) *The Worlds of Existentialism: A Critical Reader*, 3rd edn with new updating preface. Atlantic Highlands, NJ: Humanities Press International (now distributed as a Humanity Book by Prometheus Books, Amherst, NY).

—— (1992a) *Dialogue and the Human Image: Beyond Humanistic Psychology*. Newbury Park, CA: Sage.

—— (1992b) *Religion and Psychology: A Dialogical Approach*. New York: Paragon House.

—— (1995) "Constructivism, psychotherapy, and the dialogue of touchstones," *Journal of Constructivist Psychology* 8: 283–93.

Guntrip, H. (1969) *Schizoid Phenomena, Object Relations and the Self*. New York: International Universities Press.

Heard, W. H. (1993) *The Healing Between: A Clinical Guide to Dialogical Psychotherapy*, foreword by M. S. Friedman. San Francisco, CA: Jossey/Bass.

Hycner, R. C. (1991) *Between Person and Person: Toward a Dialogical Psychotherapy*. Highland, NY: Gestalt Development Center.

Hycner, R. C. in association with Jacobs, L. (1995) *The Healing Relationship in Gestalt Therapy*. Highland, NY: Gestalt Therapy Associates.

Jung, C. G. (1954) *The Practice of Psychotherapy*, trans. R. F. C. Hull, in *The Collected Works*, vol. 16. New York: Pantheon.

Kepnes, S. (1992) *The Text as Thou: Martin Buber's Dialogical Hermeneutics and Theological Narrative*. Bloomington, IN: Indiana University Press.

Laing, R. D. (1965) *The Divided Self: An Existential Study in Sanity and Madness*. London: Pelican.

—— (1971) *Self and Others*. London: Pelican.

May, R. (1969) *Love and Will*. New York: Norton.

Philipson, I. J. (1993) *On the Shoulders of Women*. New York: Guilford.

Rogers, C. R. (1961) *On Becoming a Person: A Therapist's View of Psychotherapy*. Boston, MA: Houghton Mifflin.

Rotenberg, M. (1983) *Dialogue with Deviance: The Hasidic Ethic and the Theory of Social Contraction*. Philadelphia, PA: Institute for the Study of Human Issues.

—— (1991) *Dia-logo therapy: Psychonarration and PaRDeS*. New York: Praeger.

Stierlin, H. (1974) *Separating Parents and Adolescents: A Perspective on Running Away, Schizophrenia, and Waywardness*. New York: Quadrangle/New York Times Book Co.Index

Chapter 3

Truth and freedom in psychoanalysis

William J. Richardson

Martin Heidegger was no friend of psychoanalysis. His first serious exposure to it came through the ministrations of Medard Boss, who, in effect, introduced him to Freud. Mediated through Boss's own attempt to rethink Freud's insights in what he called *Daseinsanalysis*, Heidegger's relation to Freud himself remained cool, to say the least. Several attempts in the 1950s to entice him into dialogue with the so-called "French Freud," Jacques Lacan, whose self-proclaimed "return to Freud" some found deeply consonant with certain themes of Heidegger, proved fruitless. Given this record, any new attempt to find philosophical relevance for psychoanalysis in the thought of Martin Heidegger seems ill-starred indeed. And yet . . .

Heidegger and Boss

More must be said even to understand the problems involved. First of all, who was Medard Boss (1903–90)? And how did he find his way from Freud to Heidegger (1889–1976) in the first place? A Swiss physician and psychiatrist, he felt that the training he had received proved inadequate to prepare him to deal with the kinds of clinical cases he had to face (Craig 1988). But then he stumbled on *Being and Time* (Heidegger [1927] 1996). To be sure, one would hardly call his formation impoverished. He had been trained in psychiatry by Eugen Bleuler (1857–1939) at Zurich's mental hospital and university clinic, Burghölzli. He had begun his psychoanalysis of thirty-odd sessions with an ailing Freud in 1925, finished it with Karen Horney in Berlin. He had been exposed to the teaching and supervision of Theodor Reik, Hanns Sachs, Otto Fenichel, Ernest Jones among others, and had participated for ten years in a biweekly seminar with Carl Jung. In the end, he turned to the wisdom of India for light – even tried to learn Hindi for this purpose. But then he discovered *Being and Time*, and with it Heidegger's analysis of human being (Dasein). From then on, his commitment to the consequences became total.

The earliest record we have of the relationship between the two men is a letter dating from 1947. Heidegger had been suspended from his teaching responsibilities by the ongoing denazification process, and the only published work we have from that period is the *Letter on Humanism* written in response to Jean Beaufret's questions from Paris two years earlier. When Boss requested permission to visit him that summer, we may presume that Heidegger welcomed the stimulus that would come from another inquiring mind from another country and from another discipline. At any rate, the two men –fourteen years apart in age – hit it off famously and became fast friends. They would vacation together with their wives – visiting Italy, Sicily, the Aegean Islands, and Greece – or sometimes they would simply take a work-vacation together a week at a time in Boss's getaway home at Lenzerheide in the Alps near Davos. Boss learned much from their conversations, of course, and finally decided that his experience of Heidegger the thinker should be shared with others. Heidegger agreed to lead some seminars, and several times each semester for the next ten years he would spend a week or so in Zurich offering two three-hour sessions each time to between fifty and seventy psychiatrists, most of them relatively innocent of philosophy of any kind, let alone his own.

The Zollikon Seminars

What does Heidegger do in these seminars? In a word, he offers psychiatrists a crash course in some of the fundamental concepts of *Being and Time* that had first fired Boss's enthusiasm. And who was more capable than he to do it? Those concepts by now are current coin and easily recalled. Heidegger is interested in the meaning of Being (*Sein*) as different from beings (*Seiende*) that it lets be manifest, and he proceeds by a phenomenological examination of a particular being among the rest, namely, human being that he calls *Dasein,* which must somehow know the answer to the question since it is able to ask it. Under examination, Dasein reveals itself as a phenomenon whose nature it is to-be-in-the-world. Heidegger examines first what is meant by world and then what it means to be "in" such world. As for the world itself, it is to be understood not as the sum total of everything that is but as a horizon within which beings are encountered, a matrix of relations interior to which beings have their meaning.. Eventually this matrix of meanings would be conceived of as the matrix of comprehensibility, of whatever can be articulated through speech.

For Dasein to be "in" such a world implies several different existential, that is structural, components: one structural component that discloses/projects the world as total meaningfulness (*Verstehen*: "understanding"), one that discloses beings within the world through affective disposition (*Befindlichkeit*: "state of mind"), and finally one that permits Dasein to articulate in speech what it affectively understands, This last component Heidegger calls *Rede*, but since this is his translation of the Greek *logos* it seems better simply to anglicize the Greek, hence, as "logos" – understanding thereby the structural component through which Dasein is able to let something be manifest in words. As a structural component, then, logos shares Dasein's nature as Being-with-others, and this is the foundation of its capacity to interact with other Daseins through the mediation of speech (*Mitteilung*: "communication"). It goes without saying, of course, that the structural component of logos shares in the radically temporal character of Dasein, whereby in advancing resolve Dasein lets the future come through its past, letting beings (including itself) become manifest in the present. The implications of all this are as far-reaching as the phenomenology, which justifies it, is complex.

What does Heidegger do, then, with the psychiatrists? He tries to follow the advice he gives Boss as he prepares to be a visiting professor at Harvard: "You must succeed in bringing about a change of viewpoint in your auditors, in awakening [in them] the sense in which the question must be asked" (Heidegger 2001: 258/324). He recommends a meditation on space and spatiality as a good way to start, and that is exactly how he begins his seminars. The analysis of space (and eventually time) add nothing but a certain freshness to the treatment of the issues in *Being and Time*. What is interesting is the rigor of his pedagogical method. Sessions proceed with homely examples of cups and tables. Are they here? Or there? Or where? Are they now? Or then? Or when? What is where? What is when? It is often very Socratic, and tough-minded – but also clear and sharply philosophical.

The seminars as a whole, then, resonate profoundly with *Being and Time*, but certain new themes, or at least new explications, emerge that are worth more attention than we can give them here. The first of these is the distinction, important for psychotherapy, between *Vergegenwärtigung* ("rendering something present") and *Erinnern* ("recalling" it). The first deals with what *Being and Time* refers to as Dasein's *Sein bei* other beings, that is of being able to be "near" them, not by being physically "alongside" of them but because of its privileged access to their

Being that lets them be near (2001: 70/90). This will enable him to explain certain parapraxes (like forgetting one's umbrella) without resorting to the notion of some unconscious wish.

More important is Heidegger's examination of psychosomatic phenomena, which leads him to an analysis of the human body, notably missing from *Being and Time*. Heidegger distinguishes clearly between body as *Körper* and body as *Leib*. The limit of the former is one's skin, the limit of the latter is the horizon of the world for Dasein as Being-in-the-world (2001: 86/112–13).

This permits him to give a new reading to such a phenomenon as "Stress" (e.g., 2001: 141/185). When Boss reminds him of Sartre's criticism that *Being and Time* contained only six lines about the body, Heidegger replies that this had been for him the hardest of all problems to solve and that he knew of no way to say any more about it at the time (2001: 231/292).

Let this suffice to characterize the sweep of the book as a whole. More particularly, what is to be said about the unconscious as Freud has taught us to understand it? For Heidegger, Freud is a classic example of the modern (broad sense) scientific mind, a mind that is totally oblivious to the Being-dimension of the objects it deals with, that is the mysterious process within them that lets them come to presence and reveal themselves to us as what they are. The scientific mind is interested in their object-character, their objectifiability, their capacity to be conceptualized in representations, measured, calculated, controlled. Heidegger finds the historical paradigm for this mentality jointly and, in complementary fashion, in the physics of Galileo and the philosophy of Descartes.

Heidegger takes the poor doctors through the long history that follows as a way of saying what he thinks of Freud and the unconscious. The fact is that it was Boss who introduced Heidegger to Freud's metapsychological work and, according to Boss, Heidegger "couldn't believe that such an intelligent man could write such stupid things, such fantastical things, about men and women." For Heidegger, Freud's metapsychology is merely the application of a Neo-Kantian conception of science to human being (2001: 207/260). What Freud is looking for is an explanation of human phenomena through an unbroken chain of causality (2001: 7/7). When he cannot do this on the level of consciousness, he postulates an unconscious – at best a pure hypothesis (2001: 169/214). Result: the "fatal distinction between conscious and unconscious" (2001: 254/319) is born and, alas, seems here to stay.

To stay? Well, if the Freudian unconscious is only the underside of a Cartesian conception of consciousness as an encapsulated ego-subject,

what happens if this Cartesian model is scrapped? Does not the unconscious go too? Of course it does – and that is exactly Heidegger's
position. For Dasein is not fundamentally an ego-subject. Dasein is the
clearing in which all beings (including itself) may appear and reveal
themselves as what they are. That is why for Dasein to exist "means to
hold open a domain through its power to receive/perceive (*Vernehmen-
können*) the meaningfulness of those [things] that are given to [Dasein]
and address [Dasein] in virtue of [Dasein's] own luminosity" (2001: 4/4).
Heidegger often describes this dwelling in the clearing as a "sojourn" or
Aufenthalt.

In another register, this "sojourn" is a function of the existential structures already delineated in *Being and Time*, still remarkably functional in
Heidegger's thought in the 1960s. For example:

> *Thrownness* and *understanding* belong reciprocally together in a
> correlation whose unity is determined through *language* (*Sprache*).
> Language here is to be thought of as saying (*Sagen*), in which beings
> *as* beings, i.e., from the viewpoint of their Being, show themselves.
> Only on the ground of the correlation of thrownness and understand-
> ing through language as saying is mankind able to be addressed by
> beings.
>
> (Heidegger 2001: 139/182–3, original emphasis)

Language, then, not simply in the sense of communication (*Mitteilung*)
(2001: 139/183) or even of verbal articulation (*Verlautbarung*) (2001:
185/232) but in the sense of saying (*Sagen*) is essentially a showing forth
(*zeigen*), or rather a letting show forth (*sich zeigen lassen*) or be seen
(*sehen lassen*) of the beings one encounters within the world *as* beings
(2001: 90, 96–7/117, 126). And the reverse is also true: every phenomenon shows itself [to the phenomenologist] only in the domain of
language" (2001: 96-7/83).

All of this put together adds up to the conception of Dasein as a self.
For Heidegger, the world stands for Dasein as Being-in-the-world in so
far as it remains the same through the entire historical process. But this
does not make it a substance, still less a subject. Its permanence consists
in the fact that "the self can always come back to itself and find itself in
its sojourn still the same" (2001: 175–220).

What does the word "I" add to the experience of historicizing Dasein
as a self? This is not of itself a testimony to consciousness but simply the
naming of the self as it is experienced by itself at any given moment. "For
the Greeks, 'I' is the name for a human being (*Mensch*) that adjusts to the

limits [of a given situation] and, thus at home with himself (*bei sich selbst*), is *Himself*" (2001: 188/235). To become "conscious" in such a condition will mean trying to determine "how this original being-intimate-with (*Sein bei*) [other beings] . . . hangs together with other determinations of Dasein" (2001: 110/143).

What, then, does "consciousness" mean for Heidegger? "Standing within the clearing [of Being] does not mean that human being stands in the light like a post, but the human Da-sein *takes up a sojourn* in the clearing and 'concerns' itself with things" (2001: 144/188). What are we to conclude, then, about the existence of the unconscious? If it is true that the unconscious of psychoanalysis is no more than an unbroken chain of psychic causality that by hypothesis accounts for the gaps in conscious experience, it is no wonder that Heidegger will have no part of it. But is that the only way to understand the nature of Freud's discovery?

Heidegger and Lacan

I suggest that the answer is "no." For we have now another reading of Freud that neither Heidegger nor Boss took account of, that of Jacques Lacan. For Lacan, what Freud discovered in the unconscious was not an unbroken chain of psychic causality but the hidden power of speech, which is structured not like a thermodynamic machine but like a language. If Freud's thinking had been clearly presented to Heidegger in these Lacanian terms, would he still have been so hostile to it?

I put the matter that way, because during the 1950s a strong effort was made in France to arrange a dialogue between these two lions that did not quite work. Note Heidegger's comment to Boss after the receipt of Lacan's *Ecrits*: "For my part, I am not yet ready to read the obviously baroque text. I am told, however, that it is causing the same kind of stir in Paris as (in its time) Sartre's *Being and Nothingness*" (2001: 279/348). Later (in 1967), after receiving a letter from Lacan, Heidegger comments: "I think the psychiatrist needs a psychiatrist" (2001: 281/350). A student of Heidegger was once introduced to Lacan precisely as such; Lacan's only response was: "Heidegger is not interested in psychoanalysis."

However that may be, Lacan, the psychoanalyst, was certainly interested in Heidegger, at least in the early part of his teaching career. In the famous "Discourse at Rome" of 1953, "The function and field of language and speech in psychoanalysis" (Lacan 1977: 30–113) (considered by most the *Magna Carta* of his future work), the allusion to Heidegger is explicit. For example, when discussing memory, Lacan observes: "in Heideggerian language one could say that both types of recollection constitute the subject as *gewesend* – that is to say as being the one who thus has been" and he gladly makes his own Heidegger's famous formula about "being-unto-death." Eventually, Lacan would back away from this mode of expression but he acknowledges to the end that Heidegger's work, in particular his conception of language, was "propaedeutic" to his own. In fact he translated personally into French Heidegger's landmark essay on the *Logos* of Heraclitus (1956) where Being, under the guise of Heraclitus' *Logos,* is interpreted as language itself in its origins, the aboriginal Logos. As I understand Heidegger's development, this is where it becomes clear that the language problematic of the later period is simply the natural complement to the conception of logos as an existential component of Dasein in *Being and Time*, that is after the so-called "turning (*Kehre*)" in his thought. It is this essay that permits Lacan to claim an ally in Heidegger when he says that human beings do not speak language but language speaks them.

When Lacan claims that language speaks the human subject, it is obviously the symbolic order to which he is referring as Other than the subject. There is no need to recall here that Lacan's conception of this Other of language derives from Saussure; that this Other is organized by the laws of language discovered by Saussure and his followers; that the principles of the unconscious governing dream formation discovered by Freud (e.g., displacement and condensation) follow the same pattern as the laws of metonymy and metaphor in linguistics as developed by Saussure and his followers; or that Lacan uses such facts to justify his claim that the unconscious is structured like a language. There is no need, either, to insist here that these laws – or rather *the* Law – are not abstractions but are inscribed in human culture itself and determine the subject through signifying chains forged by one's ancestral past, family history, social milieu and, as times goes on, the record of one's own personal odyssey as its frustrated desire searches for a lost object through the mediation of language.

Now it is the symbolic order, thus individuated, that Lacan claims is the structure of the unconscious that Freud discovered. This is the language that speaks the subject, rather than the reverse. For the subject of psychoanalysis, Lacan claims, is the linguistic subject. Linguists like Benveniste distinguish two modes of subject: the spoken subject, that is the subject of the spoken word as spoken that remains as part of the spoken discourse; and the speaking subject that recedes in the very act of speaking. It is the latter that for Lacan is the subject of our parapraxes, lapses, dreams, and so on – the unconscious as subject that sabotages beyond our control what we consciously intend to say and do.

All this was clear to Lacan by 1953, so if two years later he took time out of a busy teaching and clinical schedule to personally translate Heidegger's *Logos* essay, one has to surmise that he felt that this essay supported his case. In a way it certainly does. For Lacan, the id of Freud (the *Es* of *Wo Es war soll ich werden*) translates as *ça*: *ça pense, ça parle*. For Heidegger: *die Sprache spricht. C'est ça!* For both, language speaks the human thing. For Heidegger, Being-as-*Logos*, in Dasein as its clearing, speaks through beings, inviting Dasein to let them be seen as what they are by bringing them into words. For Lacan, the process is less poetic. For the symbolic order is a chain of signifiers that refer less to individual signifiers (as in the case of Saussure) than they refer to one another and as such produce the subject in language. In the words of Benveniste: "It is . . . literally true that the foundation of subjectivity is in the exercise of language" (Benveniste 1972: 262ff.). The linguistic subject as such, then, is an *effect* of the signifying chain. Thus a sign "represents something for someone," but "a signifier represents a subject for another signifier" (Lacan 1966: 840). Hence,

> the effect of language is the cause introduced into the subject. By this effect [the subject] is not cause of itself. For its cause is the signifier without which there would not be any subject in the real. But this subject is what the signifier represents, and it could not represent anything except for another signifier.
>
> (Lacan 1966: 835).

To be sure, there is a causality here, but in the order of language, not in the order of thermodynamically styled psychic energy.

What are we to infer from all this? Clearly remaining in the Cartesian tradition to the extent that he calls a human being a subject at all, Lacan in no way conceives of this subject as an encapsulated ego of consciousness. As a subject of the unconscious, it dwells in intersubjective space, in the domain of social discourse (*le lien social*), the locus of the Other. Does this mean that they are saying the same thing? Certainly not!

The case of Jennifer

Surely the two conceptions cannot be conflated, but can they throw any light on each other? My hunch is that they can. At any rate, to test the clinical viability of the foregoing parameters in a life-blood context, I propose to let them serve as general background for a brief reflection upon how the "talking cure" works . . . when it works. Highly simplified for heuristic reasons, the following record recounts the initial stages of treatment of a 15-year-old adolescent who was brought to the therapist by her mother very much against her will, I shall call her "Jennifer." This case (Simonney 2001) is cited with permission almost *verbatim*. Simonney's name for the patient is "Cherifa" for reasons that the full text makes clear, but since this part of his text does not concern us, I have changed her name to "Jennifer" as being more familiar to the Anglo-Saxon ear.

Jennifer had suffered from insulin-dependent diabetes since the age of 6. She must follow a strict diet and give herself regular insulin injections. Because she does not respect her diet, nor does she take her insulin regularly, the medical doctors became especially concerned when she began to have frequent fainting spells. She consulted with three different psychologists, all of whom urged obedience to the doctors' orders, claiming that they were only for her own good. The mother, too, became increasingly anxious, fighting constantly with her daughter in a futile effort to force her to follow medical advice. Exhausted by the struggle, the mother finally brought Jennifer to the psychotherapist, her sullen countenance testifying eloquently to her recalcitrance.

The therapist in this case was a psychoanalyst. What could he offer Jennifer that medical doctors, psychologists and an anxious mother could not? Psychoanalysis would be something that the standard therapies, whether physical, psychological or purely cognitive, would, in principle, formally ignore: access to what Freud called the "unconscious." It is common knowledge now that this for Freud was the system of psychic processes functioning outside of conscious awareness that determine, or at least radically influence, conscious human behavior and account for many forms of illness that have come to be called "mental." It was the existence of just such a system that came to be dubbed the "talking" cure; the method Freud devised for dealing with it he called "psychoanalysis." Reduced to the barest of bones, psychoanalysis consisted in: first, a method ("free association" by the subject, saying "whatever comes to mind") in conjunction with a corresponding free floating attentiveness on the part of a listener; second, a technique for interpreting thereby the unconscious desire of the subject; and third, the galvanizing of both of these in what Freud called "transference" – that unique electricity between analysand and analyst through which the subject can experience the functioning of those psychic structures, however repressed or infantile, that sabotage the subject's conscious thinking and acting.

The centrality of language in this, the foundational experience of Freud's entire enterprise, will explain why Jacques Lacan, in his celebrated "return to Freud," found the laws of structural linguistics a better paradigm with which to conceptualize the workings of the unconscious than the laws of mechanics on which Freud relied. Lacan went so far as to claim that the unconscious that Freud discovered was in fact "structured like a language." The whole process of psychoanalysis is reducible, then, to the talking of the subject to an analyst who listens – hence the etiquette "talking cure." Sure, but what makes it therapeutic? First, a bit of case history.

Quest

The mother remarried and has had a son with her second husband. Jennifer gets along well with her stepfather. On the other hand, she does not want to see her own father, nor even speak with him on the phone. She explained her refusal in the following terms: her father, who is himself a diabetic, had hidden his disease from her mother who only learned of it after the girl's birth. He used to get up at night to give himself his insulin shots, which he kept hidden in the refrigerator. We might well wonder how the mother could remain blind to such maneuvers on his part.

The girl does not forgive him for bringing her into the world with such a handicap as diabetes, so the father figure is marked with the seal of death, that possibility to which all serious illnesses may lead. It is important for her that the father figure has been divided into a second figure, represented by her reassuring and protective stepfather.

We should add that her aggressiveness towards her mother also stems from her resentment, more or less explicitly expressed, that her mother could have given birth to her in such circumstances, the daughter not having really forgiven her mother for her blindness with regards to her father's disease.

At the end of the first consultation, the mother gave me [i.e., the therapist] the addresses of the doctors who were treating the girl and asked me to get in touch with them. I told her that there was no hurry to do so, and that, if I needed to do so, I would speak about it with Jennifer first. I also said that Jennifer might be suffering from the heavy burden of her medical care.

Then, once alone with the girl, I explained the rules of the [treatment]: she was to come every week, to speak with me freely about whatever came into her head. As for me, I promised her that whatever she said to me would remain between us: confidential.

The second session arrived. Jennifer came looking extremely pleased, in marked contrast with the time before; and she told me how much she appreciated my not contacting her doctors. She added that she had already seen three different psychologists each of whom had been constantly in touch with her doctors, repeating to her that she had to take care of herself, an attitude which had been unbearable for her because it made her feel completely trapped.

She added that her mother's behavior was a source of pain for her, that her mother harassed her for not following her treatment, even going so far as to scold her in public and "to say everything in front of everybody." She added that "it's humiliating for a child to be scolded in public, and that's why I no longer take my medicine."

I think it is hardly necessary to insist on the importance of that last statement which, in some ways, gives, if not the only key, at least one of the important keys to the symptom of her refusal to accept health care. It is fitting to underline her use of the word "child," which, though she is no longer really a child, points to an infantile and old source of her disorder. In reaction to her mother's reprimands, which shows to the eyes of the world the bad daughter who does not want to be cured, might we not think that Jennifer, on the contrary, is seeking to expose her disease in much the same way as someone who would reveal a family secret, this secret being the mystery of her conception, set between the paternal lie and the maternal blindness. By exposing her illness, she is asking herself what unfathomable enjoyment (*jouissance*), with death playing a leading role, ruled over her birth. Her mother's and the doctors' reprimands place the fault on her; she is the guilty one. Here we see the [position of victim], where she suffers for two reasons: from her sickness and from the reprimands for being a bad patient. The situation is blocked since the thing she is exposing through her symptom, is not recognized. Consequently, she experiences all the care given her as a way of hushing up the truth she is trying to express.

And there, or perhaps one should say, beginning from there, the analyst, by not being totally associated with the medical discourse, by being, as Freud said, in the position of "benevolent neutrality," opens the way to the transference which is going to allow him to begin the psychoanalytic treatment. Obviously, transference is not a phenomenon arising solely within the psychoanalytic context; however, only analysis allows it to become something other than blindness, by attaching it to its unconscious roots.

Here we can say that Jennifer experienced the unit formed by the doctors and her mother as being truly persecuting and traumatizing, albeit that their conscious goal was to give her care. Conceived as an attempt to repair the damage transmitted by the father (and to a lesser degree by the mother), the care felt to her like an unbearable aggression, because she experienced it as a denial of her being and of the real meaning of her illness, a nullification of the questions she was trying to ask through the repeated fainting spells.

(Simonney 2001: 34–6)

Commentary

The neurotic symptoms (refusal of medical treatment, neglect of diet, fainting, and so on) are presented as bringing into the open not simply a repressed rage against a chronic, life-threatening disease but beyond it a question about its origin, that is the mystery of her conception, set between the paternal lie and maternal blindness in some "unfathomable enjoyment (*jouissance*), with death playing a leading role, that ruled over her birth" – all festering like a "family secret." But the sense of her question is not recognized. On the contrary, the care given her is experienced as a "hushing up" of the truth that she is trying to bring to light. "Conceived as an attempt to repair the damage transmitted by the father (and to a lesser degree by the mother), the care felt to her like an unbearable aggression, because she experienced it as a denial of her being and the real meaning of her illness." What she is seeking to uncover is this "family secret," the truth of how she has come to be what she is, the basic facts of "what is the case."

But what kind of truth can psychoanalytic experience in fact offer? Freud doesn't help much to define a psychoanalytic version of truth. In his *New Introductory Lectures on Psychoanalysis* he speaks of truth in terms of positive science:

> Its endeavor is to arrive at correspondence with reality – that is to say with what exists outside us and independently of us and, as experience has taught us, is decisive for the fulfillment or disappointment of our wishes. This correspondence with the real external world we call "truth." It remains the aim of scientific work even if we leave the practical value of that work out of account.
>
> (Freud 1933: 170)

As for truth in psychoanalysis, Freud presumably would add nuance to the term "reality" with his distinction between "psychical" and "material" reality (Freud 1900: 620), but his method would still be analogous to that of natural science, that is to search out the causes at play in any given psychic phenomenon. But all this is the language of classical positivism, where truth consists in correspondence between subject judging and object judged. What happens to truth in psychoanalysis, though, when the positivist ideal familiar to Freud is rejected out of hand? Such was the move made by Lacan.

According to the canons of scientific positivism, the rigor of scientific method demanded that every effort be made to preclude intrusion by the subject into the content (i.e., "objectivity") of that perception. In psychoanalysis, however, the subject is not *ex*cluded but *in*cluded in the research procedure. Validation of any procedure must be found elsewhere than in conformity between judgment and judged. This was one reason for Lacan's turn to formalism:

> This is the problem of grounding that must assure our discipline its place among the sciences: a problem of formalization. . . . Linguistics can serve us as a guide here, since that is the role it plays in the vanguard of contemporary anthropology. . . . And the reduction of every language to the group of a very small number of these phenomenal oppositions by initiating an equally rigorous formalization of its highest morphemes puts within our reach a precisely defined access to our own field.
>
> (Lacan 1977: 73/285)

The shift to formalism, however, meant a shift in the understanding of truth. For the primordial experience of truth will appear not in a judgment about what is the case, but what is the case itself in so far as it lets itself be seen (e-vident), that is the way things are in their very self-disclosure. The *Oxford Dictionary of English Etymology* notes "evident" from the Latin *e-videre* as having originally the sense of the middle voice as "making itself be seen." It is in this sense that I am using it here. The hyphenation is intended to call attention to the middle-voice quality of the etymology. Accordingly, the case can be made (we shall return to this later) that e-vidence in its most radical sense of [something] making (letting) itself be seen is the originary nature of truth from which all other versions (conformity, coherence, pragmatism, linguistic formalism, and so on) derive. For Lacan it is clear that the formalism he strives for is the most acceptable way of discerning – and communicating – this kind of e-vidence for the way things are.

To be sure, this is never explicated by Lacan. In fact, to the best of my knowledge Lacan never reflects formally upon the nature of truth as such (a philosophical problem, after all), but the most telling use of the term refers to the subject's relation to desire: "The whole analytical experience is no more than an invitation to the *revelation* of [the subject's] *desire*" (Lacan 1992: 221/261, emphases added). It is in that sense that from the beginning of his work, Lacan presumes that truth is essentially the e-vidence for what is the case. In the early years of his teaching, for example, he made much of the distinction between "empty" speech and "full" speech: "empty speech takes place when the subject seems to be talking in vain about someone who, even if he were his spitting image, can never become one with the assumption of his desire" (Lacan 1977: 45/254); "full" speech is achieved not by examination of the "here and now," nor by the examination of resistances, but by anamnesis:

> In psychoanalytic anamnesis it is not a question of reality, but of *truth*, because the effect of full speech is to reorder past contingencies by conferring on them the sense of necessities to come, such as they are constituted by the little freedom through which the subject makes them present. . . . It is certainly this assumption of his history by the subject, in so far as it is constituted by the speech addressed to the other, that constitutes the ground of the new method that Freud called psychoanalysis.
>
> (Lacan 1977: 48/256–7, emphasis added)

The truth of the subject (i.e., of one's desire) comes about, then, through the speaking that constitutes the psychoanalytic process. It is not based on any kind of correspondence; it is essentially revelatory in nature and takes place when meaning (sense) is discovered in an historicizing process. It has no other foundation than the efficacy of the language that utters it and prescinds completely from the "reality" that characterizes the world of its conscious activity. Founded thus in language itself, truth has an inexhaustible resilience: "Even if [language] communicates nothing, the discourse represents the existence of communication; even if it denies the evidence, it affirms that speech constitutes truth; even if it is intended to deceive, the discourse speculates on faith in testimony" (Lacan 1977: 43/251–2).

There is another element in Lacan's operative conception of truth: the negativity that permeates it. As early as 1955 in "The Freudian thing," a paper commemorating in Vienna the centenary of Freud's birth, Lacan delivered a grotesque *prosopopeia* in the name of truth to the obvious consternation of his audience. "Men, listen, I am giving you the secret. I,

Truth, will speak." His point is that there is no such thing as total truth – especially in psychoanalysis – and truth arrives at best as damaged goods. Eventually he will claim that no truth can ever be whole (Lacan 1998: 92/85). Here, however, he underlines not simply the manifestation but the inevitable distortion of truth as it comes to statement:

> For you I am the enigma of her who vanishes as soon as she appears. . . . The discourse of error, its articulation in acts, could bear witness to the truth against evidence itself. . . . For the most innocent intention is disconcerted at being unable to conceal the fact that one's unsuccessful acts are the most successful and that one's failure fulfills one's most secret wish. . . . I wander about in what you regard as being the least true in essence: in the dream, in the way the most far-fetched conceit, the most grotesque nonsense of the joke defies sense, in chance, not in its law, but in its contingence, and I never do more to change the face of the world than when I give it the profile of Cleopatra's nose.
>
> (Lacan 1977: 121–2/408–10)

Truth, then, carries the scars of negativity. In other words: "Error is the habitual incarnation of truth. Error is the usual manifestation of the truth itself – so that the paths of truth are in essence the paths of error" (1988: 263/289). Clearly, any complete account of truth must also account for the error and distortion (i.e., non-truth) that infiltrate it. So be it! We shall return to this. For Jennifer, the negative valence of truth as discovery does not appear in the therapist's undetailed record of the treatment. But no doubt it appears in the clinical work in any form of resistance to the dispelling of darkness, beginning with the recalcitrance that marked her first day. Add to this all those grab-bag banalities (e.g., parapraxes, slips of the tongue) that constitute the day labor of analytic work. Then there are dreams . . .

Quarry

In turning to Jennifer's dreams, the therapist focuses on one series in particular that is representative:

> We are going to continue now with another type of repetition, that of a dream which returned in similar forms during several sessions. The general theme of the dream is as follows: Jennifer finds herself in a boarding school where she had, in reality, spent two years before

being expelled for reasons of discipline six months ago. She feels deep regrets about no longer being in that institution intended for young people who are ill. She felt at home there, sheltered from the kind of heavy observation which she has to confront elsewhere: in that place she was not different from her peers.

Her dreams took her back to that place which she has idealized somewhat since her expulsion. Her dreams placed her once again among her favorite friends and teachers. The more often the dream came back, the more reticent she became about telling it to me: what was the use, since it was always the same thing? I pointed out to her that, first of all, a dream never repeats itself exactly the same way, and that the repetition is a sign that there is something that is insisting on being "read," in order to find a meaning. The identical dreams came one after another, session after session, but never failed to bring out some significant differences which allowed for progress in the analysis. One day, in a dream that took her once again to her former boarding school, she saw herself faint: a woman teacher, who was one of her favorites, took care of her with warmth and concern. "It's not like my mother" added Jennifer "who is aggressive and worried when she takes care of me." She went on: "Yesterday, an asthmatic friend of mine fainted. Every one hurried to take care of her. I asked them if that was the way they took care of me. They answered 'yes,' which reassured me, but I did not want to watch. I don't like to see such things; watching reminds me of myself."

We see here the development of the group of problems surrounding the Other's regard / gaze.

Jennifer needs a helpful regard / gaze, stripped of the aggressiveness that often accompanies the assistance given by someone who identifies with you, who puts his self in your shoes, such as the aggressiveness that she has often felt from her mother. She does not want her suffering to be thrown back at her as by a mirror, which was why she did not want to look at her friend who had just fainted. She would rather identify with a healthy adult who gives aid to an ill person, such as Jennifer herself. Once again we find exactly the same group of issues at stake as those involved in her wish to become a surgeon. We now understand better her nostalgia for that boarding school where, far removed from her mother, she could meet such [looks].

At the end of the session she said: "I've understood that I must be positive about things." We can interpret that statement as a wish to leave the position of victim where she had been stuck.

During the next session, she told me a dream in which she returned to the boarding school, not as an ill person, but simply to visit her friends. The principal asked her to stay but she refused.

We see this dream, in some ways, as a dream of healing. She added: "I am proud and relieved to have had this dream. Now I am less ill, I no longer have my place at the boarding school. I must leave my place to someone who needs it more."

We see here again her psyche working to free her from an identification with her illness, this idea appearing clearly in the words: "leave my place to someone else." This series of repeated dreams provided the opportunity for a psychic effort, which was concluded by the last dream. From that day on, she no longer dreamed of that boarding school; she no longer needed to do it.

(Simonney 2001: 39–41)

Commentary

This is indeed a dream of healing, and the repetitive chain is taken as a sign of progress that confirms the efficacy of the method. The dreams are disclosive in quality, for each dream deals with Jennifer's struggle to confront her regret that through her own fault she had been expelled from a boarding school where, whatever its limitations, she was more comfortable than with her mother at home. The minor differences that characterized the repetition of the same theme were significant enough to "allow for progress" (i.e., clarification) in the analysis. Three observations are in order.

First, the efficacy of the treatment clearly depends on its revelatory character. It lets the truth of Jennifer gradually disclose itself, so that the orientation of her desire begins to appear. Apparently it was the "talking" therapy that enabled this to come about.

Second, the disclosure is hampered by a built-in negativity that sabotages the process, and in dreams, distortion is one form of that negativity. In the present case the dream content works its way through the continually differentiating "details" of the dreamwork, the repetition being a sign that something still obscure is insisting on being "read" in order for meaning to appear. This slow uncovering of still to be articulated "meaning," manifested through distortion in dreams, is symptomatic, I suggest, of other negative modes of disclosure – besides Freud's favorite examples (slips of the tongue, parapraxes, and so on) – such as confusion, obscurity, ambivalence, inconsistency, contradiction, paradox, and all the ingenious subterfuges of self-deception that mark the humdrum of the psychoanalytic enterprise.

Finally, the disclosive process is liberating. The last dream in this series suggests that Jennifer wishes to dissociate herself from her role as victim of illness and to identify with a healthy adult "who gives aid to an ill person, such as Jennifer herself." Her own remark indicates the progress: "I've understood that I must be positive about things." The follow-up dream, in which she was invited to return to boarding school but chose not to because she no longer needed it, is characteristic of the normal way by which symptoms dissolve: compromise solutions to un-settled conflicts become unnecessary when the original problem is straightforwardly uncovered and dealt with in the open. The truth that the "talking" cure illumines in the subject makes possible its own kind of freedom, freedom from darkness. Psychoanalytically speaking, this type of liberation from darkness may be the most we can hope for.

All this is well and good, but none of it deals with the question of how such a process is possible. This, of course, is the philosophical question that Lacan dismisses, but Heidegger, to whom Lacan often alluded (especially in the early years but with increasing reserve as time went on), can be helpful here. Obviously the notion of originary truth as e-vidence/discovery/disclosure/ recalls Heidegger's thematizing of the Greek word for truth, *alétheia*: a combination of -*léthé* (what lies hidden in concealment) and *a*-, the alpha prefix indicating privation. Taken together, they identify truth as non-concealment (revelation, disclosure). Of course Lacan was fully aware of Heidegger's conception of truth and apparently quite comfortable with it in 1953 when describing the psycho-analytic process as the achieving of "full speech": "In psychoanalytic *anamnesis* it is not a question of reality, but of *truth*, because the effect of full speech is to reorder past contingencies by conferring on them the sense of necessities to come" (Lacan 1977: 48/256, emphasis added). Apparently he lost interest in this way of conceiving truth as he turned more and more toward the formalism, inspired by Saussure through Lévi-Strauss, that could account in a structuralist way for the "scientific" character of psychoanalysis.

Heidegger broached the question of truth already in his major work, *Being and Time* ([1927] 1996: 196–211) but shortly after thematized the issue in a complete essay, "On the essence of truth" ([1930–43] 1998). There he begins with an analysis of the classical notion of truth as conformity between judgment and judged but then proceeds phenomeno-logically:

What is stated by the presentative statement [judgment] is said of the presented thing [judged] in just such manner as that thing, as presented, is. The "such as" has to do with the presenting and what it presents. Disregarding all "psychological" preconceptions as well as those of any "theory of consciousness," to present here means to let the thing stand opposed as an object. As thus placed, what stands opposed must traverse an open field of opposedness (*Entgegen*) and nevertheless must maintain its stand as a thing and show itself as something withstanding (*ein Ständiges*). This appearing of the thing in traversing a field of opposedness takes place within an open region, the openness of which is not first created by the presenting but rather is only entered into and taken over as a domain of related-ness. The relation of the presentative statement to the thing is the accomplishment of the bearing (*Verhältnis*) that originarily and always comes to prevail as a comportment (*Verhalten*). But all comportment is distinguished by the fact that, standing in the open region, it in each case adheres to something opened up as such. What is thus opened up, solely in this strict sense, was experienced early in Western thinking as "what is present" and for a long time has been named "[a] being [*ein Seiendes*]."

(Heidegger [1930–43] 1998: 141)

It is this field of openness that Heidegger claims to be what the Greeks understood as *alétheia* ([1930–43] 1998: 145). Human comportment stands within this openness, open to beings in this way, and one's open stance varies according to the kind of comportment in question. In Heidegger's eyes, I suggest, it would be such an open stance as this that Jennifer, unknowingly of course, on the deepest level would bring into treatment in her quest for the "family secret." Heidegger's next move is to ask about the "essence" of this openness, its ultimate "nature." His answer is . . . freedom! How is such a freedom to be thought here? "Freedom for what is opened up in an open region lets beings be the beings that they are. Freedom now reveals itself as letting beings be":

The phrase required now – to let beings be – does not refer to neglect and indifference but rather the opposite. To let be is to engage one-self with beings. On the other hand, to be sure, this is not to be un-derstood only as mere management, preservation, tending and planning of beings in each case encountered or sought out. To let be – that is to let beings be the beings that they are – means to engage oneself with the open region and its openness into which every being comes to stand, bringing that openness, as it were, along with itself. To engage oneself with the disclosedness of beings is not to lose

oneself in them; rather, such engagement withdraws in the face of
beings in order that they might reveal themselves with respect to
what and how they are.

(Heidegger [1930–43] 1998: 144)

I take this to mean that in psychoanalysis, the task of the analyst would be
to let the analysand (here Jennifer) be, so that she in turn may let herself
be and thus achieve the freedom that comes with the disclosure of what
she is in truth. Practically speaking, this would mean for the analyst to let
her discourse be and have its way with her, guarding against any infiltra-
tion of his own signifying system into hers. In the case of Jennifer, the
therapist seems to have been able to do just that. Note, for example, the
sensitivity with which he hears the signifier "child" in the second session.
For him, her entire pathology resonates in it: "It is fitting to underline her
use of the word 'child', which, though she is no longer really a child,
points to an infantile and old source of her disorder." Likewise, through
the repetitive dreams and her articulation of them, despite her resistant
reticence in doing so, the truth of her relation to the hospital slowly
appears and finally lets her be free from her dependence upon it.

But an adequate conception of truth must include also the element of
non-truth that is ingredient to it. Heidegger is helpful here, too. What he
adds to the conception of truth as *alétheia* is an insistence on the negative
component of truth ingredient to it, the *léthé*. The negativity in question
is not simply an absence of manifestation but includes a mysterious
dynamic quality that Heidegger articulates as the non-essence of truth,
which takes two forms: mystery (*Geheimnis*), the concealment of what
still remains unrevealed, and errancy (*Irre*), a compounding through
forgetfulness of this double concealment:

Errancy is the essential counteressence to the originary essence of
truth. Errancy opens itself up as the open region for every counter-
play to essential truth. Errancy is the open site for and ground of
error. Error is not merely an isolated mistake but the kingdom (the
dominion) of the history of those entanglements in which all kinds of
erring get interwoven. In conformity with its openness and its relatedness to beings as a whole, every mode of comportment has its manner of erring. Error extends from the most ordinary wasting of time,
making a mistake, and mis-calculating, to going astray and venturing
too far in one's essential attitudes and decisions. . . . By leading them
astray, errancy dominates human beings through and through.

(Heidegger [1930–43] 1998: 150–1, emended)

My suggestion is that this conception of a non-essence (i.e., negativity) of truth, especially under the guise of errancy, is supple enough and comprehensive enough to accommodate Lacan's hyperbolic *prosopopeia* in which he lets Truth itself take the floor:

> For you I am the enigma of her who vanishes as soon as she appears. . . . The discourse of error, its articulation in acts, could bear witness to the truth against evidence itself. . . . For the most innocent intention is disconcerted at being unable to conceal the fact that one's unsuccessful acts are the most successful and that one's failure fulfills one's secret wish . . . etc., etc.
>
> (Lacan 1977: 121–2/408–10)

Lacan insists on one more point: the close correlation between truth and the function of language. For Heidegger, this correlation is based upon his interpretation of the meaning of *logos* for the Greeks, as we have seen, for example in the work of Heraclitus (Heidegger 1975: 59–78). Although *logos* from early on was associated with speech, the original sense of it for Heraclitus, Heidegger claims, came from *legein*, meaning "to gather" (as one gathers wood), or "to bring together" into some kind of unity, that thereby becomes manifest as what it is. Like *physis*, *logos* was from the beginning associated with the coming to pass of *alétheia*, the unconcealment of everything that is. The task of human beings would be to collaborate with the process by letting beings be seen as what they are. Eventually, it became possible to think of this gathering process (the coming-to-pass of truth) as originary language and of the vocation of human beings as bringing it to expression in words. At any rate, the vocation of human beings as such would be to bring to articulation the language of *logos* as process of *alétheia*, a task for which the poets serve as models. Psychoanalytically speaking, then, *alétheia* comes to pass through the *logos* that functions in the very speaking through which "full" speech comes about. It is in this sense that "truth is grounded in the fact that it *speaks* and it has no other means of [being grounded]" (Lacan 1989: 16/867-8, emphasis added).

Conclusion

This reflection has addressed the question about how the "talking cure" succeeds when it does succeed. It has ventured to say that the treatment succeeds because the truth it seeks is the truth of revelation (*alétheia*) which is self-validating to the extent that the e-vidence for e-vidence is e-vidence. As a liberating from darkness (*léthé*), this truth is essentially freedom, and freedom of this kind comes to pass through the functioning of language.

Is this a satisfactory answer to the initial question? Hardly. At best it serves as propaedeutic to a further examination of the real issues involved. Fundamental questions remain unaddressed, For example: What are the practical implications of the conception of truth as revelation in a concrete clinical setting? How does the conception of freedom articulated here relate to classical issues of freedom (e.g., the role of choice in the exercise of freedom, as in Jennifer's choice to forgo return to the hospital)? How are we to understand the relationship between language (*logos*) as originary and language (*logos*) as concretely functional in the clinical situation? Finally, are we really justified in introducing Heideggerian thought patterns to throw light on very conventional psychoanalytic issues as they are raised in a case such as Jennifer's? Was not the coolness toward Heidegger in Lacan's later years well advised? Is not Heidegger's question (about the meaning of Being) and the verbal apparatus that goes with it, excluded a priori from any relevance to psychoanalysis, inasmuch as, in Lacan's conception of language, "there is no Other (e.g., Being) of the Other (i.e., the symbolic order of language)" (Lacan 1977: 310–11/813)?

None of these questions has been seriously addressed here – each demands its own careful consideration. But where else can we turn? The question of "how?" will not go away.

References

Beneveniste, E. (1972) *Problèmes de la linguistique générale*. Paris: Gallimard.

Craig, E. (1988) "An encounter with Medard Boss," *The Humanistic Psychologist* 16: 24–55.

Freud, S. (1900) *The Interpretation of Dreams*, in *Standard Edition of the Complete Psychological Works of Sigmund Freud*, vols 4 and 5, ed. and trans. J. Strachey. London: Hogarth Press.

—— (1933) *New Introductory Lectures on Psychoanalysis*, in *Standard Edition of the Complete Psychological Works of Sigmund Freud*, vol 22, ed. and trans. J. Strachey. London: Hogarth Press.

Heidegger, M. ([1927] 1996) *Being and Time*, trans. J. Stambaugh. Albany, NY: State University of New York Press.

—— ([1930–43] 1998) "On the Essence of Truth," in W. McNeill. (ed.) *Pathmarks*, New York and Cambridge: Cambridge University Press.

—— ([1947] 1977) *Letter on Humanism*, in *Basic Writings*, ed. D. F. Krell. London: Routledge.

—— (1975) *Logos* (Heraclitus, Fragment B 50), *Early Greek Thinking*, ed. and trans. D. Krell and F. Capuzzi. New York: Harper and Row.

—— (2001) *Zollikon Seminar Protocols–Conversation–Letters*, ed. M. Boss, trans. F. Mayr and R. Askay. Evanston, IL: Northwestern University Press.

Lacan, J. (1956) *Logos* (Heraclit Fragment 50). *La Psychanalyse* 1, trans. M. Heidegger (1975).

—— (1966) *Ecrits*. Paris: Gallimard.

—— (1977) *Ecrits: A Selection*, trans. A. Sheridan. New York: W. W. Norton.

—— (1988) *The Seminar of Jacques Lacan. Book I (1953–1954). Freud's Papers on Technique*, ed. J-A. Miller, trans. J. Forrester. New York: W. W. Norton.

—— (1989) "Science and truth," trans. B. Fink, *News Letter of the Freudian Field* 1: 4–29.

—— (1992) *The Seminar of Jacques Lacan. Book VII (1959–1960). The Ethics of Psychoanalysis*, ed. J-A. Miller, trans. D. Porter. New York: W. W. Norton.

—— (1998) *The Seminar of Jacques Lacan. Book XX (1972–73). On Feminine Sexuality, the Limits of Love and Knowledge*, ed. J-A. Miller, trans. B. Fink. New York: W. W. Norton.

Simonney, D. (2001) "A few observations concerning a psychoanalytical cure of an adolescent," *The Letter* 23: 33–49.

Chapter 4

Beyond postmodernism

From concepts through experiencing

Eugene Gendlin

The relationship between experience and concepts is central to the theory and practice of psychotherapy. Philosophy can help us to understand this relationship. Sadly, however, few people think of combining psychotherapy and philosophy even though each has what the other most vitally needs. Psychotherapists can be immensely subtle practitioners but typically have not developed their conceptual thinking. This is because they find little use in their work for the concepts they have learned or find ready to hand. In contrast, philosophy provides a critique of the kinds of concepts psychology uses. Drawing on philosophy, we can sharpen our conceptual thinking. Without some background in philosophy, talk about kinds of concepts can seem complicated. One needs an acquaintance with talking about concepts, something that philosophers have done since Greek times. If one can see past the assumptions inherent in the usual kind of concepts we use, a new kind can be fashioned. In this chapter I will argue that psychotherapy can develop theoretical concepts directly from experiencing.

Philosophers on their side badly need to discover how *direct access* to something that could be called "experiencing" is even possible. In a long tradition most philosophers have construed "experience" as something that is always already organized by concepts. This is true, but experiencing also always goes beyond the concepts that are implicit in it. One hundred years after Freud, philosophers who are concerned with psychology still mostly go to Freud's concepts, instead of the experiential work of the whole of the twentieth century. The philosophical tendency to construe "experience" only in terms of concepts is largely reinforced by what can be found in Freud. Philosophy needs to discover that there can be a direct relation between thinking and experiencing. To discover direct experiencing opens a vast and complex philosophical field.

It is impossible to grasp the relationship between experience and concepts by concepts alone. Experiencing cannot be copied, captured, or represented. Concepts can only point toward our experience. Thus, we need to form concepts of a special kind that incorporate experiencing itself, the act to which the concept refers. We have to carry the experience along with us. Experiencing never *becomes* a concept. Since experiencing cannot be represented, the concepts can only indicate various kinds of relations between experiencing and conceptual patterns. I will present a few such concepts here.

An enormous gap called postmodernism has recently been created between experiencing and concepts. I want not only to examine the nature of this gap, but also to attempt to move beyond it. Of course there are many strands of postmodernism. It is best known for denying that there is any truth, or that one can claim to ground any statement in experience. Postmodernism is right in that one can not claim to represent or copy experiencing. But this does not mean that what we say has no relationship to what we experience – that there is no truth, that everything we say is arbitrary. In contrast to postmodernism, I show that we can have direct access to experiencing through our bodies (Gendlin 1992). I maintain that bodily experience can not be reduced to language and culture. Our bodily sense of situations is a concretely sensed interaction process that always exceeds culture, history, and language.

Not only perception

What and where is this experiencing to which we have direct access? Merleau-Ponty (1945) started in this direction with his discussion of the body, but we need to go even further. The body is not just a philosophical precondition of perception. Merleau-Ponty rescued the body from being considered one more sensed thing like all the other sensed things (as it still is in physiology). For him the body is a sensing, an internal-external orienting center of perception, not just perceived, but perceiving. But perception is not a possible starting point from which to understand ourselves and our bodies.

By beginning with perception, philosophy makes it seem that living things are in contact with reality only through perception. But plants are in contact with reality. They are interactions, quite without perception. Our own living bodies also are interactions with their environments, and that is not lost just because ours *also* have perception. Animal bodies – including ours – sense themselves, and thereby we sense the interactional living we *are*. In sensing ourselves, our bodies sense our physical environment and our inter-human situations.

It seems obvious that a situation does not consist of the perception of colors, smells, and sounds. Even the simplest situation cannot be grasped just in terms of the five senses. Every situation involves other people and their complex involvements with each other. This cannot be understood in terms of colors and smells.

Our bodies sense themselves in living in our situations. Our bodies do our living. Our bodies are interactions in the environment; they interact as bodies, not just through the five senses. We do not lurk behind a partition with five peepholes.

The living body consists of interactions with others in the world. "Perception" appears only *before* or *to* a body. But the body is an interaction also in that it breathes, not only in that it senses the cold of the air. It feeds; it does not only see and smell food. It grows and sweats. It walks; it does not only perceive the hard resistance of the ground. And it walks not just as a displacement between two points in empty space, rather to go somewhere. The body senses the whole situation, and it implies, it urges, it implicitly shapes our next action. It senses itself living the situation in its whole context.

We act in every situation, not just on the basis of colors and smells (not even all five senses crossed so each is in the others), nor just by motions in geometric space. Rather, we act from the bodily sense of each situation. Without the bodily sense of the situation we would not know where we are or what we are doing.

Not only language

It is not the body of perception that is structured by language. Nor is the body's interaction structured by culture and language alone. Rather, it is the body of interactional living in its environment. The body's interaction is always more intricate than language. It is after and with language, always again freshly ongoing and constellating this situation in the present. Language elaborates how the body implies its situation and its next behavior.

We sense our bodies not as elaborated perceptions but as the body sense of our situations, the interactional whole-body by which we orient and know what we are doing. In sensing itself the body functions as our sense of each situation. It is a gigantic omission to miss the role of the body's self-sentience, and to try to constitute the world out of percepts of the five senses.

The higher animals do much of what humans are and do. For example, Jane Goodall reports that a chimpanzee mother of an infant that has polio carefully arranges his limp arms and legs. When an adult male chimpan-zee was wounded, his small brother sat carefully pushing the lips of a gaping wound together.

The human symbolizing kind of experience is not necessary for differ-entiated communication. The animals groom each other and pick fleas even when there are no fleas, just to keep each other company. We know this also from our dogs, cats, and horses. When my cat is especially pleased about sitting next to me, he "brushes the fur" on my hand with his tongue, although he can sense that there is no fur there. This kind of com-munication happens among them and with us.

We have no difficulty answering those who think that we cannot talk of anything before language. Of course there are cultural differences once there is language. We are not concerned with a body without language. We can see the body's primacy and priority when we feel how the body now functions, always in a much wider way than language. The body functions in crucial ways, and in ways that are trans-historical. It is not the five senses but the sentient bodily interaction that takes on language and history – and then always still exceeds them. Let me show this.

The bodily felt sense of situations

Merleau-Ponty (1945) says that we sense the space behind our backs. Please notice for a moment that this is true; you can sense the space behind your back. Is that still to be called "perception?" It is not vision, hearing, or touch, nor is it just the togetherness of the five senses. It is rather a direct bodily sense that you have and use all the time.

You sense behind you not just the space, nor just space-filling visible things. You sense behind you the people to whom you could turn and speak. Those people are part of your situation just now, and you sense them as part of your sense of the situation you are in. You can sense how your present peaceful body-sense would change if you decided now to turn and say something loud to those people. That you won't do it is all included in the sense of the present situation that you now have – in a bodily way.

Suppose, for example, that you are walking home at night, and you sense a group of men following you. You don't merely perceive them. You don't merely hear them there, in the space behind you. Your body-sense instantly includes also your hope that perhaps they aren't following you. It includes your alarm and many past experiences – too many to separ-ate out – and surely also the need to do something, be it walk faster, change your course, escape into a house, get ready to fight, run, shout (.....).

My (.....) expresses the fact that your body-sense includes more than we can list, more than you can think by thinking one thing at a time. And it includes not only what is there. It also implies a next move to cope with the situation. But this implying of your next move is still a (.....) since your actual move has not yet come.

Since it includes all this, the (.....) is not just a perception, although it certainly includes many perceptions. Is it then a feeling? It is certainly felt, but "feeling" usually means emotion. The (.....) includes emotions, but also so much else. Is it then something mysterious and unfamiliar? No, we always have such a bodily sense of our situations. You have it now, or you would be disoriented as to where you are and what you are doing.

Is it not odd that no word or phrase in our language as yet says this? "Kinesthetic" refers only to movement; "proprioceptive" refers to muscles. "Sense" has many uses. So there is no common word for this utterly familiar bodily sense of the intricacy of our situations, along with the rapid weighing of more alternatives than we can think separately. We now call it a "felt sense." This phrase can say the (.....), but only if it brings the (.....) along with it so that it is part of what we mean and so that we can think further from it. Then we can also think further from the specific (.....) at any juncture of any topic, if we let a felt sense come at that juncture.

Notice that a (.....) is implicitly intricate. It is more than what is already formed or distinguished. In my example it includes many alternative moves, but more: the (.....) implies a next move – the body *is* the implying of – a next move, but after-and-with all that it includes, that move is as yet unformed.

The (.....) is interaction. It is the body's way of living its situation. Your situation and you are not two things, as if the external things were a situation without you. Nor is your bodily sense only internal. It is certainly not just an emotional reaction to the danger. It is that, but it also includes more of the intricacy of your situation than you can see or think. Your bodily (.....) is your situation. It is not a perceived object before you or even behind you. The situation isn't the things that are there, nor something internal inside you. Your intricate involvement with others is not inside you, and it is not outside you, so it is also not those two things together. The body-sense is the situation. It is inherently an interaction, not a mix of two things.

The living body *is* an ongoing interaction with its environment. Therefore, of course, it contains environmental information. The bodily (.....) also implies a further step which may not yet be capable of being done or said. We need to conceive of the living body in a new way, so as to be able to understand how it can contain (or be) information, and also be the implying of the next bit of living. It is not the usual use of the word "body." As we have seen, the body is not just an orienting center of perceiving, nor only a center of motions, but also of acting and speaking in situations.

The bodily felt sense of situation can also be related to Heidegger's (1927) concept of "being-in-the-world." The early Heidegger and Merleau-Ponty wrote powerfully about what is inherently implicit, pre-thematic. In *Being and Time* (1927), Heidegger presented a fascinating analysis of being-in-the-world that always included feeling, understanding, explication, and speech. He re-understood each and showed that they are "equally basic" to each other, and always in each other. Heidegger argued that in our felt understanding we know our reasons for an action "further than cognition can reach."

According to his hyphenated conception of the being-in-the-world, the human mode of being is really a "being in." It is a being in situations with others. Heidegger stopped here, however, and unfortunately did not understand this in a bodily way. We can go further. "Being-in" situations with others applies to the *embodied* and sentient person.

The person *is* interaction, and this includes our bodies. It can be seen in many ways. For example, the infant emerges, sucking the air, searching for the breast. The breast in turn has to be pumped if there is no infant. Thus, we are inherently interactional. This does not mean, as postmodernists say, that there is no person, just dialogue. The current rage for dialogue is an overreaction to the previous view that assumed that the person is an internal structure cut-off from interaction. Actually a person's self-responding happens within an interaction context, and is strongly affected by this context. But interpersonal relating happens within the context of a person's self-responding and is strongly affected thereby. Each can exceed the other. Therefore we try to provide maximum personal closeness with minimal intrusion of content. We call this "Focusing-oriented psychotherapy" (Gendlin 1996).

You know that there is someone there in you. And when another person looks at you, you can see that they know you are there. Sartre (1943) understood this very well. In *Being and Nothingness* he referred to it as "the look." In our theoretical concepts about persons, a person's concrete presence – and your own – have to be sensed and referred to as such. Concepts, structure, content, experience – none of these things look at you. Sartre also quite rightly said that "existence precedes essence." This is a slogan which implies that what is sitting there in the chair looking at me is more fundamental and earlier than whatever we are going to say about it. But if we take *this* (.....) along as we think, we can say quite a lot about it.

Truth and values

My postmodernist colleagues in philosophy believe that there is no truth. The fact that there is not a single truth, however, does not mean there is no truth. It means that there are many truths, and truth has many different and very important meanings. We now have objective measures to study the degree to which people's verbalizations carry forward their implicit, not yet formulated, experience. There is a kind of truth which applies when what we say has a certain kind of relationship, a certain kind of effect on what we experience. What we say and our practical choices are not just arbitrary and unrelated to what we are concretely experiencing.

Currently people consider choice arbitrary. There is disillusionment with the notion of "authenticity." It now seems to mean nothing more than some moment of decision, totally arbitrary. Value-decisions seem arbitrary when reality is thought of as value-free "facts" or "objects." But we now know that aside from arbitrarily deciding what to do, our experiencing is something else, more intricate and composed of many more implicit strands, yet sensed as one. From this come little steps such as for example: "Oh, I'm not yet together enough to decide this." The first such steps may not seem very helpful, but they create changes in how the whole situation is carried in the body. Further little steps follow in their characteristically odd and unexpected ways that go beyond the usual phrases of the common language. Instead of an arbitrariness in the process of reaching a decision, there can be a much subtler process in which you are going in a life-forward direction.

I am in favor of the kind of truth that is carried forward and elaborated. What I would not like is to consider any one kind of truth as the only kind. It is not a problem that there is more than one kind of truth. If there were, the world would be greatly impoverished. Yet postmodernists keep saying there isn't any truth. It is as though everybody just assumed that there is either just one kind of truth or no truth at all.

In fact we are always standing in a gigantic, open possibility. If you take almost anything in an experiential way and then go in a little further, it becomes much more intricate. It would really be rather boring if there were only one kind of truth. Why would anyone want that?

The zig-zag

Every way of defining is always just wrong if the definition is the end of it. Instead, let us define anything, but then sense how we are living from and speaking from our sense of that thing. Let us sense how the proposed definition affects that felt sense. With a bodily felt sense there is a different and wider sense of the self, the person, the body and the actor.

Philosophy has a long history of treating formulations as if they could be ultimate. Let us move beyond this. Instead, let us say that we *speak-from* the (.....), and that we think-from it and make concepts from it. We begin with something that needs to be said, but has been impossible to say. We now have a formulated set of steps, one way to find this "thinking at the edge" (Gendlin 1991a).

In philosophy we are moving beyond formulations alone. To take this step, I introduce a philosophy of experiencing, a philosophy of the implicit which never eliminates the actually-lived implicit. We do not "explicate" the implicit, as if to turn it into something explicit. Rather, we speak from the implicit; we take the implicit along. If we can, we carry it forward. In doing so we can also study the many relationships which can obtain between formulations on the one hand and the (.....) on the other (Gendlin [1962] 1997, 1991a, 1991b).

If we take this step, then we do not have to give up. It is not "the end of philosophy" but the opening of a large new arena. By taking this step, we arrive at very interesting conceptual patterns of an altogether new sort. There are concepts begging to be formed when you move from concepts to the (.....) , and then from it again to concepts. For example, we need and can formulate the concept of an "undivided multiplicity." I have already mentioned "carrying forward." Another concept of this sort is "crossing." When you cross two people, two things, or two cultures, they open each other's delimiting forms, reveal their intricacy, and become implicit in each other. The result is more in each than either was before. I have formulated some other concepts of this sort. Whatever we are dealing with has a capacity for more – an intricate experiential nonarbitrary capacity. Anything *is* actually an intricacy and not simply a thing over there or a diagram (Gendlin 1997a, 1997b).

I call one relationship between the (.....) and words or actions "*carrying forward*." People commonly say that the words now "match" their experience, but it must be remembered that what we formulate or claim is *never equivalent* to the (.....). *An implicitly intricate physical sense is never the same as words.* What we say is never equivalent to what we are talking about. We speak-from it. If we are lucky, what we say carries the

(.....) forward." If not, we struggle. We sense that what we say does not move the directly sensed meaning we are living. There is no static representation. Either it develops into more, or it stays stuck and perhaps shrivels.

For example, suppose you go to the theater with another person. Afterwards you discuss and analyze the play and the inchoate sense of what it meant to you. In some cases, after two or three minutes, you have nothing more to say. Now you feel that you really did not "have" much there. You have killed whatever you had taken from the play. Yet, everyone also has the other experience. In this case, as you speak you find more and more facets coming to you. You discover that you "had" much more there, than had seemed to be there at first. This is the experience I call "carrying forward." But what determines the difference? I think you can obtain the carrying forward effect if you check anything you are about to say instantly against the (.....). If it begins to shrivel, you instantly discard what you were going to say and wait for something else to come from the (.....).

The experiential mode of thinking is a zig-zag between words and felt sense. To use this mode, we need not lose our other ways of thinking. We do not lose logic, or empirical testing, or event-reporting, and we can always distinguish the zig-zag from those. *If we want to, we can almost always recognize when what we say does carry the (.....) forward, and when not.*

Experiential intricacy

Sometimes when we have a problem or an exciting insight, it may be difficult to express. We search for what to say. When no words can be found, we keep hold of the experience. We prefer staying stuck, rather than saying something that has no effect, (although what we can say might be true). We wait until new phrases or actions form themselves, to carry the sense of the situation forward.

Logic doesn't help in such instances. New phrasing does not form by deduction from what we have already formulated. On the contrary, the use of logic depends on where we position it. Logic does not tell us where to begin to institute logic. It is necessary to sense the experiential connections, and carry those forward. Once this has happened, we can formulate terms which logic can use. Then logic can arrive at its own kind of results that nothing else can achieve.

Most people do not know, nor do most philosophers assume that one can enter what I call the "implicit." At first it may be a murky zone that seems discouraging, but it soon comes into focus and then you can speak from there.

Postmodernism is telling people that there is neither a subject nor a self, and that anything we say really comes to us from public discourse. This is a reactionary stance. What we want to achieve is just the opposite. We want to empower people to speak from there – from where there are not yet any public words. Psychotherapy attempts to do this all the time. Psychotherapy can be described as a "bad poetry" – the same struggle for fresh language but without the requirement for beauty. And sometimes quite beautiful nevertheless. We can feel the language rearranging itself until new phrasing comes to speak-from newly intricate facets of experiencing that have never before been said. We want to empower people to do just that, and open up new territories.

I propose that we relate philosophy and psychology to the territory of intricacy. Without directly sensing the intricacy, I think all psychological theories and methods are false. And, they are even destructive if they are taken as representations of living people. Instead of relating to the person in front of you (and the one alive inside you), the theories tempt us to relate instead to the concepts. Then we go on from the concept, instead of the person(s). Concepts are of course valuable for what we can infer from them, but only if we use a theory *in relation* to the person right here. Then the concepts become implicitly changed by the felt sense of the person, and then the theory can help us. To understand another person is a momentary thing. In the moment when your response shows that you understand, the other person's eyes light up. You both breathe better. You both understand that you both understand. One moment later, the other person moves from there in a way you could not have imagined. No theory can generate what actually happens.

People are still very unskilled in the experiential use of theories. From a theory we generate a hypothesis, a question, or we propose a distinction, perhaps. Then we have to try it out. This means saying it – not to the mind of the person, but rather – to the concretely sensed inside of the person, *and then waiting for what comes up physically from inside.*

People usually react just to the saying. They might feel hurt, insulted, threatened, or interested. They attend to the feelings that the statement roused. People think the point of saying something from a theory is what we say, as if psychotherapy happens in the conversational process. Not in practice! In practice the point is what comes back from the intricacy in the living person. The most important success of theory-derived interpretations happens when something utterly different and unimaginable comes up from inside in response. But for this to happen one must know to await it. I insist on this with everyone with whom I work. "Look," I say, "anything *I* say about *you* cannot be right. It's only good for something right to come up in response, something that might come up from in you. Please wait for that to come."

Language has currently become the reason why philosophers feel stuck. Heidegger spent thirty years searching for a way to get the old metaphysics out of western languages. And it is true that the old phrases and the usual uses of words bring the old metaphysics whenever we say something. Yet it is precisely language – not the common phrases but the endless capacities of language – that can carry experiencing forward beyond the old metaphysics. On the general conceptual level alone there is no way out of the old metaphysics. But if you allow language to come freshly forward, then the language rearranges the old phrases and the old implicit concepts from the (.....).

The current fascination with social construction is a mistake. It is a mistake to tell people that they are only the products of culture, interaction, or their family. A human being is the person inside. You are inside you, and you can see me looking at you. But we are not just inside; we are inherently interactional. The infant arrives here, looking; a person is whatever that is, which looks at you. You cannot avoid being looked at. Nothing else does that – not a wall and not a chair. Only a person can look at you.

Being in relation is not the opposite of being a maximally self-responding individual. Interpersonal closeness and deep self-responding go together. We become more continuous inside as we become more relational. Conversely, isolation from others goes along with losing one's own inward touch with oneself. It is not true that you are either in relation or in yourself. The only real relation is when you are in touch with yourself and *thereby* can feel the mysterious other person who is looking at you and can surprise you from one moment to the next.

Currently, many philosophers say that one person can not understand another, because we bring our own meanings and interpretations to anything we understand. But if we check and correct the understanding step by step, then moments of true understanding between two people are achieved. The defining sentence that starts with "The human person is . . ." cannot be finished. But it *is* possible to feel a continuity far inside – just as it is also possible to feel no continuity inside.

The practice of focusing

In ancient times philosophy included an associated practice. We have restored this power of philosophy. My philosophy of implicit experiencing has led to the practice of focusing (Gendlin 1981). The experiential intricacy which we need for philosophical and theoretical thinking is found through focusing. Then it also has a great many other uses in life. Focusing starts with a concrete sense which can come in your body in relation to any consideration, if you invite its coming. You let your attention enter your stomach and chest. This is a kind of inward bodily attention that a few people have naturally, but which most people are not yet familiar with. I will describe the process of focusing briefly here.

In focusing one's attention moves past the usual feelings so as to reach the edge of what is sensed but not known. This is a murky but physically distinct sense of some situation or aspect of your life. Some people are very far away and dissociated from their bodies. Since everybody can feel their bottom on the chair, that is one place from which you can start. Then move your attention up into the middle of your body from there. Many people can easily feel the stomach. What is more difficult at first, is to feel the concrete physical sense. It is always this fresh bodily sense which comes in relation to this situation, or this topic at this specific juncture.

Focusing consists of precise instructions. Each instruction is for a small inner move that can be sensed in a bodily way, so that one knows when it has actually happened. To reach the entry usually requires some teaching and practice. More steps and more practice are required to become able to stay there long enough to make the further moves.

Beneath the usual feelings that everyone finds, there is a *physically sensed* murky zone which requires some training to reach. Focusing consists of certain teachable steps of bodily attention to spend time at this murky edge, until it opens and one can enter. At this level of experience one's unarticulated knowledge becomes accessible. Small steps of life-forwarding change also come at that level.

One begins by letting one's attention down into the body, attending directly in the stomach or chest. There one finds not only digestion and heart-pound, but also one's well-being or discomfort with what is just then happening. Some find this physical level immediately. Others require some time so as to gradually discover how to sense the body from inside.

If some already-known feelings are there, one passes on through them, to reach the direct sense of *what is there, but not yet known*. This might be what is not yet known behind and beneath some one feeling, or usually, the whole situation. This opaque edge is a single sense of "all that," all of what is involved in the given concern, more than one could possibly think of, separately, one by one. It is a single sense, but internally complex. At first, it may seem rather like a featureless gray wall, or a rubber pad, something concretely there but opaque. It is a "that" which seems to give one no entry. With certain steps that can be learned, one can *go in*.

When one reaches the seemingly opaque, bodily level, one attends to the distinct physically sensed *quality* of this opacity. This is the bodily version of the given situation or concern. One learns a deliberate *holding* to this access, while simultaneously *letting* new steps come from it. This combination of deliberate control and letting go at this level of experiencing leads to the emergence of previously unformulated information and newly formed entities. The implicit information and the new possibilities are characteristically more intricate than we can deliberately invent.

One can take up a number of active relationships to the concrete bodily sense of the situation. One can "place" any problem, feeling, or concern at some short or far distance from oneself. In the space that arises in focusing, the bodily sense "has a life of its own," much as another person has. Approached in certain ways, it is much more likely to open. The bodily sense can sometimes "sort itself out" into several strands. This happens not by making distinctions from the top down, but by *letting* it sort itself.

Once all this is familiar, there are other precise moves that can make a large difference. The new steps tend to take account of all the conditions of the situation that the person has experienced, certainly many more than one can have as thoughts. From the holistic sense, characteristically intricate little steps come. To speak from them, one must allow new phrases to come as well.

At the level below the so-called murky zone, the steps which come have a *sense of rightness*, an inner truth-and-value that is not infected by our conditioning and our fears. Life-forwarding steps are likely to come there. Once such steps have often been experienced, it is much easier to spend time seemingly "stuck" at the opaque level. One knows that it will usually open, and that such steps will usually come if one holds the space into which they can come.

Ultimately we find that the human body – *with and after* culture and language – senses itself in each situation in a way that exceeds the definitions, the inner and outer entities that are already formed by culture and language. The already shaped emotions, feelings, memories, images, perceptions, and thoughts have behind them the directly sensed opacity. When we move through this opacity, we find that entities actually involve an ongoing process that generates them. This living process is much more finely organized, and is in a life-forwarding motion. We can sense this process directly. In relation to any specific concern, one can stop the usual doing and thinking, and turn, so as to sense the ongoing process that is occurring at that juncture.

Focusing can show us what I call "our assumptions." Assumptions do not usually exist in an already formed way, as the word might suggest. Rather, we discover them together with their inadequacy directly in the implicit intricacy – they change in the same moment. The process brings many small changes in the whole quality of what is focused on. Small holistic shifts change the way in which the situation is carried in the body. The small shifts can lead to a large change in how the situation is felt, perceived, and understood. The small shifts in the quality of the whole scene are adaptive developments of the living organism. They move in a life-forwarding direction. They are much more intricate than our already-formed feelings, thoughts, and perceptions. Many common actions and attitudes become impossible from this much more differentiated and humane approach to oneself and others.

The space of focusing differs from the "spaciousness" which people find in meditation. If one lets one's attention down into the body, one can move on from the bodily sense in two different directions. Meditation moves from it in one direction, focusing in the other. If one lets go of the situation and divides the bodily sense off from it, and if one brings the bodily sense into the large spaciousness of meditation, the bodily sense will tend to dissolve. Meditation is an entirely positive process that one needs for many reasons. However, from the bodily sense of a particular concern one can also move in another way. Instead of going to the large spaciousness of meditation, we go *to*, and also *into* the bodily quality that is at first opaque, and then opens. One can thereby gain access to the implicit information in it, and new life-forwarding steps arise in that particular regard. We need both focusing and meditation, which are essentially two different human capacities.

Focusing is much more easily experienced than described. It requires some practice and specific instructions to become able to remain or return to this long enough to find the small steps of carrying forward and change. Focusing is best learned with a "focusing partner" with whom one takes turns, one focusing while the other listens and provides maximal presence with minimal intrusion. Over time, one can learn specific ways of staying with the bodily sense or coming back to it over and over again. It has long been known that people have an intuitive bodily kind of knowing which exceeds their consciously available knowledge, but we have only recently developed a set of reliable steps to provide an access to it.

Conclusion

First, psychologists and their public have discovered experience, but do not sufficiently recognize the role of culture, history, and language that informs our experience. Sophisticated intellectuals know this but go to the other, postmodern extreme, and argue that everything comes from culture, history, and language. Philosophically I think there needs to be a further step. The step forward would be to recognize what is *with and after* language. The body is always in a fresh situational interaction that exceeds culture, history and language.

Second, currently some thinkers are searching for "emergent" concepts and knowledge. To find this requires finding the direct access to ongoing bodily experiencing. The direct access exceeds the common phrases. But language is inherent in all human experiencing. New facets of experiencing rearrange the implicit language and can generate new sentences. These do not copy; rather they carry experiencing forward. Naïve observers believe they can "match" experience with something they say. Many postmodernists know that it is impossible to "represent," capture, or copy experience, but they take this to mean that everything is up to arbitrary interpretation. A philosophical advance is provided if we notice that we can speak-from direct access to experiencing. We can recognize the difference when we are speaking-from our direct access, and when we are not.

Third, to speak-from direct access to experience leads to a zig-zag process between speaking and access, in which experience changes, but not arbitrarily. This occurs in a sequence of small bodily sensed shifts.

Fourth, living bodies have a holistic life-forward direction that is usually called "adaptive" as if they only fit themselves to external requirements. But in fact the living systems create new and more intricate meanings and actions.

The experiencing process I have described has its own coherence. It took me a long time to affirm that the ongoing bodily experiencing has its own inherent life-forwarding implying. The little steps that arise at the edge are creative, imaginative, and always in some positive direction.

The life process is self-organizing, but much more intricately than we can conceptualize. A great undivided multiplicity is always at work. The higher animals live quite complex lives without culture. Culture does not create; it elaborates. Then we live creatively much further with and after culture. To think that we are the creation of culture is not a view one can maintain if one senses ongoing bodily experiencing directly. Culture is crude and inhuman in comparison with what we find directly. The intricacy you are now living vastly exceeds what cultural forms have contributed to you. With focusing we discover that we are much more organized from the inside out. Direct access to this intricacy enables us to think-from much more than the usual concepts and assumptions.

References

Gendlin, E.T. ([1962] 1997) *Experiencing and the Creation of Meaning: A Philosophical and Psychological Approach to the Subjective*. New York: Free Press of Glencoe (reprinted and published as paperback by Northwestern University Press, with a "Preface to the paper edition," pp. XI–XXIII).

—— (1981) *Focusing*. New York: Bantam.

—— (1991a) "Thinking beyond patterns: body, language and situations," in B. den Ouden and M. Moen (eds.) *The Presence of Feeling in Thought*. New York: Peter Lang. See also "TAE" on www.focusing.org.

—— (1991b) "Crossing and dipping: some terms for approaching the interface between natural understanding and logical formation," in M. Galbraith and W. J. Rapaport (eds.) *Subjectivity and the Debate over Computational Cognitive Science*. New York: Center for Cognitive Science (also in *Minds and Machines* 5(4) 1995).

—— (1992) : "The primacy of the body, not the primacy of perception," *Man and World* 25(3–4): 341–53.

—— (1996) *Focusing-Oriented Psychotherapy: A Manual of the Experiential Method*. New York: Guilford.

—— (1997a) "The responsive order: a new empiricism," *Man and World* 30(3): 383–411.

—— (1997b) *A Process Model*. Available from the Focusing Institute and on www.focusing.org

Heidegger, M. ([1927] 1962) *Being and Time*. Oxford: Basil Blackwell.

Levin, D.M. (ed.) (1997) *Language beyond Postmodernism: Saying and Thinking in Gendlin's Philosophy*. Evanston, IL: Northwestern University Press.

Merleau-Ponty, M. ([1945] 1962) *The Phenomenology of Perception*. London: Routledge.

Sartre, J. P. ([1943] 1956) *Being and Nothingness*. New York: Philosophical Library.

Chapter 5

A phenomenology of becoming

Reflections on authenticity

Jon Mills

We live in a time of skepticism concerning the existence of the self. While postmodernism has no unified body of theory, its one unanimous claim is the demise of the subject. Postmodernism has propitiously criticized the pervasive historical, gendered, and ethnocentric character of our understanding of the world, but it has done so at the expense of displacing key modern philosophical tenets that celebrate the nature of subjectivity, consciousness, and the teleology of the will. Consequently, the notions of freedom, autonomy, and authentic choice that comprise the fundamental activities of personal agency are altogether dismantled.

In the empirically driven world of contemporary scientific psychology, postmodernism may appear as an interesting yet marginalized phenomenon. In this sense it shares the eccentricity historically associated with existential, phenomenological, and psychoanalytic accounts that have fought for recognition in traditional psychological paradigms. Within the larger intellectual community that comprises the humanities and behavioral sciences, we may observe a divide between science on the one side, and postmodernism on the other, each with its purported critics and adherents. Strangely enough, however, scientific and postmodern approaches yield similar implications for the fate of the self. Because scientific psychology is largely entrenched in empirically and biologically based materialistic frameworks, the dynamic activities of mind – including consciousness, cognition, and subjectivity – are imperiled by reductionist strategies (Mills 2002). While postmodernism boasts to have subverted the subject, materialists have reduced it to a brain state. Either way, subjectivity, selfhood, and personal agency are displaced.

Throughout this chapter I will attempt to defend a concept of the self as an experiential process of becoming that challenges postmodern and scientific ideologies. In order to do so, I will largely draw on Heidegger's philosophy and show how his concept of *Dasein* – the concretely existing human being – constitutes a phenomenology of becoming that preserves the notions of freedom, choice, and subjective agency. Juxtaposed to Sartrean and psychoanalytic accounts, Heidegger's philosophy allows us to engage the question of authenticity, which is a central task in the process of Dasein's own becoming.

By examining the work of Heidegger and Sartre, I will seek to demonstrate the relevance of existential-phenomenological approaches to contemporary psychotherapy and psychoanalysis. The phenomenology of becoming is a fundamental pursuit of the human condition. And it is the process and quality of lived experience that becomes important within a therapeutic context. Therapy is a process of becoming, which is embraced, endured, and transcended. After examining selfhood's struggle for authenticity in the texts of Heidegger, Sartre, Winnicott, and Kohut, I will examine a detailed case study. In order to become, we must first confront the possibility of authenticity and its existential, phenomenological and psychodynamic contingencies.

The enigma of authenticity

What does it mean to be authentic? Perhaps this is a question one can never adequately answer. As allusive as the meaning of being, the question of authenticity existentially demands a response. While Heidegger was primarily concerned with the question of Being (*Sein*) rather than the nature of beings (*Seiende*), he was deeply interested in the interface between philosophy and psychology (Guignon 1993; Richardson 1993). Despite Heidegger's apathy toward Freudian psychoanalysis, his conceptualization of Dasein has direct and significant contributions for psychoanalytic thought. While there are potential conceptual quandaries between the philosophical, "ontological" discourse of Heideggerian theory and the applied, "ontical" discourse of psychodynamic approaches, Heidegger's ontology has profound implications for understanding the questions of authenticity, truth, and agency.

For Heidegger, authenticity is a uniquely temporal structure and a process of unfolding possibility. It is a state of being that is active, teleological, contemplative, and congruent – an agency with quiescent potentiality. As such, authenticity is the process of becoming one's possibilities and by nature it is idiosyncratic and uniquely subjective. Thus the pursuit of authenticity becomes a key therapeutic endeavor. Generally we might say that selfhood vacillates between authentic and inauthentic modes, that it tarries with genuine inauthenticity only to find itself genuinely authentic. Perhaps selfhood is beyond this antithetical distinction;

it merely is what it is. Perhaps authenticity is beyond the individual; it ultimately belongs to the very ontology that constitutes Being itself. This becomes particularly relevant to how Being is actualized within the process of therapy as the personal attainment of one's possibilities.

Heidegger tells us that humankind has the recalcitrant need to divulge itself as inauthenticity. Not only does Dasein unveil itself in the everyday mundane modes of existence, but also it does so in a false manner. But what does it mean for Dasein to be false, that is, what are the conditions that influence the development of inauthenticity? Is it possible that the very ontological structures of Dasein itself are false? Can the human being be thrown into a deficit world, a world tainted by fallenness and inauthenticity, so much so that it predetermines Dasein's Being-in-the-world as a falsehood? To what degree is our social environment structurally differentiated into various existential modalities that are themselves pathological, thereby affecting the very ways in which the self is disclosed? I will demonstrate that selfhood encompasses a dialectical course undulating through experiential modes of authenticity and inauthenticity, in which this very process itself is an authentic one; this is the a priori condition of Dasein as Being-toward-possibility.

Dasein and fallenness

In his philosophical treatise *Being and Time* (1927), Heidegger offers an existential ontology of selfhood as *Dasein* (being there), the actual human subject who is there, as part of the world. In Dasein's original disclosedness as Being-in-the-world, one is thrust into the ontological contingency of "Being-in" an environment (*Umwelt*) and "Being-with" others (*Mitwelt*) and with-oneself (*Eigenwelt*) which underlies all participation, engagement, and concrete involvement with the world that is *given* in one's immediate preoccupations and concerns. Thus, the world itself is constitutive of Dasein's Being for "Being-in-the-world is a state of Dasein which is necessary *a priori*, but it is far from sufficient for completely determining Dasein's Being" (Heidegger [1927] 1962: 79). As Heidegger explicates, Dasein's Being takes on a particular character a priori, and exists within the modes of authentic and inauthentic disclosedness. "Dasein exists. Furthermore, Dasein is an entity which in each case I myself am. Mineness belongs to any existent Dasein, and belongs to it as the conditions which makes authenticity and inauthenticity possible" (Heidegger [1927] 1962: 78). The modes of Dasein's disclosedness are already structurally constituted in Dasein's Being-in-the-world. However, they are only the conditions that make authenticity and inauthenticity possible. As Heidegger points out, these two modes of disclosedness must have ownership, that is, they necessarily belong to the subjective, singular Dasein. For our purposes, Dasein is to be understood within the context of *selfhood*.

As the self, Heidegger delineates the factuality of Dasein characterized by humankind's naked "thereness," one's abandonment as thrown into the publicness of "the they." As human beings disclose themselves in the everydayness of Being-in-the-world, they discover that they have been thrust into an environment without consultation or choice in the matter whatsoever, and by definition have been abandoned to chance factors which already constitute their Being. Therefore, there is a fundamental propensity of Dasein, one that belongs to everydayness, and manifests itself as *das Man*. The world is a world in which one shares with others in communal proximity. Thus, Dasein's communal structure lends itself to a participation that cannot be annulled, namely, that of *they*ness. By virtue of Dasein's communal character, one cannot *not* participate in a world determined by the pragmatics of society and the everyday concerns that structure Dasein's activities.

For Heidegger, the question of authenticity becomes intimately associated with the existential character of Dasein as concern and solicitude. Just as Dasein's relation to the environment is that of practical concern, Dasein's relation to the communal world is that of personal concern. As Heidegger explains, this form of concern belonging to everydayness by necessity will ultimately lead to modes of inauthenticity. As the "anonymous one," the uniqueness of selfhood is diffused and lost in depersonalization and "averageness."

Heidegger expounds upon another structural element in the ontological constitution of Dasein, that of "fallenness." This is the universal tendency of human beings to lose themselves in the everydayness of present concerns and preoccupations to such a degree that it does nothing but alienate them from their personal and unique future possibilities, thus reducing the fallen *das Man* to a mere "presence-at-hand." Everydayness and fallenness are ontological and natural predispositions of Dasein, therefore devoid of any value judgements attached to them; nevertheless, they are modes of inauthenticity that cannot be avoided nor refused. The degree to which one participates in these inauthentic modes has a direct bearing on the existential status of falsehood.

The fallenness of Dasein is expressed most ostensively through idle talk, curiosity, and ambiguity. Gossip is an inauthentic use of discourse that simply repeats what is heard and accepted by the public without critically examining the grounds or validity of the subject matter under question. Idle talk is merely a repetition of the conventional, an unscrutinized acceptance of the interpretations of the public. The fallen *das Man* is not concerned with understanding the ontological priorities of what is blindly accepted as truth or fact, only in reiterating the public clichés of the "anonymous one." Curiosity, which parallels gossip, underscores Dasein's hunger to explore one's environment merely for the sake of discovering novelty that provides excitement, a pleasurable distraction, and knowledge simply in order to have known. Curiosity, therefore, is not motivated out of the need for authentic understanding, it is merely an inauthentic form of solicitude. Ambiguity, on the other hand, is the dubious nature of information that is disseminated by "the they," which makes it impossible to determine what was disclosed in genuine understanding and what was not. This ambiguity is not only about the public gossip, but also in reference to Being-with-one-another, and Dasein's Being-toward-itself, hence, an inauthentic relatedness.

Fallenness leads to the "downward plunge" into the inauthentic Being of "the they" in which authentic possibility is lost in obscurity and under the guise of "ascending" and "living concretely." Is it possible, however, that this downhill plunge is a necessary one that provides the dialectical movement toward the fulfillment of Dasein's possibilities? Perhaps this turbulent necessity is the very authentic movement of Dasein toward itself as *becoming*. Rather than falling away from itself, Dasein is falling into itself. But this is possible only if Dasein becomes aware of its possibilities that it hides from itself. At this point we must ask: why does Dasein close off its possibilities in the tranquility of fallenness rather than seize them authentically? In other words, why do we hide ourselves from our own potentiality-for-Being? Perhaps Dasein is afraid of its freedom.

Dasein in bad faith

In offering an existential analysis of authenticity, we have determined that Dasein's fundamental structure is ontologically oriented toward fallenness. The false Dasein abdicates its potentiality-for-Being. While theoretically distinct from Heidegger's existential ontology, Sartre's conception of inauthenticity further contributes to our understanding of the psychological-ontical processes immersed in Dasein's falsehood.

In his magnum opus, *Being and Nothingness* (1943), Sartre introduced the notion of *mauvaise foi*, or bad faith. For Sartre, consciousness is Being, "a being, the nature of which is to question its own being, that being implying a being other than itself"; that is, "to be conscious of the nothingness of its being" (Sartre 1943: 86). In other words, authentic

Being is literally *no-thing*. Conversely, inauthenticity is defined by self-negation. Sartre asserts that "consciousness instead of directing its nega-tion outward turns it toward itself. This attitude, it seems to me, is *bad faith* (*mauvaise foi*)" (Sartre 1943: 87).

Broadly stated, bad faith is characterized by self-deception, a lie to oneself. But how can one lie to oneself? Only if one is not consciously aware of such intentions to lie or to deceive. For the individual in bad faith, the nature of such a lie "is not recognized by the liar as *his* inten-tion" (Sartre 1943: 88, original emphasis). While a genuine lie is a "behaviour of transcendence," the bad faith lie is a denial of such possi-bility. Such is the case that liars find themselves as the victim of their own self-deception and live in falsehood.

Bad faith can manifest in various existential modalities, from singular situational choices to patterns of self-deception, or as one could argue, character structure. Nevertheless, there is a double face to bad faith, namely facticity and transcendence. In the first case, bad faith is the fail-ure to accept one's facticity. In the second, it is a failure of transcendence. For example, Sartre portrays a woman who consents to go out with a man for the first time and in her bad faith she denies the intentions behind the seductions of his conduct. "She does not want to realize the urgency" of the moment and "refuses to apprehend the desire for what it is" (Sartre 1943: 96–7). Throughout the flirtations, her companion places her in such a position as to require an immediate decision, only to be protracted and disguised by the various procedures she uses to maintain herself in this self-deception. Her "aim is to postpone the moment of decision as long as possible" (Sartre 1943: 97). In Sartre's example, the woman has failed to project a future, and has allowed herself not to take notice of the reality of the situation. Her decision rests in the locus of prereflective conscious-ness: she chose not to posit a future with her suitor, thus deceiving herself of such possibility. According to Sartre, the woman has reduced herself to a thing, a passive object in which events happen to her that she can nei-ther provoke nor avoid. In bad faith, the person is in possession of the truth, but fails to acknowledge it as such, thereby avoiding the responsi-bility it requires.

The bad faith attitude is one in which the individual seeks to flee from his or her freedom and the obligations it demands by construing oneself as a thing, a Being-in-itself, rather than a Being-for-itself. Instead of, "I am in the mode of being what I am *not*," the bad faith attitude is "I am in the mode of being what I am," thus, a thing-in-itself. In short, as human agents we *must* choose. As long as one consciously chooses in freedom and accepts full responsibility for one's actions, one is in good faith.

What we are is freedom, and as freedom we are transcendence. Human beings define and redefine themselves via their choices. Decisions are made in the interest of a value or one is in bad faith. This is the case when one fails to choose, or more appropriately, when one *chooses not to choose* authentically.

Sartre's portrayal of bad faith elucidates the psychological nuances of self-deception that are structurally instantiated in Dasein's ontical practices. For Heidegger, bad faith would be a deficient mode of Dasein's Being-in-the-world; more specifically, Being-with-oneself and Being-toward one's future authentic possibilities. Within this general context, Dasein's fallenness is bad faith, a falsehood, a retreat into the everydayness of theyness, cloaked by self-deception. Furthermore, to deny our human reality as freedom by defining ourselves as a thing is Dasein's propensity to reduce itself to a mere "presence-at-hand."

If Sartre's depiction of bad faith is accurate, then every human being is in self-deception at one time or another. In fact, this is a necessary condition of Dasein itself. Due to our penchant to fall into inauthentic modes of Being-in-the-world, Dasein will inevitably engage in such deceptive practices. For Sartre, we are condemned to freedom that necessitates radical responsibility for our Being-for-itself. However, choices are made in the context of our ontological facticity and thus are affected by a milieu that, by definition, is deficient or inauthentic. Sartre's position ultimately demands for Being to transcend its ontological structures via choice. But to what degree is this possible? Furthermore, Sartre ostensibly denies the primordial motivations of the dynamic unconscious. While he rejected the psychoanalytic project, Sartre's delineation of inauthenticity contributes to the psychodynamic conceptualization of the primacy of ego organization in personality development. Again, we might say that bad faith is a defensive form of denial, a disavowal in the service of unconscious motivations, conflicts, and wishes. Sartre assumes that *every* Being has the *same* developmental capacities and intrapsychic structures to choose authentically as free agents. But what if one's freedom to recognize authentic choices has been truncated due to structural deficits in psychological development?

The false self

While the predisposition toward inauthenticity is an elemental condition of Dasein's facticity, the specific psychological dimensions of Dasein's falseness require further exploration. Dasein's psychological structures become more lucid with the assistance of a psychoanalytic explication of the self. What would it be like to not know who you are, to be alienated from your true sense of self? What would it be like to have to construct an identity that is ingenuine and artifically manufactured? What would it be like to not feel real? Within psychoanalysis, there has been a burgeoning interest in the clinical literature on the concept of the false self (Cassimatis 1984; Chescheir 1985; Khan 1971; Lerner 1985; Mitchell 1992; Schacht 1988). The inauthentic self, or the "as if" personality, further deepens our understanding of the false Dasein.

Winnicott (1960) formally introduced the notion of the false self. While some parallels exist between Heidegger's exposition of the fallen Dasein and Sartre's depiction of bad faith, Winnicott's contributions to understanding the question of authenticity deserve special merit. For Winnicott, a false self is the result of developmental conflict encountered in the child–maternal relationship. As a result, a false self is constructed as a defensive system that remains unconsciously maintained. Winnicott's theoretical framework falls within a defense model that is intimately tied to drive theory within the interpersonal context of the mother–child dyad. While having a ground in Freudian metapsychology, Winnicott's conceptualization of the false self is essentially a relational theory centering on ego defensive maneuvers that arise in response to environmental demands. More specifically, within the infant–mother milieu, the child struggles to manage libidinal/creative impulses that are solely intrapsychic; however, this takes place within the context of the relational matrix or intersubjective field. Therefore, within the stage of the first object relationships, various defenses are constructed in response to external demands, and particularly that of the maternal object. Ego organization is in the service of adaptation to the environment and pro-curement of object attachment. Repeated compliance to such demands, concomitant with a withdrawal from self-generated spontaneity, leads to an increased stifling of impulses constitutive of the natural drive for spontaneous expression, thereby culminating in a false self development.

For Winnicott, the idea of a true self originates in the capacity of the infant to recognize and enact spontaneous needs for self-expression. "Only the True Self can be creative and only the True Self can feel real" (Winnicott [1960] 1965: 148). The notion of the self as the center of spontaneity that has the "experience of aliveness" constitutes the core or heart of authenticity. However, this ability to enact such spontaneous gestures is contingent upon the responsiveness of the "good-enough mother" within an appropriate "holding environment." Thus, the etiology of the true and false self is contingent upon the quality of maternal responsiveness. The true self flourishes only in response to the repeated success of the mother's optimal responsiveness to the infant's spontaneous expressions. If the mother is "not good-enough," she does not facilitate the infant's omnipotence and repeatedly fails to meet the child's spontaneous gestures with appropriate responsiveness.

Like Heidegger's philosophical treatment of Dasein's ontology, Winnicott obviates the subject–object dichotomy with regards to the ontical structures of the self. The maternal holding environment is part of the very ontic structure of Dasein: it is constitutive of Dasein's Being. Failure in empathic attunement, mirroring, and optimal responsiveness is a deficient mode of Being-with, a precondition of the Dasein's inauthenticity. Within this context, freedom becomes abridged and affects the true self development *as it would have unfolded* if Dasein's ontological constitution of Being-with had been different. Authenticity is curtailed by the demands of others. In this sense, there is no authentic self distinct from Being-with others.

The defensive functions of the false self are constructed for one cardinal purpose, namely, "to hide and protect the True Self" (Winnicott [1960] 1965: 142). "The False Self defends the True Self; the True Self is, however, acknowledged as a potential and is allowed a secret life" (Winnicott [1960] 1965: 143). But what is the nature of this true or authentic self that is allowed a secret life? Winnicott does not offer an adequate explanation, he only points to the ability to enact spontaneous gestures of self-expression: "The True Self appears as soon as there is any mental organization of the individual at all, and it means little more than the summation of sensori-motor aliveness" (Winnicott [1960] 1965: 149). But is this a sufficient understanding of authenticity? Doesn't the notion of authenticity carry with it, if not demand of it, that Dasein *can* to some degree transcend its mere thrownness; that is, choose actively to seize upon its subjective agency despite its environment?

Clearly Dasein is more than its physiological contingencies. On one level, to be authentic or true is to act in accord with one's genuine and congruent, innate strivings and yearnings. Within the various psychoanalytic domains, authenticity may conform to the influence of unconscious drive determinants, ego mastery of the self and the environment, object relatedness and the pining for relational attachments, and the psychic need for mirroring and idealizing selfobject experiences that form the rudimentary basis of a vital and cohesive self. Whatever the nature or *being* of these authentic strivings are, Winnicott assumes they exist, are hidden, and are preserved unconsciously due to the character structure of defense.

Winnicott concludes that the false self takes on a role that appears to be "real," when in fact it is artificial. Indeed, this pseudo-real appearance takes on a "personal living through imitation" in which the child may "act a special role, that of the True Self *as it would be if it had had existence*" (Winnicott [1960] 1965: 147, original emphasis). However, for Winnicott, the true self always exists behind the mask of the false persona, lying dormant, concealed, and protected. The false self, as defense, is "a defence against that which is unthinkable, the exploitation of the True Self, which would result in its annihilation" (Winnicott [1960] 1965: 147). Thus, the etiology of the false self may be said to arise out of the deficient modes of other Daseins, which were foisted upon the child with various ontological and psychological exigencies to comply with or perish under. It may be said that a false personality constellation is constructed in reaction to the fear of death of the self. Such fear of annihilation is the most archaic form of existential anxiety, a primordial denial of Dasein's Being-toward-death.

The unconscious displacement of the emerging annihilation anxiety is organized within the interpersonal matrix of the infant's earliest object relations. Within this context, Masterson (1981) defines the false self as "a collection of behaviors, thoughts and feelings that are motivated by the need to cling to the object," and thus suppress the longings for separateness and individuation (Masterson 1981: 101). Within contemporary object relations theory, the false self operates defensively as a means to ward off separation anxiety and abandonment fears which ultimately represent the inability to integrate whole self and object representations, which in turn become the formative basis of a cohesive self. As a result, the capacity for spontaneity, autonomous self-assertion, and the expression of creativity is stymied and lost in falsehood.

Winnicott's developmental model anticipates Kohut's (1971, 1977, 1984) psychoanalytic self psychology. For Kohut, the self is a bipolar structure composed of two poles, namely: the pole of ambitions and strivings, and the pole of values and ideals. The former constitutes mirroring selfobject experiences in which the authentic core self is the center of initiative, self-assertion, autonomy, and vitality. The second pole is attained via the identification process and merger with omnipotent, calming, infallible selfobjects that are in turn internalized and become the intrapsychic structural foundation of the self. As Kohut theoretically moved away from the metapsychology of classical theory, the primacy of the self replaced the vicissitudes of the drives as "the center of our being from which all initiative springs and where all experience ends" (Kohut 1978: 95). The self, as the center of initiative and psychic motivation, depends upon the quality of selfobject experiences for its structural integrity and cohesion. Within this context, a false self would develop out of repeated failure in empathic attunement and optimal responsiveness in the early selfobject milieu. If the self becomes defined in the context of others' narcissistic needs, capacities for self-soothing and self-esteem regulation are thwarted due to a depleted or fragmented self structure.

The false self can manifest in various modalities and in degrees of its falseness. The more psychologically adjusted false self organization may be represented by the overly compliant, obsequious, acquiescent, interpersonally polite attitudes that accompany the expectations of social convention. This may be similar to Heidegger's description of Dasein's everydayness as fallenness in the modes of idle talk, curiosity, and ambiguity. In terms of Sartre's bad faith, one makes inauthentic choices that are situational, repetitive, or characterlogical in the service of avoiding one's responsibility to accept freedom. In other words, by choosing not to choose authentically, we reside in the everyday, inauthentic mode of "the they" (Heidegger 1927).

For contemporary psychoanalysis and psychotherapy, Dasein's tendency toward fallenness serves primary motivations for relational attachment, emotional-interpersonal involvement, and validation of the self. In the case of the false Dasein, such wishes are inordinately intensified due to intrapsychic structural vulnerabilities of the self. Miller (1981) discusses a particular form of false development, that of individuals who are raised by narcissistic parents and are cajoled into being responsive and attuned to everyone else's needs at the expense of their own. Children who are treated as objects to meet the narcissistic fulfillments of their parents may develop a virtuous yet tragic gift, the gift of empathy. Gifted children may develop skills of empathic attunement to anticipate, respond to, and meet the wishes of others in order to gain love and attention of their own; but only at the steep price of sacrificing their true self.

Still more toward maladjustment, one could say the false self is the "actor" who puts on his or her theatrical facade but is unable to remove such persona; the actor becomes over-identified in the role and loses his or her authenticity in one-sidedness. Under the rubric of such one-sidedness, individuals seek to make themselves into a "thing," a Being-in-itself, rather than a Being-for-Self. Winnicott asserts, "Whereas a True Self feels real, the existence of a False Self results in feeling unreal or a sense of futility" (Winnicott [1960] 1965: 148). He continues: "The best example I can give is that of a middle-aged woman who had a very successful False Self but who had the feeling all her life that she had not started to exist" (Winnicott [1960] 1965: 142). In the severe forms of the psychiatrically impaired, a false self system consists of an organization of various part-selves, none of which are so fully developed as to have a comprehensive personality of their own. This clinical phenomenon is what Laing (1969) spoke of as the *divided self*. In a divided self, there is no single false self, rather only partially elaborated fragments that might constitute a personality. In the Daseinsanalytic tradition (see Kockelmans 1978), for Laing, as well as for Ludwig Binswanger, Medard Boss, Karl Jaspers, and more contemporarily Rollo May, a false self develops out of ontological insecurity, thereby leading to an overall constricted Dasein. To the extreme, the false or divided self may experience a dissociation of personality or a radical splitting of its embodied and disembodied aspects.

The case of Chandra

Existential analysis, phenomenological approaches to therapy, and psychoanalytic thought are quite compatible to the extent that all address the psychodynamics of lived experience, unconscious conflict, the question of personal meaning and suffering, and the process of change and growth through insight and actualization of one's possibilities. Trained as both a psychoanalytic psychologist and an academic philosopher in the existential-phenomenological tradition, my approach to case conceptualization and clinical treatment conscientiously attempts to wed these respective disciplines. In order to understand the nature of authenticity and its relation to the therapeutic encounter, I will examine the case of Chandra, which has been altered to protect the patient's identity.

I saw Chandra in weekly outpatient psychotherapy for just over two years; she was 26 years of age at the start of treatment. In the beginning of her therapy she showed classic signs of depression including insomnia, depleted mood, tension headaches, sexual disinterest, and was easily brought to tears, which affected her work and her marriage. While antidepressant medication had helped to ameliorate her major symptoms, she still suffered from a severely damaged self-image. She was at times obsessionally neurotic, exhibiting self-punitive doubt and pessimistic characteristics about her self-worth and abilities, and once experienced a brief psychotic episode. She sought out therapy mainly because she was feeling hopeless about her life and her marriage.

Chandra was originally from Argentina and was raised in a very strict Roman Catholic environment by parents who were emotionally cold, unaffectionate, and callous. Her father was a local physician who was insensitive, uncaring, and stoically unresponsive to his daughters' needs for paternal attention. Since the father was the sole breadwinner of the family, his wife bore the brunt of rearing four children, all daughters. A strict disciplinarian, the patient's father demanded unquestioning obedience, hard work, and intellectual or artistic success from all four girls. Observing the doctrines of the Catholic faith, he was uncompromisingly rigid about proper rules for conduct and matters concerning sexuality. Chandra's mother, with a discernible history of depression of her own, was unable competently to attend to her maternal responsibilities and so recruited Chandra to assist her in the child rearing. Being the oldest child, Chandra became a maternal surrogate often left alone to attend to the needs and ministrations of her three younger sisters.

Because of her mother's interpersonal absence and symptomatic preoccupations, Chandra was forced to construct an internal world in which her needs became secondary to all others. Intensified by her father's physical absence and cruel emotional detachment, she became the daughter that she was expected to become – obsequious, complacent, dutiful. Not only was Chandra a depressive, but also her depression was characterlogically ingrained in the very fabric of her being. She was living a false existence alienated from her true sense of self.

Through the years from her early childhood to late adolescence, Chandra's personality developed around a chronic sense of personal inadequacy and self-loathing accompanied by punitive and irrational demands for perfection. Her father wanted her to become an accomplished violinist and she was not about to disappoint him. As a result, she conformed to the demands of her parents to such a degree that she sealed off her authentic self-strivings simply in order to survive. Because she was cajoled into being responsive and available to everyone else's needs but her own, she was used as an object to meet the narcissistic fulfillments of her parent's wishes.

In order for her to protect herself against the fear of total rejection and devaluation, Chandra defensively erected a wall of self-deception and denial by stifling her inner self and becoming the object of her parents' demands. She became a *thing*, a machine, an empty shell of emotional vacuity – all traces of personal autonomy were forfeited to the void of her parent's expectations. Yet despite the vacancy in her inner world, she had constructed an airtight fortress of self-deceit which allowed her to function and excel in her responsibilities and talents. In fact, she was an accomplished musician at a very early age.

Primarily due to her strenuous familial and musical responsibilities, Chandra was precluded from attending most social events that are common to normal childhood experience. Moreover, due to her father's obsessional control and austere moral attitudes toward sexuality, she was

never allowed to date men until she was 19 years old – and this was con-
ducted under his supervision. As a result, Chandra developed neurotic
preoccupations of guilt and shame surrounding her sexual feelings and
intense fears of being rejected by her father.

When Chandra was 22, still living at home, she met a man from the
community, nine years her senior, and fell in love. While chaperoned
by her father for the first two months of their courtship, the couple
soon made plans to marry and were wed. Approximately one year later,
Chandra received word that she had been awarded a prestigious scholarship at an urban university. The two prepared for immigration to the
United States while her husband planned to earn his MBA at the same
university. The first two years of their marriage were largely occupied by
their changing circumstances, hence Chandra's concerns about the
quality of her personal life were chalked-up to stress. Yet over the next
few months, Chandra came to realize the hole that had absorbed her
being, the abyss that consumed her identity in her self-deception. As she
became more and more depressed, life became an unbearable burden of
self-defilement and internal persecution.

The initial stages of therapy focused on the patient's dissatisfaction
in her marriage and her unrelenting depression that was inextricably
influenced by her bereft early object relations. She had come to realize
several Oedipal and pre-Oedipal dynamics that informed her choice of a
husband who she found to be selfish and unavailable, and her transference anxieties became an apparent part of our work. She further realized
how the lack of recognition, emotional attunement, and physical affec-
tion from her parents had impacted on her internal depressive-anxiety
states, somatic preoccupations, and excessive ruminations around perfection, guilt, and self-abasement. Due to her early relational depriva-
tions and selfobject failures, Chandra harbored intense yet unarticulated
needs for love and validation. While I cannot go into the details of
Chandra's treatment here, we eventually started to focus on the nature of
her personal sense of identity as a process of self-discovery.

The following segment of dialogue is from the beginning of a therapy
session approximately one year into treatment, and is provided here with
the patient's permission. We had already taken our seats. There was a
quiet agitation to Chandra's presence, as if she were rehearsing what she
wanted to say in her mind. We sat in silence for a few moments before she
began to speak:

PATIENT: I must tell you that things are different for me, things are
    great! I've been feeling great, looking forward to each morning. It's

because I've decided that I don't want to waste my time at this any longer. I no longer want to exist for his ego. I'm tired of denying myself, what is important to me. Even if he changed, I don't think I'd like him, he has spoiled his chance. I don't believe in second opportunities. It's because he's only concerned about his own dependency, not because he really cares for me. I think I should leave him. He must grow up! I no longer want to be his ornament, his prize he can dangle before others. I think it is for the best.

THERAPIST: You've told me a great deal about your dissatisfaction with him, but this is the first time you've ever mentioned thoughts of leaving him.

PATIENT: Oh I guess I'm just over-reacting. It's just that I resent his irresponsibility, his disregard for my depression. He ignores me, treats me like I was a child, like he doesn't believe I feel this way, like I'm making it up or something.

THERAPIST: It seems that during the times when he invalidates you or dismisses your feelings you feel the most rejected and angry . . . to the point that you would consider leaving him just to hurt him back . . . or to see how much he really cares for you.

PATIENT: Yes, you are right. I would like to test him to see if he cares. I know it would really hurt his pride if I left. He is so dependent, but he cares too much for himself. He doesn't like me coming here, seeing you, he thinks you put ideas in my head. He's threatened. I tell him it's important to me but all he says is that I choose extra suffering.

THERAPIST: What do you think?

PATIENT: He may be right.

THERAPIST: Why would you choose to suffer?

PATIENT: Something inside feels that it is improper to have my own needs, that it is selfish. So I am agreeable, I accommodate. That is my way. I told you that I was going home to visit with my parents this Christmas but Manuel is very mad with me because I'm leaving him behind. So he doesn't want me to go. But I'm going anyway, it is my time to relax, to be by myself. But I feel guilty for wanting to go. He says it's selfish on my part. But I need some time away. I end up taking on all the responsibility while he goes off to play and make friends. He likes to remind me that he came to this country because of me, but he has profited too. When I complain to my mother, she tells me that I can never have an ideal situation and I should just accept it. I just want him to want me to be happy. I asked him to try to understand the moods I go through. I asked if he could be happy for me to go home to relax and he said that he was happy enough to deal with my problem.

THERAPIST: I noticed that you were smiling when you said that.

PATIENT: Yes, it wasn't an adequate response; . . . he doesn't care like he should. He says he sacrificed for me but that's not true. I lived for him. I wanted him to be successful so I gave to him. I got a little in return, security, his protection, but now I don't get it. I get more from a stranger on a bus.

THERAPIST: Why do you think he has stopped caring for you?

PATIENT: I don't deserve it.

THERAPIST: Why?

PATIENT: I have always felt this, that I don't deserve to be happy. I guess this is why I buy cheap clothes.

THERAPIST: Why do you think that you don't deserve to be happy?

PATIENT: Because they – Manuel, my parents – would have treated me differently. There must be something that I am lacking, some limitation to me. That is why they show so little love – I don't deserve it.

THERAPIST: Perhaps this is a good example of how you choose extra suffering. Only now it is not your parents or your husband who tell you that you are not worthy of love, it is you. Perhaps you feel that you need to suffer . . . in order to gain their love.

PATIENT: I have had the feeling all my life that I have not yet started to exist – that I'm not a person. That I'm dead.

In this segment, we can readily observe many of the themes that illustrate the problem of authenticity. Chandra's Dasein is ontologically constricted by the fact that she was thrown into a developmentally deficient home environment that severely truncated her relation to her self, the world, and others. Chandra did not know what it meant to be real, hence authentic, and floundered for years in a depleted void attempting to construct some semblance of an identity, one that was polluted by others' desires. As a result, she chose not to choose for herself, but for others, hence she chronically tarried in bad faith. Her confession of not feeling like a person – her deadness – is the numbing alienation of turning herself into a thing, of absorbing her facticity rather than transcending. She feels the destructive tendency of denying her Self, which resonates within her as masochistic self-defilement and is identified as not being worthy of love.

Her early selfobject milieu was inhabited by deficient dependency figures, curtailing mutually responsive and regulatory attachment patterns, and thereby imperiling a cohesive self-structure. She was bound to fall prey to the repetition of unconsciously seeking out such familiar depriving objects. From the internalized phenomenal experiences of empathic failure, invalidation, affective misattunement, and lack, to her defensive false character structure designed to stave off annihilation anxiety and abandonment, Chandra shows how adaptation to developmental trauma is realized through self-deception. But it is in the wake of unconcealment that confronts emerging experience where self-denial gets excised. Chandra could no longer deny her growing self-realization. And in embracing the reality of her own internal disclosedness, she embraced her personal freedom. Let us return to a point in the therapeutic dialogue that transpired later in the same session:

PATIENT: When I get upset, I feel like I'm on the edge of a hole and I'm going to fall in. Like last week, my friend Alana was visiting me from Houston where she lives. She was driving me to run an errand and a policeman pulled us over. Her taillight was out. He was rude and gave Alana a ticket because she was not wearing her safety belt. I pleaded with him to give me a ticket instead because it was my fault for not telling her. I started to cry uncontrollably. Later, I couldn't eat and had trouble sleeping that night. He was very abrupt – What's the word? – brazen. He frightened me.

THERAPIST: What was so frightening about him?

PATIENT: I said to you once that I get frightened by men's anger. My father would yell and lose his temper when I was a little girl. I would be afraid of him. I would be at fault if my sisters did something inappropriate or if I didn't get enough practice in. My mother would not stick up for me; she would be silent, she was afraid too. She would sometimes say supportive things later after father would leave the room, but that happened rarely. She was very depressed; I felt so bad for her.

THERAPIST: You have said before that you identified with your mother's suffering, which may explain part of your depression, yet you despised her for her weakness and lack of availability. She didn't protect you from the angry policeman.

PATIENT: Yes. But as you would say, the policeman is not my father and I am no longer a little girl. Remember last year when I had those awful visions of rats coming from out of the garbage can? Well, I thought about them this week. Even though I know they were not real, I was worried. So I scrubbed the entire kitchen, the floors and all the cabinets and closets so they couldn't come out of any dirty places.

THERAPIST: What made you think of them again?

PATIENT: I don't know. Just that the apartment was dirty.

THERAPIST: Did you feel dirty?

PATIENT: No. It's like there are things from the outside that can easily get to me.

THERAPIST: Like what?

PATIENT: I don't know. I was at a bus stop and it was in the evening. This man came up to talk to me. I felt it was a dangerous situation. He asked for my phone number. I was sad when I got off the bus. I felt alone, empty. I called my mother, but she told me I was just going to have to cope.

THERAPIST: How did you feel when the man showed interest in you?

PATIENT: I felt scared; I had butterflies.

THERAPIST: Because he showed you specialness and it felt good to be wanted.

PATIENT: Yes.

THERAPIST: I imagine it's experiences like these that are most difficult for you. When you felt his desire you were put acutely in touch with your aloneness and lack of intimacy you feel with your husband, which intensified your longings to be comforted by your mother who has always failed you.

PATIENT: I keep hoping she will respond differently. The same night I cleaned the apartment, I had a dream that I had a child. It was a girl. And I loved this child. I accepted it, felt tenderness, I was content. For two days I thought about what it meant. Then I realized that the child was me . . . and I could love it. I was near water, some type of seashore. Some person was keeping my child for me. I didn't get to see it much, but I believed it existed, it was alive, and I was happy. I've been feeling more hopeful even though Manuel is so conceited. I'm prepared that if I get depressed again, it won't be that bad because I will come back, come out of it. I want to better myself. I feel I can give more to myself now. I still have a chance to exist.

This session was a turning point in Chandra's process of becoming. Just like in her dream, she was able to give birth to a new Self, one that she could love and give genuine voice to the inner, prereflective unmediated experiences that were seeking confirmation and enactment. Throughout the rest of her therapy, she continued to work hard at transcending her past and realized that she was the author of her own life. Her false Dasein underwent many significant transformations as she combated the internalized presence of her parents' excessive demands, her punitive guilt and depleted self-worth, and nurtured her own ability to allow subjective needs and genuine self-strivings to surface and speak authentically. As Chandra began to challenge the repetition of oppression, self-deprecation, and personal sacrifice for the Other, her depression abated and her self-confidence soared. Chandra realized that she *did* exist and that she was free to choose a different way of being.

Conclusion

Despite intrapsychic deficits and selfobject failures that shape character structure, Dasein is able to transcend inauthenticity by apprehending its authentic Being-toward-possibility. For Heidegger, authenticity is ultimately self-relatedness (within world-relatedness) and marked by Dasein's responsibility toward genuine *care*. This care, in other words, is an ownership of Dasein's freedom and opens a space for authenticity. For Heidegger, this process necessitates the "call of conscience," the voice of Dasein within Dasein that summons us to respond to an authentic appeal and transcend the public everydayness of Being. The false Dasein is only one mode of Being-in-the-world, and capable of recovering its authenticity in its freedom. The voice of authentic Dasein's Being-toward possibility summons me toward myself. Such authentic relationship to our true possibilities is borne out of our experience. Dasein is called to a new possibility of Being.

Chandra eventually heard her call of conscience as invigorating self-care, discovery, and love. Through the empowerment of her personal agency, she began making better choices on how she wanted to live her life, derived through authentic self-reflection. Recall that postmodernism allegedly denies the existence of the individual subject; thus the notion of the self and that of authenticity are merely illusions. But Chandra's case is a pragmatic example of how reductionistic versions of postmodernism delude themselves into thinking that there is no individuality or teleology of conscious agency. For all practical purposes, this claim is absurd: I exist by virtue of the fact that I posit myself and contemplate my thoughts, feelings, and actions through determinate choice and negation. And just as I exist as a subject who reflects on my existence, Chandra chose a different existence through laborious self-analysis facilitated by the therapeutic, relational encounter. She did so by increasingly embracing her emerging sense of self as freedom, which first revealed itself as self-knowledge: in order to be, we must become.

Despite the vogue postmodern trend that displaces personal agency and the self, I have attempted to show that human subjectivity is an indispensable and experiential process of becoming. Heidegger is very clear that "Dasein exists" (Heidegger [1927] 1962: 78), not as an epiphenomenon of larger cultural and linguistic forces, but as a subject who emerges within them equiprimordially. Dasein is the human being who lives in a world composed of multiple dynamic organizations that are psychologically, socially, and temporally realized in relation to the past, the present, and future possibilities. And just as Sartre (1943) emphasizes our subjectivity as radical freedom, and psychoanalysis as the pursuit of bringing to light that which lies hidden from our immediate conscious awareness, we exist in relation to what we can become. Ultimately in both the existential and psychoanalytic traditions, we can only become free through knowledge.

References

Cassimatis, E. G. (1984) "The false self," *International Review of Psycho-Analysis* 11: 69–77.

Chescheir, M. W. (1985) "Some implications of Winnicott's concept for clinical practice," *Clinical Social Work Journal* 13: 218–33.

Freud, S. ([1923] 1961) *The Ego and the Id*, in *The Standard Edition of the Complete Psychological Works of Sigmund Freud*, vol. 19, ed. and trans. J. Strachey. London: Hogarth Press.

Guignon, C. (1993) "Authenticity, moral values, and psychotherapy," in C. Guignon (ed.) *Cambridge Companion to Heidegger*. Cambridge: Cambridge University Press.

Heidegger, M. ([1927] 1962) *Being and Time*, trans. J. Macquarrie and E. Robinson. San Francisco, CA: HarperCollins.

—— ([1949] 1977) "On the essence of truth," in *Martin Heidegger: Basic Writings*, ed. D. F. Krell. San Francisco, CA: HarperCollins.

Khan, M. M. (1971) "Infantile neurosis as a false self organization," *Psychoanalytic Quarterly* 40: 245–63.

Kockelmans, J. (1978) "Daseinsanalysis and Freud's unconscious," *Review of Existential Psychology and Psychiatry* 16: 21–42.

Kohut, H. (1971) *The Analysis of the Self*. New York: International Universities Press.

—— (1977) *The Restoration of the Self*. New York: International Universities Press.

—— (1978) *The Search for the Self: Selected Writings of Heinz Kohut: 1950–1978*, 2 vols, ed. P. Ornstein. New York: International Universities Press.

—— (1984) *How does Analysis Cure?* Chicago: University of Chicago Press.

Laing, R. D. (1969) *The Divided Self*. London: Pelican.

Lerner, P. M. (1985) "The false self concept and its measurement," *Ontario Psychologist* 17: 3–6.

Masterson, J. F. (1981) *The Narcissistic and Borderline Disorders*. New York: Brunner/Mazel.

Miller, A. (1981) *The Drama of the Gifted Child*. New York: Basic Books.

Mills, Jon (2002) "Five dangers of materialism," *Genetic, Social, and General Psychology Monographs*, 128(1): 5–27.

Mitchell, S. A. (1992) "True selves, false selves, and the ambiguity of authenticity," in N. J. Skolnick and S. C. Warshaw (eds.) *Relational Perspectives in Psychoanalysis*. Hillsdale, NJ: Analytic Press.

Richardson, W. J. (1993). "Heidegger among the doctors," in J. Sallis (ed.) *Reading Heidegger*. Bloomington, IN: Indiana University Press.

Sartre, J. P. (1943) *Being and Nothingness*, trans. H. E. Barnes. New York: Washington Square Press.

Schacht, L. (1988) "Winnicott's position in regard to the self with special reference to childhood," *International Review of Psycho-Analysis* 15: 515–29.

Winnicott, D. W. ([1960] 1965) Ego distortions in terms of true and false self, in *The Maturational Processes and the Facilitating Environment*. New York: International Universities Press.

Chapter 6

Language and subjectivity
From Binswanger through Lacan

Roger Frie

It was Anna O., the famous patient of Breuer and Freud, who first referred to the psychoanalytic method as a "talking cure." Language continues to be central to the practice of psychotherapy and psychoanalysis because it is through language that we communicate and express ourselves. Contemporary theory asserts that the human being, or subject, exists not only in relationship to others, but also within language itself. In recent discussions of the role of language in clinical theory and practice, the traditional view of the subject as a "speaker" of language has given way to the postmodern notion that the human subject is dependent upon the language that it speaks. Postmodernism not only highlights the ambivalence of meaning in language, but also demonstrates that understanding is mediated by the symbolic world of culture and tradition in which we exist. While the rise of postmodernism has undoubtedly enriched our understanding of human experience, its account of language and subjectivity is open to question. As a result of postmodernism's overriding emphasis on language, prelinguistic, nonverbal, and bodily realms of experience have been pushed to the margins of theoretical and clinical discourse. In fact, for some postmodernists, there is nothing prior to or outside of language

In an attempt to address this development, this chapter begins with a brief examination of the work of Jacques Lacan, the French psychoanalyst whose work underlies much of the current focus on language. Lacan recognizes the reality of nonverbal and bodily experience, yet in line with poststructuralism he privileges the symbolic realm. My aim is to assess the role of the linguistic dimension in recent theory and practice in terms of Lacan's assertion that the human subject is an "effect of the signifier." Following this examination, I turn to the existential-phenomenological tradition as an alternative approach for understanding the relationship between language and subjectivity.

In light of postmodernism's attempt to reduce subjectivity to its articulation in language, the perspectives on language and subjectivity developed by existential-phenomenological psychoanalysts and philosophers are particularly germane. To this end, this chapter will focus chiefly on the work of the Swiss psychiatrist and psychoanalyst, Ludwig Binswanger, since he bridged the divide between psychiatry, psychoanalysis, and philosophy in a way that others did not. Only a small number of Binswanger's writings (Binswanger 1958, 1963) have ever been translated, however, and as a result he remains largely unknown to English-speaking readers. In seeking to demonstrate the relevance of his work, my discussion will rely primarily on untranslated texts; all translations are my own. I will elaborate the extensive connections between Binswanger and the work of Martin Buber and Martin Heidegger. And I will show the way in which Binswanger's emphasis on bodily experience parallels Maurice Merleau-Ponty's development of lived experience and considerably predates current clinical interest in the body. Ultimately each of these thinkers sought to achieve an account of human experience that included both the centrality of language *and* the reality of prelinguistic, nonverbal, and bodily experience.

Psychoanalysis and the symbolic order

Postmodernism and poststructuralism operate within diverse disciplines and do not constitute a coherent body of thought, yet their proponents are largely united in the assertion that the subject's encounter with language is always deforming. Implicit in poststructuralist theory is the subordination of the subject to language, which is famously expressed by Roland Barthes, who states:

> Linguistically, the author is never more than the instance of writing, just as I is nothing other than the instance of saying I: language knows "subject," not a "person," and this subject, empty outside of the very enunciation which defines it, suffices to make language "hold together," suffices, that is to say, to exhaust it.
>
> (Barthes 1984: 145).

A related argument is developed in the earlier work of Michel Foucault, whose declaration of a radically new era beyond subjectivity is central to the postmodern movement. According to Foucault, the subject is fragmented by language, concepts, and history and our bodies themselves are actually destroyed in the process (Foucault 1977: 148, 153).

In order to question the view of human subjectivity as dependent upon the language we speak, I will briefly examine the work of Lacan, whose ideas have been influential in bringing about the linguistic turn in recent psychoanalysis (Frie 1999b). Unlike many poststructuralists, Lacan does not reject the human subject altogether. His aim, rather, is to illustrate the decentering of subjectivity that takes place through the subject's encounter with language. Lacan thus retains a conception of subjectivity, however minimal.

Lacan's career as a psychiatrist and psychoanalyst went through numerous stages. Early on he allied his work with Binswanger's phenomenological psychiatry and drew on the existential-phenomenological philosophies of Heidegger and Sartre. His avid interest in disciplines beyond medicine and psychiatry was evident throughout his career. Yet Lacan's many internal contradictions and shifts in position seem to betray any attempt to coax a coherent system out of his work. His philosophical influences are many and the later Lacan was as likely to reject or deny his early interests in phenomenology as he was to identify his work with mathematics. My aim in talking about Lacan is not to elaborate a constructive interpretation, but rather, to sketch an outline of his approach to language and subjectivity.

For Lacan, the human being is from the very start linguistic, social, and intersubjective. He starts from the premise that the human being is embedded not only in relationships, but also in language itself. From this perspective, I would suggest that Lacan's ideas are relevant to recent interpersonal, relational, and intersubjective perspectives in psychoanalysis, which explore and elucidate the dynamics at work in the dyads between parent and child, analyst and analysand, self and other. Lacan can be understood as adding a further dimension to the dyad, namely a semiotic code of language and culturally entrenched behavior, which he refers to as the symbolic order.

Lacan developed three orders or dimensions to interpret human experience: the imaginary, the symbolic and the Real. The imaginary register is made up of visual and reflected images. The symbolic register is the intersubjective field of language and ritual. The third and most elusive register, the Real, refers to the realm of human experience that is beyond symbolization. It describes such experiences as sexuality and death which, according to Lacan, subsist outside of language.

For Lacan, the decentering of the subject begins very early in the realm of the imaginary, in what he refers to as the "mirror stage." The newly born infant first experiences a sense of bodily unity through an encounter with its own reflection. Its self-reflection is necessarily a misrecognition, however, because the infant does not have control over its bodily functions.

This discrepancy between the infant and its imagined unity results in a fundamental splitting, which is soon exacerbated by its entry into language. Imaginary identifications in the mirror stage thus give way to a more profound splitting of the subject in the symbolic order.

The importance of language for psychoanalysis was recognized early on by Freud, who wrote extensively about slips of the tongue, jokes, and the theory and practice of free association. Yet Freud never elaborated the role of language in human development and paid scant attention to its signifying power. In order to account for the primacy of language, Lacan "reread" Freud from the perspective of structuralism and linguistics. As a psychoanalyst, Lacan was probably most influential in his assertion that the unconscious is structured like language. Whereas Freud's discovery of the unconscious undermined the autonomy of the self because it implied a inalterable tension between the ego and id, for Lacan, subjectivity is ultimately fractured and decentered by its insertion in, and ultimate dependence upon language.

Lacan's theory of language and his emphasis on the instability of linguistic meaning derives its fundamental insights from Ferdinand de Saussure's concept of the linguistic sign. Saussure (1916) argued that meaning is dependent not upon fixed symbols and concepts, but upon the relation and difference between symbols. In addition, Lacan turned to the structuralist anthropology of Claude Lévi-Strauss. Following Lévi-Strauss, Lacan argues that before the subject is born, it already has a position within a kinship order, which he refers to as the symbolic order.

For Lacan, the symbolic is only one of three orders, yet he insists on its primacy. He argues that the subject's reality *is* the symbolic order. Lacan (1977) maintains that the subject is inserted into a pre-existing symbolic order and can be understood as an "effect" of the signifier. Implicit in Lacan's work is the belief that we exist in a language that we neither invent nor fully control. Thus in order for the infant to express its needs, it must learn a linguistic code and articulate its demands in words that are not its own. Language is the medium through which we communicate our desires and needs. Yet when we talk to one another, we can never be certain that the meaning of our communication is understood in the way we intend. It is this interminable shifting of meaning in language which, according to Lacan, divides the subject.

What does this mean clinically? As a psychoanalyst, Lacan is primarily concerned with what can be articulated within the linguistic paradigm of the symbolic order. He therefore attributes relatively little importance to a theory of affect, depriving such phenomena of any force that might escape absorption into symbolic interaction. According to Lacan, the transference of affect is actually a transference of image, referred to as imaginary transference. The emotional relationship within the analytic session between analysand and analyst is presented as a relationship of identification. Lacan is interested in affects chiefly as transmitted, that is, as exteriorized in intersubjective communication.

According to Lacan, the analysand's affect becomes important to the course of analysis when the analysand is able to articulate the affect's meaning. Only thus is the movement from the imaginary to the symbolic achieved. And for Lacan, as we have seen, the effectiveness of an analysis is dependent upon the primacy of the symbolic. As such, the function and structure of language must remain at the forefront of analytic experience.

It is certainly true that the experience of analysis is verbal, but the psychoanalyst also deals with much that is nonverbal. Because the emphasis in psychoanalysis has historically been on the patient's free associations, however, nonverbal communication has often been neglected. Freud observed nonverbal behavior in his patients, but he did not elaborate on, or develop this aspect of analytic work.

Nonverbal communication includes such elements as facial expression, gesture, posture, and vocal prosodic elements such as quality of speech, rhythm, and tone (Ekman 1993). Clearly there is much analytic territory that cannot be defined in terms of free association and interlocution (see Frie 1999b.) Indeed, it is probably not too daring to suggest that nonverbal communication is as important to the analytic process as verbal communication. We need only think about such issues as a patient's facial expression at the beginning or end of a session, the timing and length of silences, or the mood in which interaction is undertaken and achieved to realize that the nonverbal communication is always implicit in the analytic dyad.

Psychoanalytic researchers have recently sought to define and elaborate the nonverbal realm. Examination of dyadic interaction has shown that much communication takes place nonverbally. Linguistic communication within a dyad is actually framed by a so-called paralinguistic communication that is often outside of our awareness. According to Bloom, this aspect of communication conveys "the affective quality of the relationship . . . through observation of rhythm sharing, body movement, timing of speech and silences" (Bloom 1983: 84). Research on infant–mother interaction (Beebe and Lachmann 1988) suggests that infants and mothers continually attune to one another's emotional states by matching facial expressions, tone of voice, and behavior. When one individual in a dyad matches the other's nonverbal emotion cues, whether body posture or facial expression, that individual recreates the autonomic changes and body sensations associated with the other's emotional state.

Emotion also plays a fundamental role in the coordination of the mind and body. Emotions are both an intrapsychic and an interpersonal phenomenon since they "connect not only the mind and body of one individual but minds and bodies between individuals" (Pally 1998: 349). Nonverbal communication of emotion is often unconscious. It can cause autonomic changes in the body such as blushing or blanching, and can alter bodily behaviors such as facial expressions and gestures. Emotions thus regulate minds and bodies between participants in the psychoanalytic dyad.

And it is well known, though perhaps less well accepted, that the analyst's "felt-sense" is an essential form of understanding in analytic work. My felt-sense, or intuition, is crucial for perceiving and deciphering the contents of a nonverbal communication, and not by chance relates to the disclosure of meaning in artistic endeavors. Indeed, the complexities of articulating and expressing emotion are known to artists and psychoanalysts alike, and point to the need to move beyond a linguistic framework for interpreting and understanding human experience.

World-designs and language

The nonverbal realm of human behavior and its role in communication was of particular interest to the Swiss psychiatrist and psychoanalyst, Ludwig Binswanger. He sought to develop a conception of the human being that was not reductionistic and would account for the wider context of human behavior. An early student and colleague of Freud, Binswanger crossed the disciplinary divide between psychiatry, psychoanalysis, and philosophy with relative ease. Binswanger was a proficient writer, but much of his work is steeped in continental philosophy and literature. Largely as a result of this interdisciplinary approach, I believe, most of his work has remained untranslated, thus receiving little attention from English-speaking readers. I will begin by providing a brief background to his ideas on prelinguistic, nonverbal, and bodily experience and will also draw extensive connections to similar perspectives developed by the early Heidegger, Buber, and Merleau-Ponty. As a result of the existing translations of his work (1958, 1963), Binswanger became known somewhat erroneously as a "Heideggerian" psychiatrist and psychoanalyst. By drawing connections to Buber, Merleau-Ponty and others I will aim to demonstrate that Binswanger's work has a much broader base than is generally realized.

Binswanger was the director of the Bellevue Sanatorium in Kreuzlingen, Switzerland, from 1910 until 1956. He trained as a psychiatrist under Eugen Bleuler at the Burghölzli Psychiatric Hospital in Zurich, where he first became acquainted with psychoanalysis. Binswanger was offered the directorship of the Burghölzli when Bleuler stepped down, but chose instead to remain director of Bellevue, which was founded by his grandfather in 1857. Binswanger dedicated much of his time to the integration of theoretical and clinical insights from philosophy, psychoanalysis and psychiatry. Binswanger's broad theoretical interests were reflected in his personal associations with major thinkers of the time. Among the prominent figures who visited Binswanger in Kreuzlingen were Freud, Husserl, Heidegger, Buber, Karl Löwith, Ernst Cassirer, Alexander Pfänder, and Max Scheler. Bellevue Sanatorium itself became a famous center for psychiatric treatment. Included among its patients were such well-known personalities as the Swiss artist Ernst Ludwig Kirchner, the Russian dancer Vaslav Nijinsky, and the German sociologist Max Weber. Binswanger retired in 1956, but remained an active writer, publishing his last work just one year before his death in 1966.

Binswanger and Freud first met in 1907 and entered into a voluminous correspondence, punctuated by personal visits, which lasted until Freud's death in 1939 (Binswanger 1957a; Fichtner 1992). Binswanger was attracted to Freud because of the insights that psychoanalysis provided into human behavior. At the same time, he was critical of the proto-physiological basis on which Freud's drive theory and models of the mind were based. Indeed, Binswanger was the only serious critic of psychoanalysis with whom Freud maintained a collegial relationship. Binswanger was simply unable to accept the notion that human behavior is causally determined by the instinctual energy of the id. Although he never questioned the explanatory potential of natural science, Binswanger sought to understand and explain human beings in the totality of their existence, not as natural objects constructed from various parts.

In an attempt to place psychoanalysis on a wider footing, Binswanger incorporated the findings of philosophy into his clinical work. Husserl's project of phenomenology provided him with a method to explain the "visual reality" of the mentally ill person. It was, however, Heidegger's move beyond Husserl in *Being and Time* (1927), that influenced Binswanger's thinking most directly. Heidegger's notion of being-in-the-world enabled Binswanger to develop a philosophically oriented approach to psychiatry that sought to understand the context in which the individual exists and discovers meaning. According to Binswanger, the goal of psychopathology was to see how we structure our world and thus, how we relate to our environment and the people around us.

According to Binswanger, Heidegger's conception of world – the matrix of relations in which the human being, or Dasein, exists and discovers meaning – provides the clinician with a key conceptual tool for understanding and describing human experience. "In thus indicating the basic structure of Dasein," Binswanger writes, "Heidegger places in the psychiatrist's hands a methodological key by means of which he can, free of the prejudice of scientific theory, ascertain and describe the phenomena he investigates in their full phenomenal content and context" (Binswanger 1955: 264). Binswanger's aim was to apply concepts such as "world" and "Dasein" to clinical case material in order to provide a more satisfactory method of interpreting human behavior. Following Heidegger, Binswanger also adopted the term "Daseinsanalysis" to describe his work, though as we shall see, he never became a Heideggerian and remained critical of key aspects of the philosopher's work.

As interpreted by Binswanger, the notion of being-in-the-world signified that we are not isolated, encapsulated egos, but rather, beings who are always in relation to other humans and the world around us. He thus enlarged Heidegger's ontological conception of world to include the horizon in which human beings live and through which they understand themselves. At the same time, Binswanger recognized three simultaneous modes of being-in-the-world: the *Umwelt*, constituting the environment within which a person exists; the *Mitwelt*, or world of social relations; and the *Eigenwelt*, the private world of self. According to Binswanger, the three modes together constitute a person's world-design – the general context of meaning within which a person exists.

Binswanger sought to achieve knowledge and scientific description of the world-designs of his patients: that is, to see how they would relate to the people and social environment around them, and thus to understand how they structure the world in which they exist. In other words, Binswanger did not interpret a patient's experiences in terms of intrapsychic drives or a mental apparatus. Nor did he simply elaborate the physical reality of the patient's world. For Binswanger, person and world are one.

Like Heidegger, Binswanger also maintains that the human being always develops in a shared and articulated world. Human development takes place through dialogue with the other. As Binswanger puts it:

> The human being is only human in speaking with one another, in the communication of I and Thou as we, on the basis of a shared linguistic world . . . a shared linguistic world design. Language is not a mere

"medium of exchange," but a being-with-one-another in a world that makes understanding possible.

(Binswanger 1955: 350).

By stressing the linguistic and social nature of the self, Binswanger lends cogency to the post-Cartesian conception of the subject, according to which the self comes to be in language. He specifically rejects the notion of an isolated individual and argues that the subject must always be understood to exist within a shared world of language.

Yet, in contrast to the linguistic turn that has come to dominate much recent psychoanalytic theory and continental philosophy, Binswanger maintains that subjectivity can never be entirely reduced to language (Frie 1997). To put it differently, although we may think in words, the fact remains that words themselves do not think. Meanings are not simply added to senseless experience. According to Binswanger, language does not in itself create the existence of world. Rather, language is the manifestation of the prelinguistic awareness we have of ourselves and the world around us. The experience of world precedes its articulation in language.

The case of Lola Voss

Binswanger explored the spatial, temporal, and verbal structures of human existence in a study entitled *Schizophrenia* (1957b). One of these case studies, "The case of Lola Voss," illustrates his clinical perspective on language. Unlike "The case of Ellen West" (Binswanger 1958), which rightly generated much debate as well as criticism (Chernin 1981; Laing 1982), Binswanger's discussion of Lola Voss has been relatively neglected. The case was first published in 1949, but the actual events took place several decades earlier; it is also one of the few to have been translated into English (Binswanger 1963: 266-341). Binswanger's discussion illuminates the role and function of language in Lola's experience of incipient schizophrenia. My purpose in examining the case is to demonstrate how Binswanger's perspective on language and world translates into a clinical understanding of the patient as a subject of language.

Lola entered the Bellevue Sanatorium at the age of 24 and stayed for a period of fourteen months. Binswanger continued to receive reports on her condition for several years after her departure. Lola was referred to the sanatorium by her parents, who were concerned with what they described as Lola's increasingly erratic and withdrawn behavior. Binswanger elaborates the way in which Lola's experience of world is ever more determined by her bounded and idiosyncratic world-designs.

Her experience of incipient schizophrenia exemplifies the process of "mundanization," in which Dasein gives itself over to a specific world-design, and is, in effect, overwhelmed and possessed by it. Binswanger refers to the state of surrendering to a particular world-design as "thrown-ness." Lola, he tells us, "sought cover from the world," which threatened to become "uncanny."

Lola's schizophrenia becomes evident as her existence is more and more overwhelmed by a single world-design. Binswanger explains that being overwhelmed is itself expressed through the experience of delusion. According to Binswanger, Lola tried to protect herself against the onslaught of the "dreadful" by seeking to guess its intentions in an oracle of symbols and words:

> As Lola, in her interpretations, resorts to various languages, compositions of syllables and inversions of letters, she reveals the basic features of all superstition: fixation upon the most inconspicuous, unimportant and innocent details, and their elevation into the sphere of the decisive majesty of fate.
>
> (Binswanger 1963: 292–3).

Thus, Binswanger talks of Lola's "near-psychotic superstitious language-oracle" as providing her with a bridge between her anxiety of the "uncanny and horrid," on the one hand, and her surrender of herself to the "secret conspiracy of personalized enemies," on the other. What is involved, according to Binswanger, is a withdrawal of life from its own decisional context by making all decisions dependent upon another. As such, Lola has essentially "renounced her own particular power to decide and lets herself be advised only by 'things,' which, for their part, are not objects or things as they are in themselves, but rather things as linguistically modeled and created by her" (Binswanger 1963: 289).

Lola's existence thus is no longer one of becoming and evolving. On the contrary, the temporalization of her existence is determined by the way in which she is continually on the alert for a danger that might suddenly threaten and possibly overwhelm her, whether it be the uncanny or fear of persecution. The spacialization of Lola's existence can be understood in relation to her overwhelming anxieties. Lola's superstitions provide her with the only means to salvage a space in which she can move freely. Her existence is now determined in every way by her entirely individualized world-design. She has, as such, given up her agency.

The extremity of Lola's world-design is most apparent in terms of its verbal structure. In her delusional state, Lola develops a superstitious faith in "the omnipotence of words" (Binswanger 1963: 263) and creates a closed system of signs, which includes its own grammar and syntax. In essence, Lola surrenders herself to a self-created system of signs and thereby divides herself from other people and the world around her. Thus, while Lola continues to reside within language, language has itself been transformed into a closed system that she uses to insulate herself from meaningful human interaction. Here we can see that the loss of related-ness described by Binswanger is closely associated with Jacques Lacan's conception of "the Real," in which psychotic experience is characterized by the loss of meaningful speech (Lacan 1977).

Binswanger, however, goes a step further to suggest that even in the absence of meaningful vocal language and communication, the patient's experience of world is disclosed through attunement to her surroundings. Indeed, a person will rely on a bodily experience of her environment, even when she is able to express her experience in words. Language, as we know, allows for the articulation of self-consciousness, and consti-tutes a necessary condition of human development in the context of a shared world. During her paranoid delusions Lola Voss was fully im-mersed in her own closed world of symbols that effectively shut her off from others. Yet for Binswanger, the point remains the same. Language does not create the existence of world. It is, rather, a manifestation of our prior world disclosure that takes place through an implicit, bodily attune-ment to one's surroundings. Implicit, bodily awareness is a basic facet of human experience. Our prelinguistic experience of world is always in-herent to our use and understanding of language.

At the height of Lola's delusions, Binswanger appears to have been the only person with whom Lola was able to maintain a relationship. In con-trast to most psychiatry of the day, Binswanger emphasized the need for clinicians to use empathy and intuition in relating to their patients. Significantly, then, their communication was not based only, or even chiefly, on Lola's use of spoken language. Rather, in order to relate to his patient, Binswanger relied as much on Lola's affect, bodily expression, and the feeling-tone in what she said, as he did on the actual words she used. At the same time, it was precisely Lola's use of language that pro-vided an important, indeed, key insight into her experience of world.

Binswanger recognized the vital importance of maintaining a relation-ship with Lola. For Binswanger, Lola's well-being was dependent upon the return of meaningful speech and concomitant relatedness to others. In his view, Lola would be able to return from her state of paranoid delusion only through the repair of her relations with other people and the world in which she lived. This is also reminiscent of Harry Stack Sullivan and

Frieda Fromm-Reichmann, who both argued that pathology was a specific problem neither of the id nor of the superego, but of the relation of the self to its reality. Binswanger thus underlines the linguistic nature of our existence and suggests that relatedness is crucial to well-being (Frie 2000). In order to regain her sense of self, Lola would have to acknowledge and act on her agency by using language as a means of communicating her needs, wishes, and desires with others.

Binswanger was sensitive to the myriad ways in which his patients expressed themselves nonverbally through their bodies. In reflecting on the role of the bodily communication, he suggests that physical symptoms are not mere substitutions for verbal language, but constitute a form of language on their own:

> One must realize that . . . under certain circumstances [the body] remains the only form of expression left to people, and that the human being henceforth also uses the language of the body: that is, instead of scolding and raging, the human being chortles, belches, screeches and vomits.
>
> (Binswanger 1935: 146).

Bodily expression, however, is not limited to situations in which a person experiences loss of speech. On the contrary, bodily behavior is a significant form of nonverbal communication. Blushing or blanching, like laughing or crying, are nonverbal reactions that constitute a part of the affective dimension of human interaction. These varied behavioral, affective expressions are relevant to intersubjective communication precisely because of their reactive character.

To reduce prelinguistic and nonverbal experience to that which can be verbally articulated is to neglect a crucial fact: the nonverbal realm exists precisely because there is a dimension of human experience that cannot be adequately represented in, or expressed through language. This does not imply that what cannot be linguistically articulated can be disregarded. On the contrary, the nonverbal affective dimension specifically resists being drawn into discourse.

Implicit communication and therapeutic interaction

For Binswanger, the nature of our dialogue determines the structure of our relationships with other people. The problem of relation is central to Binswanger's work. In his attempt to develop a theory of human interaction that was not reductionistic, Binswanger was equally critical of both Freud and Heidegger. Binswanger argued that Freud's attempt to account for interpersonal love through a causally determined theory of drives was fundamentally flawed. Indeed, Binswanger's rejection of any form of biological determinism leads him to dismiss outright the proto-biological basis of the libido. To this end, Binswanger remarks:

> The monstrous difference between the *genetic derivation* of all forms of love from a single source and the disclosure of love as a unified anthropological originary phenomenon, forbids any attempt to even compare our concept with that of psychoanalysis.
>
> (Binswanger [1942] 1993: 234–5).

Referring to the psychoanalytic explanation of love, Binswanger states further that if love were simply an "*illusion*, in the explanatory sense of . . . Freud, then it would be difficult to conceive how love can constitute a 'reality'; a reality cannot be based upon something 'unreal'" (Binswanger [1942] 1993: 140). In Binswanger's view, Freud's theory of libido plainly fails to account for the phenomenological reality of love, which is central to the interpersonal field of psychotherapy and psychoanalysis.

Binswanger initially turned to Heidegger in search of developing a more satisfactory conception of human interaction. However, just as he dismissed Freud's concept of libido, Binswanger also found Heidegger's conception of interpersonal interaction to be lacking. In his chief theoretical work, *Basic Forms and Knowledge of Human Existence* (1942), Binswanger argues that Heidegger's treatment of social dimension in *Being and Time* does not sufficiently account for the role of other human beings in the achievement of authenticity or self-understanding, and entirely omits the notion of interpersonal love. Binswanger's argument follows the earlier critique made by Heidegger's one-time student, Karl Löwith (1981), and has more recently been elaborated by the German philosophers Michael Theunissen (1977) and Jürgen Habermas (1985).

Binswanger's critique of Heidegger led to a split between himself and the philosopher, the roots of which can be traced to the early 1930s, when Binswanger first began to apply the philosopher's ideas (Frie 1999a). While Binswanger was an innovative thinker and clinician, he was never trained in philosophy and his reading of Heidegger's work sometimes revealed this fact. Heidegger initially supported Binswanger's endeavors, but eventually took offence. By the late 1940s, he began to work together with the Swiss psychiatrist and psychoanalyst, Medard Boss, who in contrast to Binswanger was not inclined to be critical.

There is also another side to the differences between Binswanger and Heidegger, namely the philosopher's political past. In my view, Binswanger's critique of Heidegger places him largely outside of the debate over the philosopher's activities under National Socialism in Germany. Binswanger was himself of Jewish heritage; his grandfather, a well-known psychiatrist, left Bavaria for Switzerland because anti-semitism prohibited him from setting up a sanatorium there. Binswanger's chief work, *Basic Forms and Knowledge of Human Existence* was published in 1942, in the midst of World War II, and can be read as an outcry against the unfolding horrors of the time (Frie and Hoffmann 2002). In addition, during the war Binswanger's Bellevue Sanatorium in Kreuzlingen became a haven for a number of local German Jewish intellectuals. Curiously, though, Binswanger appears never to have questioned Heidegger about his political involvement, even though the philosopher's political views must have been known to him when they took up contact again after the war. Instead, Binswanger seems to have portrayed the apolitical attitude typical of many other Swiss of his social and economic stature.

Although Binswanger's argument against Heidegger is philosophical in nature, it is worth examining briefly because of its clinical implications. The problem with Heidegger's perspective, as Binswanger saw it, was not that Heidegger overlooked human sociality. Rather, the difficulty lay in the fact that Dasein achieved its authenticity in essential isolation from others. As Binswanger states: Heidegger "sees only the inauthentic They-self besides the authentic self, and omits the authentic positive possibility of Being-with-one-another: that is, the being in one another of first and second person, of I and Thou, the We-self" (Binswanger [1942] 1993: 217). In other words, Heidegger does not include the possibility of achieving authenticity through dialogue with another. As we shall see, it is precisely the I–Thou relationship that Binswanger sees as crucial to the psychoanalytic process. As a clinician, he believed that psychoanalysis was dependent upon the emergence of a type of loving I–Thou relationship between psychoanalyst and patient.

Binswanger's critique of Heidegger provided the stimulus for his own elaboration of the interpersonal dimension. To this end, Binswanger turned to the work of Buber. As with Freud, Binswanger carried on a long correspondence and friendship with Buber and in 1936 wrote to Buber stating that:

> I not only follow in your every step, but see in you an ally, not only against Kierkegaard, but also against Heidegger. Although I am

methodologically deeply indebted to Heidegger, I take exception to his conception of Dasein (as mine). . . . It is very important that you want to achieve a conceptualization of the public that is not limited to the multitude and the They.

(Buber 1973: 621)

The impact of Buber's philosophy of dialogue on Binswanger is most apparent in *Basic Forms and Knowledge of Human Existence*. In the preface to that text, Binswanger acknowledges an equal indebtedness to Buber's short treatise, *I and Thou* (1923), and to Heidegger's *Being and Time* (1927). Not by chance, I believe, Binswanger's clinical interest in the work of Buber is shared by a number of contemporary interpersonal and relational psychoanalysts, who have discussed the relevance of Buber's ideas (Aron 1996; Ehrenberg 1992).

The problem of relation, or dialogical life, is central to Buber's entire philosophy. Buber argues that the human being can never be fully understood apart from relation. As Buber states, each component of a relation "considered by itself is a mighty abstraction. The individual is a fact of existence insofar as he steps into a living relation with another individual. . . . The fundamental fact of human existence is human being with human being" (Buber 1965: 203). Buber maintains that the character of a relationship is always determined by which of the basic words is spoken: when I–Thou is said, the I is different from the I that speaks the primary word I–It. As Buber puts it, the "I–Thou can only be spoken with the whole being. The primary word I–It can never be spoken with the whole being" (Buber 1923: 54). Dialogue, in this sense, not only is a mode of linguistic communication, but also denotes the interhuman dimension generally.

Buber's theory of relation provided Binswanger with a more adequate conceptual underpinning from which to elaborate his conception of self-realization in a loving I–Thou relationship. Not by chance, Binswanger also sees the I–Thou relationship as crucial to the therapeutic process. As a clinician, he believed that psychoanalysis was dependent upon the emergence of a type of loving I–Thou relationship between therapist and patient. Binswanger (1942) delineates different forms of social existence – dual, plural and singular modes – that are oriented towards the achievement of authenticity in loving dialogue with another person. Binswanger's aim is to elaborate the anthropological structure of a loving I–Thou relationship that permits that achievement of authenticity. And for Binswanger, it is precisely in and through a loving I–Thou relationship, or dual mode of love, that growth and change become possible.

Binswanger's conception of the dual mode is indebted to Wilhelm von Humboldt's notion of the *dualis*. According to Humboldt (1983), the very possibility of speaking is conditioned by address and response. The *dualis* constitutes a unique linguistic mode in which the speaker and addressee are always posited together. A similar perspective is expressed by Merleau-Ponty in *Phenomenology of Perception* (1945):

> There is one particular cultural object that is destined to play a crucial role in the perception of other people. In the experience of dialogue, there is constituted between the other person and myself a common ground; my thought and his are inter-woven into a single fabric, my words and those of my interlocutor are called forth by the state of the discussion, and they are inserted into a shared operation of which neither of us is the creator. We have here a dual being, where the other is for me no longer a mere bit of behavior in my transcendental field, nor I in his; we are collaborators for each other in consummate reciprocity. Our perspectives merge into each other, and we co-exist through a common world.
>
> (Merleau-Ponty [1945] 1989: 354)

Merleau-Ponty suggests, in a manner akin to Humboldt, that dialogue takes the form of a "dual being" and results in the experience of a common world, in which I and the Other coexist. It is this notion of a unity, or common world, which also forms the basis of Binswanger's theory of communication.

For Binswanger, the experience of dialogue with another will not always be open to articulation. This was a theme that was of particular interest to him, since he wrote extensively about romantic, interpersonal love. Binswanger argued that because speakers can never be certain that what they say is understood in the way they wish, only nonverbal communication can fully express the human emotions. "For that reason," insists Binswanger, "the real expression of love is not language, but rather, the 'silent' look . . . the silent embrace of love" (Binswanger [1942] 1993: 69). In other words, love is disclosed not through linguistic articulation, but immediately in silence itself. According to Binswanger, communication in the interpersonal love relation reaches its highest form in silence. Binswanger writes that only thus is it possible "to reveal oneself to the other entirely . . . in uninterrupted conversation, exactly that form of conversation which is not even interrupted by silence" (Binswanger [1942] 1993: 146).

This insight into the nature of communication is also related to the analytic setting in which understanding can be implicit. For example, the attempt to express implicit understanding or a felt sense in words can result in a loss of the fullness of meaning that was grasped by analyst and analysand just a moment before. In such situations, words may appear oddly insufficient and the process of analysis takes the form of a "tortured poetry" in which both analyst and analysand search for metaphors to adequately convey what was implicitly understood.

The mutual silence described by Binswanger does not exist outside of language, however. In fact silence is itself a form of signification. In the practice of psychoanalysis, we know that silence can be as significant as speech. It is just as important to listen to and intuit the meaning of silences as it is to understand and interpret the meaning of speech. For this reason, the role of silence can also be likened to art and aesthetic experience. Artists have long known that words are a poor medium for expressing emotions. To this end, Merleau-Ponty argues that it is precisely through silence that aesthetic communication is attained: "Language speaks, and the voices of paintings are the voices of silence" (Merleau-Ponty 1964: 42). In aesthetics as in psychoanalysis, communication is often through feeling and intuition and therefore precedes or may even appear to transcend language.

Binswanger's (1942) distinction between different forms of dialogue leads him to differentiate between two different types of speech. The first is the "ordinary speech" of our everyday dealings with others. The second is "conversation" that occurs between partners in an I–Thou relationship, and forms the basis for analytic interaction. In ordinary speech, one person is dependent upon and will direct his or her actions according to what the other says. As Binswanger puts it, one person "takes the other by his or her word," and identifies that person by what he or she says. Ordinary speech is characterized by misunderstanding and uncertainty in communication, as each partner sees the other as an object or means to an end. In conversation, however, speakers do not rely only on the articulated words of the other person. Rather, the relationship is characterized by a direct, immediate form of communication that allows each participant to look beyond individual utterances to comprehend the meaning of what is said.

For Binswanger, the dynamic interaction in "conversation" implies that the self does not seek the particular conveyed in language, but rather, the *being* of the other as it is expressed through love. Binswanger maintains that I–Thou love "has nothing to do with isolated individuality, nor with 'details,' nor with determination, nor consequently with negation or division . . . it is only as wholeness and achieves wholeness" (Binswanger

[1942] 1993: 177). Binswanger states further that whereas ordinary speech always has a specific purpose in mind, conversation is noninstrumental.

It is important to note that the distinction made by Binswanger between ordinary speech and conversation is also present in the work of Heidegger and Lacan. In *Being and Time*, Heidegger (1927) differentiates between "idle talk" and "discourse." Idle talk denotes the inauthentic, anonymous chatter of the They, whereas discourse refers to Dasein's authentic response to the voice of Being. Lacan, who like Binswanger draws extensively on Heidegger's philosophy, repeats this distinction. Lacan (1977) draws a distinction between "empty speech" and "full speech." According to Lacan, empty speech designates the discourse of the illusory ego and belongs to the register of the imaginary. Full speech is attained when the subject abandons the imaginary autonomy of the ego and "hears" what it says in the intersubjective domain of the analytic session. However, whereas Binswanger's notion of conversation is characterized by the reciprocity between its participants, Heidegger's notion of discourse and Lacan's full speech both tend to marginalize the participatory role of the other. The point, for Binswanger, is that therapeutic interaction always involves *both* participants. The therapeutic dyad is intersubjective in the sense that the subjectivities of both the therapist and patient determine the nature of the interaction.

Binswanger's emphasis on mutuality was generated both by his rejection of the traditional psychiatrist–patient relationship, and in reaction to the classical psychoanalytic relationship. It is on this point that Binswanger's perspective is surprisingly close to interpersonal and recent relational psychoanalytic theorists. Binswanger enables us to see how mutuality (Aron 1996) in the therapeutic relationship can be a vehicle for change. On this view, moments of face-to-face meeting in the therapeutic relationship which allow for self-realization are not ends in themselves, but that which enables future mutuality and self-awareness to take place.

When the other person is described simply as an object for self-reflection or as the means to self-discovery, the relationship is drained of attachment, intimacy, and engagement (Ehrenberg 1992). When applied to the therapeutic relationship, this insight suggests that therapist and patient meet face-to-face and come to know each other as two interacting human beings. If this is not the case, then the self, though placed in a context of a relationship, is defined only in terms of separation. The emphasis, then, is on increasing self-understanding through continuing relationship to others.

The theory of therapeutic interaction I am outlining here suggests that the work of therapy does not simply stop when contact with the other is made or when both participants in the relationship are touched in some way by the interaction. Rather, as Darlene Ehrenberg (1992) points out, the relationship takes on new dimensions as the affective complexity of what gets activated in the moments of shared meeting can be further clarified and explored. And it is precisely the expanded awareness achieved through an authentic, reciprocal relation that is crucial to self-understanding and continued growth.

Bodily experience

For Binswanger, then, implicit in our use of language is an emotional and bodily awareness that facilitates communication and understanding. The body has become a topic of considerable interest among psychoanalysts and philosophers alike. The role of the body in psychoanalysis has traditionally been discussed under the rubric of "instinct" or by Lacan (1981) in terms of "illusory desire." For Freud, as we know, "the ego is first and foremost a bodily ego" (Freud [1923] 1961: 26). Binswanger essentially agreed with this position, maintaining that "the human being not only has a body but is a body and expresses him/herself through the body" (Binswanger [1935] 1947: 146). Binswanger nevertheless objected to Freud's tripartite division of the mind and all but rejected the determinism implicit in Freud's theory of drives.

According to Freud, drives are first and foremost bodily phenomena. Drives make demands on the mind, which, broadly speaking, attempts to assimilate them. In the terminology of Freud's structural theory, the ego, as a synthesizing agency of the psyche, seeks to integrate the demands of the blind drives of the id, with the exigencies of external reality. The purpose of psychoanalysis, according to Freud, is to facilitate this process.

Debate over drive theory has not detracted from the basic recognition of the body's clinical importance. Whether one accepts the notion of bodily based drives or seeks to reformulate them, the experience of the body is central to psychological life and clinical interaction. Current psychoanalytic research illustrates the body's relevance in the treatment of psychic trauma and affective disturbances. Feminist psychoanalysts (Benjamin 1995; Harris 1998) demonstrate the importance of the body in the construction of gender and sexual identity, and examine its clinical relevance within the psychoanalytic dyad. Joyce McDougall (1989) argues that psychoanalysts need to assess psychosomatic disorders because the mind's distress is often evident in somatic manifestations. And Henry Krystal's (1988) work with alexithymic patients suggests that affect is both a mental and bodily phenomenon, which is developed through emotional processing with caregivers.

The recent increase in psychoanalytic discussion of bodily existence is predated by existential-phenomenological philosophy. It was Merleau-Ponty who famously maintained that the mind can be understood only in terms of the body: "The perceiving mind is an incarnated body" (Merleau-Ponty 1962: 3). He sought to undercut the Cartesian distinction between mind and body by arguing that the subject essentially *is* a body. To this end, Merleau-Ponty (1945) developed the notion of the "body-subject," which drew on Binswanger's (1935) earlier exploration of the same theme. Both argue the mind can only be understood in terms of its body and its world. As Merleau-Ponty notes: "We grasp external space through our bodily situation. . . . For us the body is much more than an instrument or a means; it is our expression in the world, the visible form of our intentions" (Merleau-Ponty 1962: 5).

On this view, language elaborates our bodily sensations, but does not create them; the process of sensing one's environment through the body always exists prior to and alongside the use of language. Merleau-Ponty's basic insight that "the perceiving mind is an incarnated body" suggests that our bodies continually provide us with a sense of the situations and contexts in which we exist and interact. We sense what is behind and in front of us. This bodily, or felt, sense is not a product of reflective thought. Rather, it is prereflective and helps us to orient ourselves and know what we are doing. "Bodily sensing" is neither external observation nor subjective and internal, but a form of interaction with our environment. Speaking, in turn, "carries forward" (Gendlin 1992) our bodily interaction.

This view of the body and language is not limited to psychoanalysts or philosophers. Indeed, among neuroscientists currently reflecting on the mind–body problem, Antonio Damasio (1994) provides a similar perspective. Damasio argues that the body is a "ground reference" for understanding the world around us:

> The body, as represented in the brain, may constitute the indispensable frame of reference for the neural processes that we experience as the mind; that our very organism rather than some absolute external reality is used as the ground reference for the constructions we make of the world around us and for the construction of the ever-present sense of subjectivity that is part and parcel of our experiences; that our most refined thoughts and best actions, our greatest joys and deepest sorrows, use the body as a yardstick.
>
> (Damasio 1994: xvi)

In a manner akin to Merleau-Ponty, Damasio is describing the fundamental involvement of the body in all human experience. His insights are particularly germane, since the body, as we know, plays a crucial role in the psychoanalytic dyad.

Reflecting on Damasio's view of the body, Edgar Levenson proposes that "it may well be that the mind is not master, but is formed and molded by the body . . . [and] that our psychoanalytic desideratum, understanding, is neither entirely verbal nor intellectual, but more a limited reflection on an ineffable felt experience" (Levenson 1998: 240). The notion of felt experience points to the role of affects, which are themselves bodily sensations. And, as the psychoanalytic process suggests, affective experience only gradually reaches the point at which it can be articulated or named.

Psychoanalysis has traditionally relied on language: the articulation of thought, affect, fantasy, and dreams in words. I am suggesting that the emphasis on language and the intellect in psychoanalysis implicitly sustains the mind–body separation. As a result, the embodiment of understanding and cognition elaborated by Binswanger, Merleau-Ponty, and others remains outside the purview of traditional psychoanalytic theory and practice. According to Merleau-Ponty, our perception and understanding of the world is always and already grounded in our fundamentally embodied selves. He shows us that any attempt to separate intellect and soma is an artificial distinction of a whole. When applied to the psychoanalytic setting, we see that our foundations for self-reflexivity, understanding, knowledge, and articulation lie in our bodily sensations. Language, on this view, is a necessary, but not sufficient condition of subjectivity.

Conclusion

Although language and subjectivity are intrinsically linked, our understanding of subjectivity is curtailed if we do not also account for prelinguistic and nonverbal experience. Following Binswanger and Merleau-Ponty, I have argued that our bodily experience forms the basis of subjectivity and makes reflective thought and articulation possible. To view subjectivity only in terms of its articulation in language is problematic precisely because it does not account for our implicit self-awareness or bodily sense.

Because language is always inherent in meaning, there has understandably been an overemphasis on language and context in recent clinical theory and practice. Yet we also experience meaning through our bodily participation in the world. From this perspective, language and the body are indelibly related to one another, each being dependent upon the other. The fact remains, however, that we always speak from the body. And it is precisely for this reason that bodily experience provides a way of conceptualizing subjectivity and agency.

In developing this view of subjectivity, I am not arguing that the mind is indelibly private or self-enclosed. On the contrary, self-experience is always grounded in the body and language. As such, the nature of subjectivity is not only dependent upon, but also enhanced by history, culture, and community. We exist in language and are always fundamentally embedded in multiple contexts. Yet we are not simply subverted by the language we speak. The notion of a "decentered self" seems naïve unless we also account for the fact that we maintain a sense of continuity and cohesion as we engage others and transform the social field in which we exist. This requires a concept of agency (Frie 2002). By accounting for the body and bodily experience, we can begin to address the complex issue of personal agency – the person as an embodied, active being – which has been banished from current debate by postmodernism's wholesale rejection of the subject.

References

Aron, L. (1996) *A Meeting of Minds: Mutuality in Psychoanalysis*. Hillsdale, NJ: Analytic Press.

Barthes, R. (1984) *Image, Music, Text*. New York: Hill and Wang.

Beebe, B. and Lachmann, F. M. (1988) "The contributions of mother–infant mutual influence to the origins of self and object representations," *Psychoanalytic Psychology* 5: 305–37.

Benjamin, J. (1995) *Like Subject, Love Object*. New Haven, CT: Yale University Press.

Binswanger, L. ([1935] 1947) *Über Psychotherapie: Ausgewählte Vorträge und Aufsätze, Bd. I*. Bern: Francke.

—— ([1942] 1993) *Grundformen und Erkenntnis menschlichen Daseins: Ausgewählte Werke, Bd 2*. Heidelberg: Asanger Verlag. [Translation of title: Basic Forms and Knowledge of Human Existence.]

—— (1955) *Ausgewählte Vorträge und Aufsätze, bd. II: Zur Problematic der psychiatrischen Forschung und zum Problem der Psychiatrie*. Bern: Francke.

—— (1957a) *Sigmund Freud: Reminiscences of a Friendship*. New York: Grune and Stratton.

—— (1957b) *Schizophrenie*. Pfullingen: Neske.

—— (1958) "The case of Ellen West," in R. May, E. Angel and H. Ellenberger (eds.) *Existence: A New Dimension in Psychiatry and Psychology*. New York: Basic Books.

—— (1959) "Sprache, Welt und Bildung," *Sprachspiegel* 15: 65–73 and 97–106.

—— (1963) "The case of Lola Voss," in J. Needleman (ed.) *Being-in-the-world: The Selected Papers of Ludwig Binswanger*. New York: Basic Books.

Bloom, L. (1983) "Of continuity and discontinuity and the magic of language development," in R. Gollinkoff (ed.) *The Transition from Prelinguistic to Linguistic Communication*. Hillsdale, NJ: Lawrence Erlbaum.

Buber, M. ([1923] 1970) *I and Thou*. New York: Charles Scribner's Sons.

—— (1965) *Between Man and Men*. New York: Macmillan.

—— (1973). *Martin Buber Briefwechsel aus sieben Jahrzehnten, bd II: 1918–1938*. Ed. Grete Schaeder. Heidelberg: Lambert Schneider.

Chernin, K. (1981) *The Obsession: Reflections on the Tyranny of Slenderness*. New York: Harper and Row.

Damasio, A. (1994) *Descartes' Error: Emotion, Reason, and the Human Brain*. New York: Avon.

Eckman, P. (1993) "Facial expression and emotion," *American Psychologist* 48: 384–92.

Ehrenberg, D. (1992) *The Intimate Edge*. New York: W. W. Norton.

Fichtner, G. (ed.) (1992) *Sigmund Freud – Ludwig Binswanger: Briefwechsel, 1908–1938*. Frankfurt a. M.: Fischer Verlag.

Foucault, M. (1977) *Language, Counter-Memory, Practice: Selected Essays*. Ithaca, NY: Cornell University Press.

Freud, S. ([1923] 1961) *The Ego and the Id*, in *The Standard Edition of the Complete Psychological Works of Sigmund Freud*, vol. 19, ed. and trans. J. Strachey. London: Hogarth Press.

Frie, R. (1997) *Subjectivity and Intersubjectivity in Modern Philosophy and Psychoanalysis: A Study of Sartre, Binswanger, Lacan, and Habermas*. Lanham, MD: Rowman and Littlefield.

—— (1999a) "Interpreting a misinterpretation: Ludwig Binswanger and Martin Heidegger," *Journal of the British Society for Phenomenology*. 29: 244–58.

—— (1999b) "Psychoanalysis and the linguistic turn," *Contemporary Psychoanalysis* 35: 673–97.

—— (2000) "The existential and the interpersonal: Ludwig Binswanger and Harry Stack Sullivan," *Journal of Humanistic Psychology* 40: 108–30.

—— (2002) "Modernism or postmodernism? Binswanger, Sullivan and the problem of agency in contemporary psychoanalysis," *Contemporary Pyschoanalysis* 38: 635–74.

Frie, R. and Hoffmann, K. (2002) "Binswanger, Heidegger, and antisemitism," *Journal of the British Society for Phenomenology* 33: 221–8.

Gendlin, E. (1992) "The primacy of the body, not the primacy of perception," *Man and World* 25: 341–53.

Habermas, J. (1985) *The Philosophical Discourse of Modernity*. Cambridge, MA: MIT Press.

Harris, A. (1998) "Psychic envelopes and sonorous baths," in L. Aron and F. Sommer Anderson (eds.) *Relational Perspectives on the Body*. Hillsdale, NJ: Analytic Press.

Heidegger, M. ([1927] 1962) *Being and Time*. Oxford: Basil Blackwell.

Humbolt, Wilhelm von (1983) *Schriften zur Sprache*. Ed. Michael Böhler. Stuttgart: Reclam.

Krystal, H. (1988) *Integration and Self-Healing*. Hillsdale, NJ: Analytic Press.

Lacan, J. (1977) *Ecrits: A Selection*. New York: W. W. Norton.

—— (1981) *The Four Fundamental Concepts of Psycho-Analysis*. New York: W. W. Norton.

Laing, R. (1982) *The Voice of Experience*. New York: Pantheon.

Levenson, E. (1998) "Awareness, insight, learning," *Contemporary Psychoanalysis* 34: 239–49.

Löwith, K. (1981) "Das Individuum in der Rolle des Mitmenschen", in K. Stichweh (ed.) *Sämtliche Schriften, Bd. I*. Stuttgart: J. B. Metzler.

McDougall, J. (1989) *Theaters of the Body: A Psychoanalytic Approach to Psychosomatic Illness*. New York: W. W. Norton.

Merleau-Ponty, M. ([1945] 1989) *Phenomenology of Perception*. London: Routledge.

—— (1962) *The Primacy of Perception*. Evanston, IL: Northwestern University Press.

—— (1964) *Signs*. Evanston, IL: Northwestern University Press.

Pally, R. (1998) "Emotional processing: the mind–body connection," *International Journal of Psycho-Analysis* 79: 349–62.

Saussure, F. de ([1916] 1966) *Course in General Linguistics*. New York: McGraw-Hill.

Theunissen, M. (1977) *Der Andere*. Berlin: de Gruyter.

Chapter 7

Psychoanalysis and subjectivity in the work of Erich Fromm

Daniel Burston

Psychoanalysis began as an implausible profession that sought to study human subjectivity through the lens of the natural sciences. For the first sixty-odd years of its existence, the theoretical underpinnings of analytic discourse were overwhelmingly positivistic and reductionistic. The protean properties of desire, the qualities and intensities of despair, rage, guilt, anxiety, and faith were all construed as the overt expression of specific quanta of sexual and aggressive energy circulating in a biological system, whose interactions with kindred systems were regulated by motives and mechanisms that are largely outside of domain of consciousness. The whole aim of psychoanalytic technique was to disclose the patient to him- or herself, by "making the unconscious conscious," in the hope and expectation that becoming reacquainted with disowned or dissociated subjectivity would afford some leverage against symptoms by making the patient more "objective." But the term "objectivity" had a peculiar meaning in this context, since the ultimate in "insight" was presumed to be the ability to transpose the experience of raw, irrational passions glimpsed or released in clinical work into this utterly impersonal, mechanistic frame of reference.

Of course, there were "dissident" or "heretical" thinkers and schools who challenged Freud's positivism, among them Erich Fromm, who is the subject of this chapter. Fromm argued that our conflicted and irrational passions, including but not limited to sex and aggression, are actually expressions of *diverse modes of relatedness*, which are designed to address and overcome the problem of our "existential aloneness." Fromm was ignored by the analytic mainstream in North America until the early 1960s, when the work of Fairbairn and Winnicott, George Klein, Heinz Kohut, Roy Schafer and many others openly or implicitly called Freud's philosophical anthropology into question. Empathy and relatedness were emphasized, and it became acceptable, even advantageous, to

disparage Freudian instinctivism. But then, as now, Fromm, who anticipated many of the newer breed, never really got his due (Burston 1991).

Today we have reached a new threshold in the development of analytic
theory. Analysts do not merely question the cogency or relevance of the
metapsychology, but the very existence of the psychological subject it
was ostensibly intended to illumine. The goals of fostering autonomy
and a truth-loving disposition, which Fromm shared with Freud, and
vigorously commended him for, have become deeply suspect to many.
Spurred on by developments in continental philosophy, many psychoanalysts now proclaim the nullity or non-existence of the human subject,
and regard *this* hollow dictum as the pinnacle of insight or emancipation.
It never occurs to them that without the existence of human subjectivity,
and of real human subjects, however conflicted or unconscious they may
be, psychoanalysis lacks a domain of competence, even a subject matter.
In the absence of human experience and human intentions toward the
world, symptoms ultimately lose their intelligibility, and psychoanalysis
becomes a truly *impossible* profession.

Though he was never accepted in the analytic mainstream, and is still
somewhat overlooked today, Erich Fromm was unusually prescient in his
critique of the positivist underpinnings of Freudian theory. Moreover, his
implicit understanding of human subjectivity, which I attempt to elucidate
here, furnishes a useful alternative to the sweeping and totalistic denials of
human subjectivity that have been made fashionable by postmodernism.

Fromm and Freud: on method and the goals of therapy

Erich Pinchas Fromm was born in Frankfurt in 1900, and died in 1980,
in Locarno, Switzerland. He was descended from illustrious rabbinic
families, and was an avid student of Torah and Talmud. In 1920, he
helped found the *Freies Judisches Lehrhaus,* directed by Martin Buber
and Franz Rosenzweig, in Frankfurt, and in 1922, completed a doctorate
(in sociology) on Jewish law under Alfred Weber in Heidelberg. In 1924,
Fromm abandoned the rabbinic vocation to become a psychoanalyst,
studying one year with Wilhelm Witenberg in Munich, another with Karl
Landauer in Frankfurt, and finishing with two more under Hanns Sachs
and Theodor Reik in Berlin. In 1927, Fromm, Karl Landauer, Georg
Groddeck, Heinrich Meng, and Ernest Schneider founded the Frankfurt
Psychoanalytic Institute. And later that year, at Max Horkheimer's invitation, Fromm joined the Frankfurt Institute for Social Research, becoming their director for social psychology (Funk 1982).

Fromm's first papers on psychoanalysis sought to effect a theoretical synthesis of Marx, Freud, and Max Weber, and appeared in the *Zeitschrift für Sozialforschung,* the Frankfurt School's house organ, circa 1930 to 1937 (e.g. Fromm 1932, 1934; Jay 1973). In 1938 Fromm left the Frankfurt School, which had relocated to Columbia University during World War II, because Horkheimer refused to publish Fromm's (1929) study of pro-fascist sympathies among ostensibly left-leaning German workers. Published posthumously, it is the historic forerunner of Theodor Adorno's *The Authoritarian Personality* (Fromm [1929] 1984; Burston 1991). Another reason Fromm left, evidently, was that his evolving critique of Freud's positivism and strong patriarchal bias against women alienated the emerging analytic elite that Horkheimer was eagerly courting at the time (Burston 1991).

In 1946, Fromm co-founded the William Alanson White Institute with ex-wife Frieda Fromm-Reichmann, Clara Thompson, and Harry Stack Sullivan. He served as clinical director there from 1946 till 1950, when he founded the Mexican Institute of Psychoanalysis (Funk 1982). Though it has achieved considerable stature in the intervening years, at the time, the William Alanson White was a somewhat marginal training institute, and Fromm had little influence on the analytic mainstream as a result. His real impact was not on clinicians, in the first instance, but on the general, educated public and on academics keen to apply analytic perspectives to the study of social, cultural and political trends and processes, for example David Riesman, whose book *The Lonely Crowd* was a lengthy meditation on and dialogue with Frommian themes and perspectives (Riesman 1950; Roazen 1990).

Fromm's first bestseller, *Escape from Freedom*, was published in 1941. In it, Fromm adopted the existentialist thesis that freedom is not always longed for unambiguously, since it inevitably engenders anxiety in its wake. This insight was then applied to the study of fascist collectivism and trends toward banality, conformity, and consumerism, which were construed as various mechanisms of "escape." But though it reached a wide and receptive audience in North America, it alienated the psychoanalytic establishment. Apart from its blunt critique of American culture, and the whole psychology of "adaptation" preached by many ego-psychologists, Fromm was also quite critical of Freud's insistent positivism, and attempted to recast psychoanalytic theory in terms of the *Geisteswissenschaften*, or "sciences of the human spirit," that is the human sciences, long before this currently commonplace project became respectable in mainstream circles. In a variety of papers that preceded and followed *Escape from Freedom*, Fromm argued that the methods of the natural sciences are simply unsuited to the study of human subjectivity, because the formation (and/or deformation) of the psyche is shaped as much (or more) by social and historical forces as it is by biological processes (Fromm 1932, 1941). Moreover, the natural sciences employ experimental and quantitative research methods, which seek to predict and control the behavior of objects. The study of human minds requires a distinctive methodology which does not seek to predict or control the behavior of objects, but to *understand* a human subject's conscious attitudes and behavior, and their unconscious social and historical determinants (e.g. Fromm 1957).

To grasp what is at issue here, ponder the distinction between the German words "*erklaren*" and "*verstehen*." *Erklaren* denotes a mode of explanation in which the theorist tries to explain appearances in terms of antecedent causes in naturalistic, scientific terms. It applies equally to the behavior of inanimate matter, other animal species, and to human beings, considered from a materialistic and deterministic point of view. It seeks to render appearances intelligible by minimizing, abolishing or transcending human subjectivity, or to explain the contents and qualities of experience in terms of natural processes that go on outside of it. So, for example, gravity, gamma rays, and natural selection are objects of scientific inquiry, though they are not objects of experience as such. Still, they do shape human subjectivity and the world we experience, and we can talk and reason about them objectively, as it were, at least in principle.

Verstehen, by contrast, is a mode of explanation that applies only to human behavior, and the attempt to render human subjectivity intelligible in its own terms. It is what R. D. Laing would call an *interexperiential* process of understanding the other person in terms of the meanings with which they themselves endow their situation or surroundings, and their own intentions, relative to their cultural and historical situation. This calls for the creation of qualitative research techniques, such as those that Fromm pioneered in his study of blue collar workers in Weimar, and which he revised and expanded in *Social Character in a Mexican Village*, coauthored with Michael Maccoby (Fromm and Maccoby 1970). By contrast with *erklaren*, which seeks to bracket or eliminate subjective experience in order to explain phenomena objectively, *verstehen* addresses itself directly to the phenomenon of subjectivity, including the tacit or "lived" meanings that shape a person's behavior, but either precede or elude the subject's conscious ratiocination, "the unconscious."

To his credit then, Fromm appreciated the absurdity of trying to elucidate the qualities and contradictions of human subjectivity by deploying the methods and models of the natural sciences, as Freud claimed to do. From a human science perspective, Freud's whole theoretical project sounds rather implausible, like trying to make ice by boiling water. And in addition to basic questions of method, where Fromm's views were quite controversial, there was a subtle but profound shift in the overall focus of Fromm's *social psychology* that alienated the analytic elite as well.

Freud's studies on "the pathology of civilized communities" focused on how civilization engenders neurotic conflicts, yet sustains strong social bonds by sublimating surplus libido and displacing our latent envy of our intimates and peers into aggression against outsiders – "the Other." Conflicts between Eros and aggression, society and the individual, and so on, said Freud, are rooted in biology, and therefore intractable, and our collective efforts to contain and diffuse them — through religion, morality and cultural evolution – are the result of the progressive elaboration of a single, nuclear conflict relating to the incest taboo (Freud 1913, 1930).

Even before *Escape from Freedom*, Fromm found Freud's Oedipal monism quite contrived and bourgeois; evidence of an inability to appreciate the specificity of other cultures, and to "explain" normal ideas and attitudes in other milieus by analogy to those of neurotics in our own (Fromm 1932, 1934). And by contrast with Freud, who tried to make the Oedipus complex culture-constitutive, Fromm emphasized the depth and universality of pre-Oedipal issues, both clinically and culturally, long before it was popular to do so (Fromm 1932, 1934; Burston 1991).

Moreover, and more importantly, with the passage of time, Fromm's social psychology focused less on the vicissitudes of the instincts and more on statistically normal character traits that actually enhance, rather than hinder the person's adaptation to society, and which diminish, rather than aggravate, inner conflict (Fromm 1932). These culturally congruent patterns of conduct and belief, termed "socially patterned defects" (Fromm 1941), diminish our capacity to think critically, to experience and express solidarity with out-group members, and to develop and maintain loving, intimate relationships with others in our own milieu (Fromm 1955; Burston and Olfman 1996).

Unlike Freud, who recommended "everyday unhappiness" as an alternative to neurotic suffering, Fromm recognized that statistical normality may minimize inner and interpersonal conflict, but may also be inimical to the real goals of human development, which were articulated in the great spiritual and philosophical traditions of the East and West. And rather than explaining these widespread deformations of human subjectivity – which he once termed "the pathology of normalcy" (Fromm 1955)

– in light of the contradictory aims of Eros and Thanatos, society and the individual, and so on, Fromm looked to the specific *contradictions within a society* that rendered these defects "adaptive" (e.g. Fromm 1955, 1961a, 1968).

Fromm's call to elucidate the specific constellation of historical, socio-logical and economic processes which envelop an individual's existence was not merely a methodological precept for social psychology. On the contrary, Fromm brought these issues into the clinical setting, and devoted what some consider an inordinate amount of time to dwelling on the "social construction" of his patient's subjectivity. Moreover, he did not stop there. According to Fromm, it was not merely history and class consciousness, but the language and logic of a particular cultural group that shape the conscious experience of the subject, by imparting cogni-tive templates through which experience is "filtered," shaping their apprehension of both "inner" and "outer" reality, thereby "normalizing" or homogenizing their experience.

For example, take the words "objective" and "subjective" in vernacular English. To the vast majority of educated people in the Anglo-American world, the terms "objectivity" and "subjectivity" denote mutually exclu-sive or antagonistic states of mind. The more "subjective" one's attitude, presumably, the more it is colored by emotion, bias, projection, and so on, and therefore the less "in touch" with reality one is. And correlatively, the more "objective" one's attitude, the more impersonal and less in-formed by feelings it is presumed to be. In short, our language is struc-tured in terms of mutually exclusive alternatives that ordinarily preclude thinking in terms of a *grounded* subjectivity that is closer to reality as a result of being more deeply reflexive than average – one of the aims of analytic treatment, presumably. When language is riddled with false antinomies that promote a kind of cultural alexythemia, one cannot blame the ordinary person for one dimensional thinking, or an inability to con-ceive of growing in objectivity by becoming *more* subjective, as it were. The problem is that, until recently at least, many psychoanalysts who should know better, habitually invoked this way of thinking, because of Freud's own positivist leanings.

Though Fromm emphasized the primacy of pre-Oedipal issues, as indi-cated earlier, his countervailing emphasis on the specificity of cultures stipulated that there is no single, nuclear conflict underpinning the great diversity of cultures and faiths. Nevertheless, he allowed that since the advent of agriculture, and of gender and class hierarchies, prevailing modes of production and of authority constrain us to meet our material needs in ways that are often at variance with our human or *existential* needs (Fromm 1951, 1961a). This discrepancy, which is usually disguised and/or rationalized by the prevailing ideology, results in the gradual atrophy of "humanistic conscience," which in turn fosters apathy, indifference greed and violence (Fromm 1955, 1962). Moreover, in the capitalist era, said Fromm, the ideology of rugged individualism offers its adherents a handy instrument for self-deception, the perfect cover for abject conformity, an unwitting flight into collectivism (Fromm 1941).

That being so, said Fromm, analysis should never treat normalization or mere symptom alleviation as a goal of treatment. Normality as such is not the goal (Fromm 1970). Instead, analysis should aim for a full restoration of the analysand's humanity, by granting or restoring access to depths and facets of the analysand's own mind that are normally cut-off or proscribed by conventional "social filters" that comprise the "social unconscious" (Fromm 1962). But just what are these "social filters"?

Subjectivity and "social filters"

Though Fromm never dwelt on this, to my knowledge, the antagonism between the "objective" and "subjective" attitudes alluded to earlier is part of a more sweeping series of binary oppositions that structure how our language defines and describes ways of being-in-the-world. This binary code for thinking about thought, and for defining and describing different modes and qualities of experience, provides a splendid illustration of what Fromm meant by "social filters." Consider the following diagram, in which "Type A" represents "objectivity" and "Type B" represents "subjectivity," as these two orientations are commonly conceived.

Type A	*Type B*
1 Objectivity	Subjectivity
2 Facts	Values
3 Thought	Feeling
4 Quantitative measurement	Sense of quality, meaning, pattern
5 Detached observation and classification of phenomena	Empathic, participant identification
6 Impersonal, impartial judgment	Personal, biased judgment
7 Scientific attitude	Artistic and/or religious orientation

Anyone versed in history or anthropology knows very well that this popular way of bifurcating human experience is not grounded in ontological necessity, but in sociohistorical contingencies that valorize instrumental rationality above all other human values. But in our scientistic culture, this notion of objectivity is taken to be merely "objective," while subjectivity (and all that it entails) is generally deemed to be a backward, deficient or frankly *irrational* orientation toward reality. And as long as that is the case, an appeal to "objectivity" can always be used to invalidate or repress certain thoughts, feelings, and experiences that are deemed inconsistent with prevailing cultural codes and procedures.

In truth, the ideology of objectivity – objectivism, for lack of a better word – is neither fully objective nor value free. It is useful in the production of knowledge, when the latter is defined as mere information. But pursued systematically, without being balanced and informed by a "Type B" orientation, the objectivist mentality is sterile or frankly counterproductive in the production of wisdom, considered as a developmental goal whose chief prerequisite is *self-knowledge*.

To his lasting credit, Albert Einstein realized this. And so do many other gifted natural scientists, who decry the pseudo-objectivity of much that masquerades as "hard-headed" science. In recent years, many accomplished natural scientists have argued that the objectivist mentality has long since outlived its usefulness, or was even a mistake to begin with, even where the natural sciences are concerned. Meanwhile, practitioners of the human sciences have always realized that objectivism often masks other attitudes and agendas, and that a deep grasp of human reality requires a judicious synthesis of Type A and Type B orientations. The failure to integrate thought and feeling, facts and values, and to understand "the Other" in empathic, intersubjective terms fosters what Fromm once termed "a chronic low grade schizophrenia" (Fromm 1970) that is pervasive, and furthermore, quite dangerous, especially among leaders and policy makers. Reading his critique of American foreign policy circa 1961, one is reminded of C. Wright Mills' evocative term "crackpot realism" (Fromm 1961b).

In any case, perhaps the best way to describe a "social filter" is by contrast to an idea that enjoys greater currency. Like the Freudian superego, Erich Fromm's "social filters" perform a kind of routine censorship over certain domains of thought and feeling, hindering the entrance of certain things into consciousness, the difference being that these social filters are not merely "intrapsychic" systems or processes, but are diffusely distributed through society at large. Moreover, they serve to sustain the status quo, rather than an individual's neurotic equilibrium, and are the product of relatively recent sociohistorical processes and constraints, rather than hypothetical events in remote prehistory that supposedly shape our "phylogenetic inheritance." Finally, unlike the Freudian superego, social filters do not punish those whose experiences are deemed odd, transgressive or invalid by the cultural mainstream. Society itself takes care of that. People who lack conventional social filters are apt to experience the world rather differently than the majority of their peers, and the resulting inner and interpersonal conflict, if it is deep or acute enough, may imperil their sanity, or put them at risk for some form of punishment or excommunication unless they conform. That being so, said Fromm, one task of analysis should be to enable analysands to embrace a more grounded, ethically centered nonconformist stance, to "live soundly against the stream."

These ideas, which were developed at length in numerous publications during the 1940s, 1950s and 1960s, did not endear Fromm to most of his analytic colleagues. Despite its earlier radicalism, in the Cold War era, psychoanalysis sought acceptance in the American mainstream, and to that end, professed to be politically neutral while preaching a gospel of "adaptation" – contradictions that Fromm addressed candidly, and often, in his writing (e.g. Fromm 1970).

Epistemology, self-authorship and the search for truth

But while Fromm deviated sharply from Freud and his followers on many issues, he was not a thorough-going constructivist. In some respects, he remained faithful to the Enlightenment rationalism that inspired Freud. Though he showed a prescient appreciation of the role of language, culture and historicity in the "constitution" of the subject, Fromm shared Freud's belief that the truth, in many instances, can be reliably discriminated from fiction, illusion, and error. In *Beyond the Chains of Illusion* (1962), Fromm strongly commended Freud for emphasizing the disillusioning function of the analytic dialogue, arguing that unless or until an analysand is able to relinquish his cherished illusions, he cannot experience or embrace the truth about himself or the world – a condition Fromm likened to the biblical concept of idolatry. Giving up idols/illusions is therefore a precondition of freedom, and a hallmark of a truth-loving disposition (Fromm 1962, 1966).

Now, at the risk of stating the obvious, the word "illusion" implies the existence of its opposite, namely truth. And the same is true of word pairs like "truth" and "error," "truth" and "fiction." Yet strange to say, in our times, the status and indeed, the very meaning of these terms has become moot in many circles. The recent rise of poststructuralism, social constructivism, deconstructionism and other postmodern discourses that have made inroads in psychoanalysis is largely responsible for this state of affairs.

For purposes of our discussion, let us define truth as parsimoniously as possible, as what actually is the case. Thanks to the aforementioned schools of thought, it is widely believed that we have no way of reliably ascertaining what is (or is *not*) the case, of discriminating between truth and error, between illusions and truth, and so on. People who stubbornly cling to the belief that we can, and indeed, *must* make such judgments on theoretical, as well as practical grounds, are often accused of being narrow, "reactionary" or even positivistic.

But in truth – if I may say so *without* irony – one need not be a positivist or a political conservative to believe in the existence of non-relative truths, and more importantly, perhaps, in our ability to discover them – in principle, at any rate. Edmund Husserl is a good example of a human science theorist who commended natural scientists for their search for non-relative truths, though he categorically rejected the applicability of their methods to the study of the mind.

In a similar spirit, Fromm commended Freud for his pursuit of objective truth, even though he critiqued his positivistic metapsychology. Fromm believed that the kind of candid self-scrutiny engendered by analytic treatment fosters a kind of de-centration – in Piaget's sense – that enables individuals to be more "objective" about themselves, but without nullifying or denying their own subjectivity, or somehow capitulating to the subjectivity of another. Objectivity in this sense does not mean identifying with the observing (i.e. the analyst's) ego, which is how this process is often formulated. It is a process of rediscovering and reclaiming one's subjectivity – overcoming one's alienation, becoming more conscious and self-possessed. And as a result, one's thought processes become more realistic, because less distorted by vanity, fear and greed, more attentive to complexity and more tolerant of ambiguity.

In addition to embracing certain strains of rationalism, there is an element of realism that enters into Fromm's notion of truth. And yet contrary to prevailing misconception, Fromm was not a naïve realist. Fromm was as aware as anyone that truth is always apprehended from the standpoint of a thinking, feeling, experiencing human subject, who is embedded, in turn, in the discourses of his or her cultural milieu. Moreover, he acknowledged that there are deep psychological truths that can be expressed *only* in symbolic language, that is in mythological or theological imagery, at certain stages of social development (Fromm 1951, 1966). And since all discourses, symbolic systems, even scientific ones, are cultural/historical products, and subject to change and development, at any given moment in time, they may afford us only a partial or distorted premonition of the truth (Fromm 1962). We may not have the *whole* picture.

Like any good novelist or playwright, Fromm was aware that in consciousness, as well as the unconscious, truth and fiction are sometimes intricately intertwined, and that there are riddles regarding one's own past and current motivations that can never be completely unraveled; there are instances where it is best to suspend judgment, rather than force closure through self-deception or pseudo-certainties issuing from theoretical preconceptions. Moreover, as a seasoned psychoanalyst, Fromm knew that we do not always embrace or espouse the truth from disinterested motives. We often have multiple (and sometimes conflicting) agendas, and regardless of what actually is (or is not) the case, our reasons for thinking as we do can be complexly determined by very diverse motives, some of which are entirely obscure to ourselves (Fromm 1962).

Finally, Fromm distinguished different ways of knowing or "possessing" truth. People who accumulate information or ideas second-hand may be in possession of information that is factually correct about some entity or process "out there." But the way in which they acquired it was essentially passive, and their reliance on "the experts" in the field makes them less genuinely "informed" than those who have acquired their knowledge first hand, and been transformed in the process. So, for example, someone who has "learned" everything there is to know about the principles and techniques of carpentry, music, celestial navigation, or love-making by reading books, viewing instructional videos, and so on, is invariably less competent and trustworthy than a truly seasoned practitioner. Acquiring knowledge by actively engaging with reality, rather than learning "about" it, affects one's whole being, and is vastly superior to merely accumulating knowledge passively and vicariously, through what Fromm called the "having" mode. Active, experientially based learning promotes the growth of reason, and of respect for the thing (and oneself), a process of self-authorship the Germans call *Bildung*. Mere rote learning or information gathering, by contrast, promotes tendencies toward passivity, alienation, abstractification and quantification that are already dangerously advanced in contemporary society, and threaten to stifle the genuine love of truth (Fromm 1955, 1976).

All of these caveats apply to (and are embedded in) Fromm's notion of truth. Nevertheless, like Husserl, Fromm maintained that the human sciences need not abandon the search for truth, and that in the absence of a committed, collaborative search for truth, psychoanalytic treatment is analytic in name only, having abandoned Freud's radical spirit. Fromm never embraced the old scientistic fallacy that reality is *completely* knowable, and would be known one day in its entirety. On the contrary, he supposed that the project of exploring "inner" and "outer" reality, and acquiring greater "objectivity" about them both commits us to a process of *endless inquiry*. Moreover, said Fromm – citing Marx and Freud as examples – it takes great courage to relinquish illusions, to step outside prevailing consensus, and the ability to do so is predicated on faith in reason and *a passionate pursuit of truth,* regardless of how that squares with prevailing prejudices. In short, Fromm favored a truth-loving or truth-seeking disposition, and was actually more concerned with the process of *truth-seeking* than with its final, and perforce provisional, results.

Skeptics counter that if all knowledge is provisional, and there is no final reckoning, how can we have faith in "reason" to discriminate truth from error, reality from illusion? How can we even say that one theory is more accurate or adequate or complete than any other, if each and every theory is destined to be revised or discarded in turn? Unfortunately, Fromm never addressed this vexing issue head on. But Fromm's discussion of the role of imagination and "generative perception" in "the productive character" clearly implies that the growth of objectivity *vis-à-vis* the self, or genuine self-knowledge inevitably entails a deepening and strengthening of subjectivity, rather than its overcoming or erasure (Fromm 1947).

Of course, none of this means that we must make a fetish of individual subjectivity, or sever it from the cultural and linguistic landscape in which it emerges and takes shape. But contrary to prevailing usage in philosophy, the human sciences and mental health professions, for Fromm, reason, objectivity, and so on are not inherently *opposed* to subjectivity. The pertinent question here is: what *kind* of subjectivity are we talking about? The kind of subjectivity Fromm associated with "productivity" in *Man for Himself* (1947) is liberating and life-enhancing, and stands in marked contrast to the sweeping *subjectivism* and belligerent *irrationalism* that Fromm said is characteristic of fascism and "the syndrome of decay" that he discussed in *The Heart of Man* (1964) and *The Anatomy of Human Aggression* (1973).

Just as many psychoanalysts now deny the existence of truth, or our ability to discover it, so there are now many popular postmodern trends within the human sciences – structuralism, poststructuralism, deconstructionism – that seek to nullify human subjectivity completely. And here is a stunning irony. Formerly, it was the *natural* scientists who attempted to banish or deny subjectivity, or to explain it as a mere ephiphenomenon of more basic, physical processes that can be apprehended – and manipulated – in a purely "objective" fashion. Now, however, it is the avant-garde in the *human* sciences who are telling us that the sense of selfhood, subjectivity, and so on, is epiphenomenal, though by their reckoning, it is either an error or ruse of language or a social machinery of power – rather than naturalistic, physical processes – that generates these appearances. Though some of these theorists still quote Marx or Freud in their writings, the new wave of theorists tend to disparage them, or to see them merely as a propaedeutic to their own approach, which they regard as vastly superior, and as emancipatory, in some sense (O'Neill 1999).

At the risk of sounding obtuse to postmodern proponents, I must point out that in the absence of real, suffering human subjects, just who or what is being liberated, by whom, and for what purpose, is always perforce unclear. Abolish the subject, or subjectivity in general, and there is really nothing left to discuss, and nothing left to strive for – or against, for that matter. Though many self-styled "radicals" may pretend otherwise, if they wish, the existence of actual or potential persons is a basic and non-negotiable precondition for any truly human science, whether the task of that science is construed as being emancipatory or as merely hermeneutic in nature. And you cannot address a person *as* a person, either theoretically or practically, unless you, in turn are a personal presence, who bears respectful witness to their subjectivity. Dismissing these objections as symptoms of lingering fallacies like "humanism," "essentialism," and so on — especially among psychotherapists, who really should know better – does *not* address the problem at hand. It is merely an emotional – dare I say "subjective"? – excuse for *not* dealing with it.

Fromm, fascism and the postmodern mentality

Having said all that, we can now address ourselves to the question: what would Fromm have made of contemporary trends? Fromm died in 1980, just as they were beginning to take root here, and while he doubtless heard their names, and read a little about them, Fromm never commented on them publicly, to my knowledge. That being so, anything we can offer by way of response to this question is bound to be somewhat conjectural. Still, had Fromm lived long enough, he might have attributed the appeal of structuralism, poststructuralism, deconstructionism, and postmodernism in general to a deep but understandable disenchantment with the objectivistic mindset of the "Type A" mentality, and less hopefully, perhaps, to the proliferation of crypto-fascist and "marketing" trends in the "social unconscious."

Let us begin with "marketing" trends. Fromm's first discussion of the marketing character appeared in *Man for Himself* in 1947. Fromm cited Karl Polanyi's observation that the modern market is no longer a place of meeting, where producers and consumers typically know each other, negotiate directly, and where goods and services are appraised and exchanged in terms of their actual use value. In truth, the modern market is not even a place, but an utterly impersonal mechanism in which commodities and services are bought, sold, and traded on the basis of their *exchange* value, which is determined by the vagaries of fashion, of chance and the market machinations of transnational corporations.

That being so, Fromm stressed that the "marketing" mentality proliferates when, regardless of their ability (or lack of it), people must "market" their skills and personality aggressively to avert failure and unemployment. At the same time, this mentality spreads where the tendencies to abstraction, quantification, and alienation accompanying the headlong advance of technology promote a tendency to experience oneself and others as commodities for sale on the labor market. In short, the more or less obligatory transformation of one's skills and personality into commodities for sale insures that workers do not experience themselves as active, human subjects, but as bundles of attributes bereft of any intrinsic value, and desperately dependent on others to confer value and bestow meaning and direction on their increasingly hollow, aimless consumeristic existences (Fromm 1955).

Fromm's "marketing" mentality was predicated on the belief that the conditions of work for the average worker, the quality and intensity of alienation associated with work and its rewards, shape prevailing social character, and filter down to the upcoming generation through the various agencies of socialization. As society reproduces itself, parents and schools collaborate in producing a new cohort of workers who are well adapted to prevailing conditions. If those conditions happen to include low job security, and ceaseless technical innovation and change, the resulting "social character" will not feature a rigid authoritarian, but a protean shape shifter with a permanent identity crisis and little by way of core convictions or beliefs. While preferable to fascism, of course, it still compromises human integrity. One salient consideration is the way marketing trends erode our capacity to think critically. By critical thinking, Fromm meant the capacity for rational doubt, and not intelligence as measured by IQ tests. On the contrary, according to Fromm, a person can be highly intelligent, IQ-wise, and still lack the ability to question or consider matters deeply, freed from conventional prejudices and beliefs. In fact, Fromm noted, highly intelligent people generally come up with cleverer reasons for distorting reality than less intelligent people do. Intelligence as measured by conventional methods has little to do with the ability to reason critically. It may be a help or a hindrance (Fromm 1955).

Another potent threat to the ability to think critically comes from submission to irrational authority, evidenced, for example, in the resurgent appeal of fascism, in both its overt and hidden forms. Had Fromm lived after 1980, he would have followed the disclosures and debates about Martin Heidegger's Nazism and Paul De Man's avid collaboration with the Nazis very closely. Moreover, he would have deplored the fact that so many of their ardent supporters are on the Left. Having already called attention to latent pro-fascist sympathies among the Left in the 1920s, Fromm would have lamented the bizarre spectacle of intellectual capital that originates on the Right in the first half of the twentieth century migrating leftward in the latter half of the century. And it continues to dazzle the left-wing intelligentsia at the opening of the twenty-first century (Rockmore 1995).

At the very least, Fromm would have urged people who are interested in these issues to reflect deeply on the claims made on behalf of theorists of an *overtly* fascist stripe by influential theorists on the Left. For example, take the following quote from Jacques Derrida's (1989) defense of Heidegger, *Of Spirit: Heidegger and the Question*:

> I shall explain in conclusion why what I am presenting politely as a hypothesis must necessarily turn out to be true. I know that this hypothesis is true, as though in advance. Its verification appears to me to be as paradoxical as it is fated. At stake in it is the truth of truth for Heidegger, a truth the tautology of which does not even have to be discovered or invented. It belongs to the beyond and to the possibility of any question, to the unquestionable itself in any question.
>
> (Derrida 1989: 9)

If instead of employing his elusive eloquence, Derrida actually spoke his mind in a straightforward fashion at this juncture, many people who revere him might question this excuse for a "defense."

A hypothesis that is "necessarily true," as Derrida says, is not a hypothesis but an *axiom*. And an axiom, by definition, is beyond proof or refutation. Derrida is saying, in effect, that for him, at any rate, Heidegger's intellectual integrity, innocence, and so on, are axiomatic. Moreover, the oracular phrase "the truth of truth" implies that in addition to containing or encompassing itself, truth harbors non-truth, that is accidental or extrinsic elements that are either irrelevant or opposed to it in some fashion. This is a paradoxical, provocative, and potentially useful assertion that is left dangling in the air, unclarified and unsupported by what immediately follows. I will not venture to speculate what Derrida means by his cryptic allusion to "the unquestionable . . . in any question," but if he is really asserting anything here, in his elliptical way, Derrida is probably affirming that "the Question" is *not* a question, but the occasion for uttering a foregone conclusion. In other words, that Heidegger is beyond criticism or reproach *because* he is Heidegger. Or in effect, that the fact that Heidegger *is* Heidegger authorizes us to stifle all rational doubt and to repose unquestioning faith in the view that Heidegger was in possession of "the truth of truth," while the critics who put "the Question" to Heidegger (for example, Farias 1989; Wolin 1990; Rockmore 1995; Bronner 1994) merely tear at truth's trappings.

Everyone is entitled to their own opinion, of course. But make no mistake. This is not just clever obfuscation. At issue here is the deification of a man – in short, a species of (post)modern *idolatry*. And sadly, Heidegger and Derrida are not the only thinkers who are accorded such latitude nowadays. Lacan, Althusser, Foucault, Baudrillard, and many others have been dubbed "Master Thinkers," and have loyal followings who hang on their every word (Borch-Jacobsen 1991; Rockmore 1995; O'Neill 1999).

Of course, to those who value critical thinking, the very phrase "Master Thinker" – with capital letters – is apt to give one pause. And this occasions the reflection that Fromm was also quite capable of referring to Freud, Marx, Spinoza, or Meister Ekhardt as a "master." But that never deterred him from engaging in forthright criticism of their work. In fairness to his critics, myself included, Fromm was not above a bit of idolatry himself, especially where Freud and Marx were concerned (Burston 1991). But even in his most idolatrous moods and moments, Fromm never declared any of his intellectual role models as being above or beyond criticism, and never invited us to follow his example by taking their ideas or integrity on faith. This runs completely counter to Fromm's intellectual ethos. According to Fromm, the willingness or desire to succumb to the blandishments of irrational authority are an integral part of the whole fascist phenomenon – something we must vigilantly guard against.

At this point, the reader may wonder whether I am merely explicating Fromm's position on recent trends in academia and psychoanalysis, or whether I actually share it. The answer, I confess, is "yes and no." As regards the rise of relativism and the proliferation of the "marketing" character, there is no denying that the two trends coincide in space and time. They share a historical moment, and could plausibly be construed as diverse manifestations of the self-same *Zeitgeist*. However, this interpretation of cultural trends is problematic because it is predicated on two assumptions: first, that ethical or epistemological relativism are symptoms of a widespread social pathology, rather than legitimize positions in their own right; and second, that the intelligentsia is as deeply affected by mass culture as "the masses" themselves.

Of these two propositions, the latter certainly rings true, especially when contemporary academia is embracing, indeed, gorging itself on popular culture. The first one, however, is demonstrably false. While it may be more popular at present than formerly, relativism has been around since the dawn of civilization. Sophists like Protagoras were challenging Socrates and Plato with relativistic arguments more than two millennia ago (Guthrie 1968). Moreover, if you survey the history of philosophy, you soon discover that arguments in favor of ethical and/or epistemological relativism vary considerably in the degree of cogency and depth that they achieve. They are not all of a piece, and do not deserve to be lumped together indiscriminately as the by-products of social pathology – a curiously Platonic move, incidentally.

Conclusion

Fromm's elaboration of subjectivity in the human sciences is clearly complex. He opposed the tendency to pit objectivity against subjectivity in an adversarial fashion, as positivism was wont to do, yet also rejected a sweeping and indiscriminate subjectivism that fosters a climate of irrational authority. Fromm "believed" in reason, though reason, for him, was not the detached, computational intelligence of instrumental reason. For Fromm, reason engages the world from a position of grounded subjectivity – an integrative, dialectical movement that unifies, rather than severs or splits mind and body, thoughts and feelings, facts and values. He would question whether an analyst or therapist who embraces a postmodern worldview is likely to achieve the kind of "core to core" relatedness that is necessary to restore hope and build a solid, working rapport with "hard" cases. And if so, whether this fortunate outcome was not the product of an unwitting inconsistency, a gap between theory and practice, in which the therapist does not credit the existence and/or experience of the person as subject, but acts *as if* he or she believed in it. Fromm would have regarded the fashionable tendency to nullify the human subject as being deeply estranged from human reality, and no better than the radical behaviorist program of bracketing "subjective" experience off in a theoretical "black box," even if the theoretical rationale for expunging subjectivity from our epistemic framework is based on different premises.

References

Borch-Jacobsen, M. (1991) *Lacan: The Absolute Master*. Stanford, CA: Stanford University Press.

Bronner, S. (1994) "Unorthodox remarks on Heidegger's philosophy," in *Of Critical Theory and its Theorists*. Oxford: Blackwell.

Burston, D. (1991) *The Legacy of Erich Fromm*. Cambridge, MA: Harvard University Press.

Burston, D. and Olfman, S. (1996) "Freud, Fromm and the pathology of normalcy," in M. Cortina and M. Maccoby (eds.) *A Prophetic Analyst*. Northvale, NJ: Jason Aronson.

Derrida, J. (1989) *Of Spirit: Heidegger and the Question*. Chicago: University of Chicago Press.

Farias, V. (1989) *Heidegger and Nazism*. Philadelphia, PA: Temple University Press.

Freud, S. ([1913] 1950) *Totem and Taboo*. New York: W. W. Norton.

—— ([1930] 1961) *Civilization and its Discontents*. New York: W. W. Norton.

Fromm, E. ([1929] 1984). *The Working Class in Weimar Germany: A Psychological and Sociological Study*. Cambridge, MA: Harvard University Press.

—— (1932) "On the method and aims of an analytic social psychology," translated in E. Fromm (1970) *The Crisis of Psychoanalysis*. Greenwich, CT: Fawcett Premier.

—— (1934) "The social psychological significance of mother right," translated in E. Fromm (1970) *The Crisis of Psychoanalysis*. Greenwich, CT: Fawcett Premier.

—— ([1941] 1965) *Escape from Freedom*. New York: Avon.

—— (1947) *Man for Himself: An Inquiry into Psychology and Ethics*. Greenwich, CT: Fawcett Premier.

—— ([1951] 1957) *The Forgotten Language*. New York: Grove Press.

—— (1955) *The Sane Society*. Greenwich, CT: Fawcett Premier.

—— ([1957] 1995) "Notes on the Institute of Man," reprinted in the *Bulletin of the International Erich Fromm Society*. Tubingen: The International Erich Fromm Society.

—— (1961a) *Marx's Concept of Man*. New York: Frederick Ungar.

—— (1961b) *May Man Prevail? An Inquiry into the Facts and Fictions of Foreign Policy*. Garden City, NY: Doubleday.

—— (1962) *Beyond the Chains of Illusion: My Encounter with Marx and Freud*. New York: Simon & Schuster.

—— ([1964] 1968). *The Heart of Man: Its Genius for Good and Evil*. New York: Harper & Row.

—— (1966) *You Shall Be as Gods: A Radical Interpretation of the Old Testament and its Tradition*. Greenwich, CT: Fawcett Premier.

—— (1968 [1974]) *The Revolution of Hope*. New York: Harper & Row.

—— (1970) *The Crisis of Psychoanalysis: Essays on Marx, Freud & Social Psychology*. Greenwich, CT: Fawcett Premier.

—— (1973) *The Anatomy of Human Aggression*. Greenwich, CT: Fawcett Premier.

—— ([1976] 1981) *To Have or to Be?* New York: Bantam.

Fromm, E. and Maccoby, M. (1970) *Social Character in a Mexican Village: A Sociopsychoanalytic Study*. Englewood Cliffs, NJ: Prentice Hall.

Funk, R. (1982) *Erich Fromm*. Hamburg: Rowohlt Taschenbuch Verlag.

Guthrie, W. K. C. (1968) *The Sophists*. Cambridge: Cambridge University Press.

Jay, M. (1973) *The Dialectical Imagination*. Boston, MA: Beacon.

O'Neill, J. (1999) *The Poverty of Postmodernism*. New York: Routledge.

Riesman, D. (1950) *The Lonely Crowd*. New Haven, CT: Yale University Press.

Roazen, P. (1990) *Encountering Freud: The Politics and Histories of Psychoanalysis*. New Brunswick, NJ: Transaction.

Rockmore, T. (1995) *Heidegger and French Philosophy: Humanism, Anti-Humanism and Being*. New York: Routledge.

Wolin, R. (1990) *The Politics of Being: The Political Thought of Martin Heidegger*. New York: New York University Press.

Chapter 8

The primacy of experience in R. D. Laing's approach to psychoanalysis

M. Guy Thompson

The recent interface between psychoanalysis and other disciplines, which were traditionally held at arm's length by the analytic community, has led to a sea change in psychoanalytic theory and technique. These trends have primarily occurred in North America under the rubric of so-called relational psychoanalysis, an amalgam of disparate and even contradictory perspectives including hermeneutics, constructivism, deconstructionism, and intersubjectivity. Largely a creature of the American psychoanalytic community, virtually all of these postmodern theories filtered into North American culture from Europeans, including the French psychoanalyst Jacques Lacan, who first identified the linguistic element of psychoanalysis with structuralism, and French poststructuralist philosophers such as Jacques Derrida, Jean-François Lyotard, and Michel Foucault. American analysts who are identified with the relational perspective have tended to eschew the more theoretical preoccupations of the French school and focus instead on a relaxation of classical psychoanalytic technique (e.g. neutrality and abstinence) emphasizing the so-called real and personal aspects of the analyst–patient relationship.

Ironically, many of these efforts to relax the technical rules of psychoanalysis were anticipated in the 1950s and 1960s by European psychoanalysts and psychiatrists who were identified with existentialism and phenomenology, including Ludwig Binswanger, Medard Boss, and R. D. Laing. Yet analysts who are identified with the relational perspective and sympathetic with postmodernism rarely cite the existential analysts as either forerunners to or influences on their work. It is nevertheless striking how similar the so-called innovations in technique are to the work of Laing and other existential psychoanalysts. Perhaps Laing's estrangement from the British psychoanalytic community plays a role in this anomaly as well as Laing's inherently philosophical perspective, a feature of his work that also accounts for the limited influence Lacan has exerted on the North American psychoanalytic community.

The purpose of this chapter is to examine Laing's complicated and enigmatic relationship with psychoanalysis with a view to emphasizing those features of his perspective that comply with the interpersonal and derivative relational schools of analysis. In so doing I shall emphasize Laing's debt not only to existentialism and phenomenology but especially to skepticism, the basis of the postmodern critique of contemporary culture (Thompson 2003).

Any endeavor to situate Laing's work in the context of psychoanalysis immediately places the author in a quandary, not the least because Laing had relatively little impact on the psychoanalytic community in Britain or the United States, the two countries where he enjoyed most of his popularity. Indeed, despite his enormous contribution to contemporary thought, there is neither a Laingian theory nor technique that pertains to his way of conducting psychoanalytic treatment or, for that matter, any form of psychotherapy. In fact, Laing's refusal to couch his clinical perspective in either theoretical or technical terms was an important feature of his debt to the skeptical philosophical tradition, which impacted not only Nietzsche and Heidegger (both of whom influenced Laing's thinking) but also many of the exponents of the contemporary postmodern perspective. Yet Laing was trained as a psychoanalyst at the British Psychoanalytic Society and though he drifted away from the psychoanalytic community following the completion of his training, Laing continued to call himself a psychoanalyst for the rest of his life.

If Laing thought of himself as a psychoanalyst then what kind of an analyst was he? How did Laing apply what he conceived psychoanalysis to be in his work as a psychoanalytic practitioner? Moreover, what manner of psychoanalysis did he practice and who were the principal influences on his clinical philosophy? Although Laing trained at the British institute he has traditionally been associated with the so-called existential school of psychoanalysts instead of the object relations school, the classical perspective, or the hermeneutic. Already this presents us with a paradox, because existential psychoanalysis is not now nor ever was officially affiliated with the International Psychoanalytical Association, the principal psychoanalytic accrediting body. Thus it would be useful to examine what existential psychoanalysis is presumed to entail, in what manner it can be deemed psychoanalytic, and in what measure Laing can be said to represent this school of analysis.

Laing's relationship with existentialism

Existential psychoanalysis is typically depicted as a clinical perspective that derives from a wide range of loosely associated theorists who have only marginally influenced the mainstream of psychoanalytic theory and practice. For example, Roy Schafer's (1976) rejection of Freud's motivational mechanisms that are said to be driven by instinct, in favor of a view that emphasizes the individual's agency implies the influence of existentialism in Schafer's work, though he would probably deny this. Moreover, Hans Loewald (1980) explicitly acknowledged his debt to Heidegger in the development of his views about psychoanalytic theory and practice, and Stanley Leavy (1980, 1988) has acknowledged his debt to phenomenology in virtually all of his psychoanalytic publications. Touchstones with the existential and phenomenological perspective include the interpersonalists, intersubjectivists, and hermeneuticians, though none of these camps can be said to adhere to strictly existential preoccupations.

Existential analysis was conceived by Ludwig Binswanger and Medard Boss, each of whom drew on the philosophical tradition of Martin Heidegger (1962, 1992). Although Binswanger and Boss found a great deal of value in Freud's clinical philosophy, their work can be best understood as a reaction to, and in large measure a rejection of, Freudian psychoanalysis. Whereas Freud saw human beings as harboring a dark continent of disavowed motives, intentions, and lust that he believed occupies a part of the mind that is unconscious, Binswanger and Boss viewed existence from a Heideggerian perspective, situating existence "in-the-world," so that mind and world are so merged that the intelligibility of each is discernible only in terms of the other.

It was not until 1960 with the publication of Laing's first book, *The Divided Self* that, in the words of Jean-Paul Sartre, existentialism finally found its Freud. Laing's conception of psychoanalysis was derived from a synthesis of numerous philosophers, including Heidegger, Sartre, Søren Kierkegaard, Friedrich Nietzsche, Maurice Merleau-Ponty, Max Scheler, Paul Tillich, Eugene Minkowski, Martin Buber, G. W. F. Hegel, and even Michel de Montaigne, the sixteenth-century skeptic. Laing was also indebted to the classical philosophers, Christian theology and mysticism, and the considerable influence of eastern philosophy. Laing's debt to the work of the American psychiatrist, Harry Stack Sullivan, and the American family therapy movement that flourished during the 1960s has been noted by numerous commentators (Friedenberg 1973; Burston 1996; Kotowicz 1997).

When one takes the breadth of Laing's intellectual résumé into account it becomes immediately apparent that it is misleading to characterize him as simply an existential analyst, in spite of his having become one of the most prominent proponents of existential analysis in Europe in its heyday that culminated in the 1970s. On some occasions Laing also characterized himself as a phenomenologist and at other times a skeptic, either of which more closely approximates his intellectual position. It is perhaps for this reason that, in spite of his debt to and identification with the existential tradition, the only label to which I am comfortable assigning Laing's analytic bias is that of simply psychoanalyst, the precise nature of which, because of his skeptical bent, resists categorization.

Ironically, despite their devotion to Heidegger, Laing felt that Binswanger and Boss failed to grasp the essence of Heidegger's philosophy, embodied in Heidegger's enigmatic conception of truth which Laing characterized as, "that which is literally without secrecy" (Laing [1961] 1969: 111). Laing also derived from Heidegger his preoccupation with the notion of authenticity and its correlate, inauthenticity, or self-deception. For Laing, the basic thrust of any effort to situate psychoanalysis in existential and phenomenological principles must necessarily be rooted in the relationship between truth and falsehood. It is our inescapable conflict between them that accounts for the split in the self and engenders forms of human suffering that are customarily labeled as editions of psychopathology, though Laing was uncomfortable with this label and affected an ambivalent relationship with it throughout his clinical career.

A skeptic at heart, Laing believed that knowledge is intrinsically personal and that everything we believe is rooted in our experience, which is unique to each person alone. In turn, experience engenders suffering, so it is our nature to mitigate our suffering by deceiving ourselves about what our experience tells us. Due to our efforts to deny our experience we inevitably adopt false truths that are more acceptable (and less painful) than the ones we actually experience and split ourselves accordingly. It was on this basis that Laing emphasized the "political" (or social) nature of psychical suffering and why psychoanalysis is an inherently subversive endeavor. When effective, psychoanalysis undermines established truths, whether such truths assume the form of edicts that are popularized by culture or are the manifestations of neurotic fantasies that become substitutes for a more painful reality. Hence, Laing's conception of psychoanalysis is characterized by two fundamental principles: first, all human knowledge is rooted in personal experience; and second, the weight of experience is so painful that we seek to relieve it through self-deception.

Laing's relationship with psychoanalysis

What makes Laing's clinical philosophy specifically psychoanalytic is the affinity between Laing's philosophical assumptions and his subversive deconstruction of Freud's technical recommendations. Like Laing, Freud believed that virtually all forms of psychopathology are the consequence of secrets that human beings conceal from themselves. Freud concluded that we harbor such secrets due to the overwhelming weight of experience, at the point that its commensurate suffering becomes insupportable. In fact, Freud's treatment method was the model on which Laing fashioned his clinical philosophy, though it was less doctrinaire than Freud's. In fact, Laing's and Freud's respective styles diverged considerably. Whereas Freud insisted that his patients use a couch so they could not stare at him for eight hours a day, Laing made a couch available for those who wanted to use it but he did not require it. Laing achieved the same purpose (of not being stared at) by employing comfortable chairs that were situated at opposite ends of his darkened consulting room. This made it difficult, given the distance between them, for his patients to make eye-contact or even to determine whether or not he was looking their way. Whereas Freud depicted these considerations as matters of technique, Laing was more prone to characterizing them as matters of style, an aspect of Laing's personality emphasized by Heaton (2000: 511–15).

A psychoanalyst's style is not to be confused with being stylish, a matter of aesthetics and fashion. One can follow a fashion but one's style is unique because it derives from one's being and is a determinant of how we experience ourselves and other people. The closest approximation to style in Freud would be his emphasis on the analyst's *character*, which emanates from one's moral code and is conscious. On the other hand, style is a matter of ethics and is unconscious. Foucault regarded ethics as the practice of freedom, so it is not something we think about because it is manifested spontaneously, from the person one is. Thus one's style embues one with the freedom to be oneself when working with patients, but without imposing oneself on them. Laing put a great deal of emphasis on cultivating one's style when in training instead of learning technical interventions by rote. Freud apparently had style in his work with patients and felt free to be himself. Yet his technical principles have been adopted in the strictest terms by succeeding generations of analysts who have treated them as a code of conduct, constricting their freedom to develop their own style, an anomaly that Laing was acutely aware of.

If these distinctions indicate some of the differences in style between

Laing and Freud, the similarities they shared were more substantial. Like Freud, Laing believed that the only way to undo the consequences of self-deception is to take part in a therapeutic relationship wherein the two participants endeavor to be as honest with each other as they can. Whereas Freud believed that psychopathology is caused by the difficulty every human being has with an intrinsically harsh reality, Laing concluded that some realities are harsher than others and that the difference between your reality and mine has vast implications for how we experience each other, and ourselves. In fact, Laing was so uncomfortable with the very concept of psychopathology and its nomenclature that he found it impossible to draw a sharp line between the normal and the pathological. This aspect of Laing's style was particularly evident in his treatment of patients who had been diagnosed as schizophrenic at one time or other, a diagnostic category Laing never entirely embraced.

Laing's emphasis on the interpersonal basis of reality and the capacity every human being possesses to subvert the other's experience through the use of lies and deception characterizes the specifically existential aspect of Laing's conception of psychoanalysis, derived to a significant degree from his debt to Nietzsche. This assessment of psychological suffering led Laing to endorse in even stronger terms than Freud's the latter's observation that the therapeutic relationship must be rooted in a strict adherence to truthfulness. Laing not only embraced Freud's insistence on fidelity to the fundamental rule – that patients should endeavor to be as honest as they are able – but also endorsed its correlate, the rule of neutrality, to an even higher level. In Laing's assessment this technical principle, in spite of the current tide of opinion against it in analytic circles, means nothing more onerous than to be unequivocally open minded and sensitive toward the person one is treating, no matter how trying or difficult a patient may be (Thompson 1994, 1996a, 1996b, 1997).

The primacy of experience

Having examined the manner in which Laing situated himself in the psychoanalytic tradition, I now turn to his views on the therapeutic process itself, specifically one's experience of it. I employ the term experience because this deceptively simple if ambiguous term was the foundation of Laing's treatment philosophy. It should be apparent to anyone who is familiar with Laing's work that experience plays a principal role in his thinking. Two of his books – *The Politics of Experience* (1967) and *The Voice of Experience* (1982) – even include the word in their titles.

Yet, just because a term is included in the title of one's books does not guarantee that the author gives it much weight. Other psychoanalysts have included this term in the title of their books, though the concept plays no discernible role in their thinking. Wilfried Bion (*Experiences in Groups* 1961, *Learning from Experience* [1962] 1983), Neville Symington (*The Analytic Experience* 1986); and Thomas Ogden (*The Primitive Edge of Experience* 1989), for example, included experience in the title of their books, but they have summarily rejected the notion that experience should be equated with consciousness and substitute in its place the notion of "unconscious experience," a contradiction in terms (a point I examine in greater detail later).

What Laing intended by experience is of immeasurable importance because no other term more poignantly demonstrates the differences between the psychoanalytic tradition and Laing's phenomenological rendering of it. Because Laing's interpretation of experience is rooted in phenomenology, his conception of this term serves, more than any other, to differentiate his approach to psychoanalysis from more conventional schools of thought, including recent trends in the interpersonal, relational, and intersubjective perspectives. In order to demonstrate the inherently enigmatic nature of experience it is important to review the etymology of the term and how it has been typically conceived.

The English term for experience is derived from the Latin *peritus*, cognate with the word peril, meaning risk, jeopardy, or danger. The Greek root of experience, which is older than the Latin, derives from the word *empeiria* which gives us the word empirical, a term that was adopted by the British empiricists (e.g. John Locke and David Hume) who founded their philosophy on the primacy of sensual experience. *Pathos*, meaning suffering, is yet another Greek antecedent to the English experience, which gives us the term pathology, the study of passion. According to the *Oxford English Dictionary*, to experience something means to feel, suffer, and undergo, in the sense that what we experience is not of our own making. The term experience also gives us experiment, which serves as a technical term for the empirical scientific method, connoting the means by which one endeavors to test a theory through practical application. In the twenty-first century, the words empirical, experiment, and experience are often used interchangeably, though each has vastly different connotations when invoked outside a scientific framework.

Over the past two centuries the German language has offered subtle variations on the specific types of experience of which we are capable that the English language subsumes under the one term. It should not be surprising then that German philosophers have dominated nineteenth-

and twentieth-century investigations into the nature of experience that subsequently influenced other European cultures such as France, Great Britain, Switzerland, and Spain. Most relevant are the German philosophers Hegel, Schopenhauer, Nietzsche, Dilthey, Husserl, and Heidegger, each of whom elaborated on the meaning of experience in their respective philosophies, granting the concept a pivotal role in phenomenology and existential philosophy. These philosophers, in turn, influenced the French existentialists, including Jean-Paul Sartre, Simone de Beauvoir, Maurice Merleau-Ponty, and Gabriel Marcel, and the Spanish philosophers, Miguel Unamuno and Jose Ortega Y. Gasset. I shall say more about phenomenology later, but first I review the German treatment of experience and the etymology from which their conception of it is derived.

The first is the German *Erfahrung*, derived from *Fahrt*, meaning journey. Hence, *Erfahrung* suggests the notion of temporal duration, such as when one accumulates experience over time and the accruing of wisdom from old age. The other German word for experience is *Erlebnis*, derived from *Leben*, meaning life. Hence, *Erlebnis* connotes a vital immediacy in contrast to the predominantly historical (or temporal) *Erfahrung*. When invoking *Erlebnis*, the speaker is referring to a primitive unity that precedes intellectual reflection. When one integrates these nuances into the other etymological references to the word listed above we can appreciate the inherent subtlety of the concept that is often overlooked. For example, in the scientific community experience entails the accumulation of empirical knowledge through the use of experimentation, an inherently active emphasis. On the other hand, experience may suggest something that happens to us passively when we are sensitive to stimuli, such as the experience of watching a movie in a darkened theater. Experience also refers to the process whereby one submits to education, including the accumulation and memorization of knowledge over time. Moreover, the term may also connote a journey I have taken when traveling to a foreign country, perhaps in wartime when faced with great peril and danger, the experience of which may have expedited my journey into manhood. In other words, experiences are essentially transformative, depending on how deeply I permit a given experience to move me.

One can appreciate from this excursion into the etymology of experience that even though it offers tantalizing hints as to what the word is often taken to mean, there remains something ineffable about the concept that defies categorization and definition. This presents us with yet another paradox since the word is often employed, according to Martin Jay, "to gesture towards precisely that which exceeds concepts and even language itself" (Jay 1998: 3). In fact, the notion of experience has often been employed as a marker for what is so private or personal that it cannot be rendered in words. One's experience of love, for example, is a type of experience that some insist is impossible to express or grasp in words alone, because it is experienced long before it is ever understood. Even when I try to communicate my experience to others, only I can know what my experience is. Hence, just as experience resists definition, our efforts to convey the particular features of our experience are imperfect because experience is impossible to convey in words, let alone reduce to them. This ineffable dimension to experience made a profound impression on Laing and many of his clinical vignettes emphasize the power that silence often plays in the treatment situation.

This observation has significant implications for the psychoanalytic experience for patient and analyst alike who rely almost entirely on the passage of words between them. This also raises questions as to the nature of nonverbal and even preverbal experience, as well as so-called unconscious experience. Experience also plays a pivotal role in analytic interpretations because whenever analysts interpret what they take their patient's utterances to mean they are raising an important question: is the analyst in a better position to determine the nature of the patient's experience than the patient him- or herself? Moreover, are there dimensions to experience that the patient is resistant to experiencing because patients are inclined to intellectualize their experience instead of allowing themselves to take it in and experience it, fundamentally? In other words, is there is a *meta*-level to experience beyond the mere feeling or thinking about something that involves finally *experiencing* one's experience, even serving as a precondition to free associating? These questions defy conclusive explanations, yet we grapple with the consequences of them at each moment of the treatment situation.

The phenomenology of experience

Despite our commonsense appreciation of the role experience plays in our lives, such considerations pale when contrasted with the contribution that phenomenology has made to our understanding of potential experience and what experience specifically entails when we make it the focus of our attention. No psychoanalyst has given more thought to the primacy of experience than Laing himself. In order to appreciate the contribution of phenomenology to our understanding of experience it is necessary to return to the distinction between the two kinds of experience that are delineated by the German terms, *Erfahrung* and *Erlebnis*. Phenomenology is concerned with determining the significance of the relationship between *Erfahrung* and *Erlebnis*; in other words, with the question: what does it mean to genuinely experience something? As noted earlier, empiricist philosophers such as Hume separated experience from rationality by consigning to experience sensual data alone. Hence scientific methodology, which endeavors to combine the experience we derive from our senses with our capacity to think about and reflect upon the nature of such experiences through objective experimentation, is unable to account for the human subject's experience of ideas, thoughts, and imagination. This is because philosophers have traditionally split human beings in two, assigning one portion of the human project to rationality (the mind) and the other portion to sense experience (the body). Though the notion of reflecting on the data provided by our senses is supposed to bring the two together, this does not explain how the two can be reconnected given the presumed disparity between them. Indeed, given the underlying assumptions of this schema, reconciling the two would be theoretically impossible.

The singular contribution of Husserl at the turn of the twentieth century was to reconcile the split between sense experience and rationality. He suggested that all experience is already inherently thoughtful because the nature of consciousness is intentional, which is to say the act of consciousness and its object are given in one stroke. One is not "related" to the other because each is irrevocably dependent on the other, so that neither can stand alone. As Buddhists have traditionally argued, the presumed split to which western thought has been devoted is illusory because the two are actually one. Hence, phenomenology is able to claim that there are *levels* of experience, just as there are levels of awareness (or consciousness) depending on how diligently I set out to *see* (rather than comprehend) what my experience discloses to me through the painstaking activity of critiquing my experience as it unfolds. This thesis is especially relevant to psychoanalysts who endeavor to direct the patient's attention to the patient's experience by interpreting what it means. Viewed from this angle, a good interpretation is not intended to explain one's experience, but to deepen it, in the phenomenological sense. Many psychoanalysts are puzzled with the phenomenological preoccupation with experience and confuse phenomenology with cognitive psychology, assuming (mistakenly) that consciousness is simply a matter of cognition when in fact many of our cognitive acts, though conscious, are not necessarily experienced in the manner that phenomenologists emphasize.

Not all phenomenologists, however, conceive experience the same way. Husserl, for example, was concerned with finding a means through subjective experience to absolute knowledge, whereas Heidegger rejected absolute knowledge in principle and adopted a more skeptical approach to what experience makes available to us (Thompson 2000a, 2000b). For Heidegger, experience is essentially the revealing of Being. In other words, my experience discloses who I am and the world I inhabit: the two are interdependent because each serves to constitute the other. By anticipating my experiences with a specific aim in mind I can make use of my experience to gain insight into the person I am because experience is always *my own*. In other words, there are degrees to experience; it is not all or nothing. This is why I am also capable of resisting experience, avoiding it, and even forgetting experiences (due to repression) that are too painful to bear. In turn, the degree to which I am even capable of experiencing anything, whether a piece of music, a work of art, even a psychoanalysis, is determined by how willing I am to submit to the experience in question. According to Heidegger, this notion of "submission," an essential feature of eastern philosophy, is vital to the role experience plays in my life and the use I am able to make of it.

The psychoanalytic experience

What role does experience specifically entail in the psychoanalytic treatment situation? Is experience antithetical to my capacity to reason, as some have suggested? Or does my ability to reason depend on my capacity to experience the very thoughts my words endeavor to reveal? Moreover, how do these considerations pertain to Laing's employment of the term in his conception of psychoanalysis? First, it should be acknowledged that Freud also allowed experience a critical role in the evolution of pathogenic symptoms, even if his conception of experience relied on the commonsense notion of the term. For example, Freud believed that our capacity to bear painful experience as children determines whether we develop neurotic symptoms or worse when we grow up. According to Freud, when a child is faced with an experience that is too painful to bear, the child simply expels the experience from consciousness via one defense mechanism or the other, allowing the experience of frustration to magically disappear as though it had never occurred in the first place. The only problem with this solution is that the repressed memory finds an alternate means of expression when it is transformed into a symptom. The adult subsequently suffers and even complains about such symptoms though he or she hasn't a clue what caused the symptom or what purpose it serves.

For Freud, the purpose of a pathogenic symptom is simple, though diabolically ingenious. It shields the individual from a painful disappointment that the person who suffers the symptom wants desperately to forget, minimize, or ignore. Because the disappointment in question was only repressed but not entirely eradicated, the individual instinctively avoids experiencing the disappointment and anything that subsequently reminds him of it. The irony of Freud's thesis is that so-called traumatic experiences are never actually *experienced* as such, but are deferred until a later date when, with the help of a psychoanalyst, perhaps, the repressed (or projected, denied, etc.) memory can be elicited and finally experienced, but for the first time. In other words, it is the belated *experience* of trauma, not its mere "recollection" or comprehension, which gives the psychoanalytic moment its power.

Based on this hypothesis, psychoanalysis is nothing more than an investigation into the patient's experience, suffered over the entirety of one's life. Hence, analysts seek to learn about the experiences (*Erfahrung*) that patients remember over the course of their history, and they also seek to understand the patient's experience of the analytic situation (*Erlebnis*) which is to say, the patient's experience of the relationship with the analyst – so-called transference phenomena. But analysts are also interested in eliciting what may be characterized as lost experience (or what Heidegger would call potential experience) through the patient's free associations. Change comes about through patients' ability to speak of their experience instead of concealing it, as they have in the past. In other words, giving voice to experience serves to deepen it (in the Heideggerian sense), but only if the kind of speech elicited succeeds in plunging patients to the depths of their suffering.

What I have said about psychoanalysis so far may sound more like phenomenology than psychoanalysis, per se. All I can say in response to this observation is that, in its latency, psychoanalysis is already phenomenological, at least in the way Laing conceived it. On the other hand, there is something about Freud's notion of the unconscious that is adverse to the phenomenological perspective when it alludes to experiences occurring "in" a person's unconscious that the patient has no awareness of experiencing. These areas of contention notwithstanding, the phenomenologist and the psychoanalyst both recognize that we are perfectly capable of engaging in acts that we claim no awareness of and, hence, that we have no experience of either. Awareness and experience, from a phenomenological perspective, are necessarily interdependent concepts. According to Husserl, experience presupposes an I who *suffers* his or her experience, so that no matter how decentered or obscure one's I or ego may be, experience is a determinant of subjectivity. Yet we saw in Heidegger how it is possible to account for levels or degrees of experience, depending on whether one is prepared to undergo the suffering that is entailed in determining what one's experience is.

The proposition that there are levels of experience and, hence, levels of consciousness as well offers important implications for what Freud depicted as unconscious motivation and intentions which, when interpreted in the treatment situation, are seldom remembered by the patient to whom such intentions are attributed. Yet, there are undeniable moments in every patient's treatment when one does remember or realizes one's part in a drama that had heretofore been inaccessible to recollection. Laing accounted for this phenomenon by suggesting that Freud's conception of the unconscious is nothing more than a mode of thinking (consciousness) that patients are "unaware" of thinking. In other words, patients have no experience of *thinking* the thoughts attributed to them because they did not hear themselves thinking the thoughts in question. At the moment such thoughts occurred to them, their mind was "somewhere else." Psychoanalysts say they were unconscious of what they were thinking, whereas phenomenologists say they simply failed to listen to, and hence *experience*, what they were saying, though the thoughts no doubt occurred to them on an intuitive, pre-experiential level. Hence, the psychoanalytic experience is designed to reacquaint us with that dimension of our Being that we typically abhor and endeavor to conceal. By actually listening to what we say to the analyst *when* we say it, we reflect on our free associations at the moment they are uttered and hear them for the first time, by *experiencing* them.

Whereas Laing says that the ambiguous aspect of experience should be assigned to its inherently mysterious nature and treated with appropriate attentiveness, Freud argues that experience is subject to repression when a person's anxiety becomes insupportable and renders it "unconscious." In Freud's schema, something must be done to retrieve and finally return such repressions to consciousness by giving voice to experience as it becomes manifest in the analytic situation. The *raison d'être* of psychoanalytic theory assumes that neurotics live in their heads and have lost touch with what they think is so and how they genuinely feel about their existence. Consequently, the purpose of psychoanalytic treatment is to return to the ground of an originary experience from which the patient has become estranged, allowing such patients to finally claim their experience *as their own*, as they recount it to the analyst. Are these two perspectives hopelessly at odds with each other or are they simply speaking to the same phenomena with different terminology? Laing's phenomenological rendering of the psychoanalytic concept of defense mechanisms offers an apt example of how he incorporated the basic tenets of phenomenology into his psychoanalytic perspective. According to Laing,

> Under the heading of "defense mechanism," psychoanalysis describes a number of ways in which a person becomes alienated from himself. For example, repression, denial, splitting, projection, introjection. These "mechanisms" are often described in psychoanalytic terms as themselves "unconscious," that is, the person himself appears to be unaware that he is doing this to himself. Even when a person develops sufficient insight to see that "splitting," for example, is going on, he usually *experiences* this splitting as indeed a mechanism, an impersonal process, *so to speak*, which has taken over and which he can observe but cannot control or stop. [Hence] there is some phenomenological validity in referring to such "defenses" by the term "mechanism."
>
> (Laing 1967: 17, emphases added)

Laing uses phenomenology to emphasize what the patient *actually experiences* in relation to the analyst, not what the analyst believes, supposes, or imagines is going on in the patient's (unconscious) mind. Analytic patients, Laing allows, may indeed have a sense of themselves as living "in a fog," "out of it," "going through the numbers," "on automatic pilot," and so on. Hence, when the analyst suggests that such experience (or non-experience) may be construed as a mechanism, the patient is perfectly capable of appreciating the metaphoric quality of this terminology. Laing's point, however, is that psychoanalysts tend to take this notion, not metaphorically but literally, as though there are indeed mechanisms and the like controlling our behavior, of the nature of which we are unaware and may never become aware, no matter how much analysis we have experienced.

Laing emphasizes the importance of extending this notion further by examining the ways in which so-called unconscious aspects of a person's behavior (as well as "unformulated" experience) must be accounted for *in terms* of what one experiences and how. This is in contrast to speculating what a given patient may be said to be experiencing, when the experience in question is inaccessible to the patient and, for that matter, the patient's analyst as well. Laing proposes, for example, that the patient's defenses "have this mechanical quality because the person as he experiences himself is dissociated from them," because he is alienated from his own experience and, hence, "himself" (Laing 1967: 17). Indeed, what are defenses if not *protective maneuvers against the immediacy of experiencing one's experience*? Hence, phenomenologically speaking, repression would characterize the patient's capacity to forget painful experience; denial is essentially the denial of one's experience; projection is the means by which the person attributes his or her experience to others; splitting characterizes the person's ability to divide experience into two isolated worlds whereby the existence of the one is kept in abeyance from the other. And so on.

This reading of psychoanalysis is probably unfamiliar to most analysts because it is entails an existentialist reading of Freud from the perspective of phenomenology. Unfortunately, this reading of Freud – and, by extension, of psychoanalysis generally – is hardly evident in the psychoanalytic community, though there have been recent attempts to address the situation by incorporating some of the basic tenets of phenomenology into psychoanalytic theory (e.g. Loewald 1980: viii; Leavy 1980, 1988; Atwood and Stolorow 1984; Schafer 1976.) In the main, however, such efforts have fallen short of reframing the corpus of psychoanalytic theory and practice along phenomenological lines, which would necessitate greater emphasis on the immediacy of experience from a phenomenological perspective. Indeed, the mainstream of psychoanalysis, including adherents of the postmodern perspective, has virtually factored the very notion of experience out of play, despite recent claims to the contrary.

Ironically, recent efforts to incorporate the phenomenological conception of intersubjectivity into the psychoanalytic landscape (e.g. Atwood and Stolorow 1984; Stolorow 1997; Stolorow and Atwood 1992; Benjamin 1990) have misconstrued phenomenology's aim as that of doing away with subjectivity altogether. Although Heidegger has played a principal role in replacing the Cartesian preoccupation with subjectivity with the decentered component to personal existence, Heidegger never did away with the subject entirely and even deemed that the self is the instrument *through* which conscious experience comes into being. On the contrary, the specific focus of phenomenology is and always has been to delineate *the precise features of experience as they become manifest in the here and now of the situation one is in*. Any form of intersubjectivity that proposes to dispense with this critical component of the phenomenological perspective ceases to be intersubjective, properly speaking, and withdraws into a theory-heavy *rationalization* of the therapeutic process that is closer to the Cartesian tradition than a, properly speaking, phenomenological one.

On the other hand, American analysts who are sympathetic with postmodernism tend to emphasize matters of technique over theory. Elliott and Spezzano (1998: 73), for example, suggest that the work of Irwin

Hoffman is postmodern due to his lack of certainty about what is going on between himself and his patients, in contrast to analysts who are more invested in determining what is allegedly happening in the analyst's and patient's unconscious. This is a point well taken and consistent with the skeptical outlook in contrast to the dogmatic assertions of previous generations of analysts. Similarly, the work of Schafer is said to be consistent with the postmodern perspective when Schafer questions whether patients should be characterized as "deceiving" themselves simply because the analyst suspects it is so. Of course, these features of Hoffman's and Schafer's respective work could just as easily be characterized as existentialist in nature, so they are neither necessarily nor essentially postmodern (Thompson 1998: 332–5). Elliott and Spezzano argue, moreover, that just because postmodernism embraces a perspectivist framework does not necessarily imply that one interpretation is just as good as any other, a frequent criticism among analysts who reject postmodernism. Thus Elliott and Spezzano conceive a mitigated version of postmodernism. In contrast to the more radical position of French psychoanalysts such as Lacan and Kristeva, they offer a pragmatic interpretation of the postmodernist principles common among American analysts who identify with the relational perspective.

The question of authenticity

Despite similarities between the postmodern and phenomenological perspectives (due to their respective roots in a skeptical sensibility) the principal difference between them is the postmodernist rejection of authenticity, a principal feature of both Nietzsche's and Heidegger's philosophies as well as Laing's clinical perspective. Although Heidegger was the first philosopher to employ authenticity as a technical term, Nietzsche's and Kierkegaard's respective philosophies were important sources for this component of Heidegger's philosophy. For Nietzsche, authenticity characterizes the person who is not afraid to face up to the fundamental anxieties of living. Such an individual is embodied in Nietzsche's conception of the *Übermensch*, usually translated into English as overman or superman, who is capable of coming to grips with his or her fears and overcome the weight of his or her existence by accepting reality for what it is, unbowed and unafraid. Such a person would permit the more passionate, Dionysian aspect of his being to dominate over his more rationalistic, Apollonian side.

Postmodernists have rejected Nietzsche's ideal as merely one more edition in a long history of such mythic figures (e.g., the Marxist proletarian,

Freud's perfectly analyzed individual, Sartre's existentialist hero). For postmodernists, Nietzsche's ideal fails to take into account the severe limitations that human beings must contend with and ultimately accept. While there is some truth to this assessment of Nietzsche's hero, one would be mistaken to construe Heidegger's authentic individual as nothing more than a twentieth-century edition of Nietzsche's so-called superman who would appear in the future as an exemplar in overcoming human weakness and hypocrisy.

One of the principal differences between Nietzsche's superman and Heidegger's conception of authenticity is that for Heidegger there is no such person who epitomizes the "authentic hero" in juxtaposition to people who are inauthentic. Authenticity is characterized instead as a specific act or moment in any individual's life where the context in which a situation arises offers an opportunity to behave authentically or not. Indeed, the concept is so central to Heidegger's philosophy that it is difficult to appreciate what authenticity entails without an understanding of his philosophical outlook.

In contrast to Nietzsche, Heidegger was not talking about an ideal person who would some day emerge to replace the stereotypical contemporary neurotic, a view that is moralistic as well as pathogenic. Instead, Heidegger argues, all human creatures are inauthentic by their nature, but sometimes behave authentically when they rise to the occasion, or as Laing would observe, when they are capable of being honest with themselves. Of course, we are challenged to do so virtually every moment of our lives, but too distracted or anxious to give it much thought. So how do we manage to act authentically in spite of our condition and, more to the point, what would doing so entail?

In order to understand what authenticity entails it is helpful to know what it means to be inauthentic. Carman (2000) observes that there are two depictions of inauthenticity in Heidegger's magnum opus, *Being and Time* (1962), that on the surface appear to contradict each other but in fact are complementary. Both are aspects of "fallenness" (*Verfallenheit*), a fundamental component of inauthenticity, which characterizes the individual who sells out to public opinion in order to curry favor and success.

A central theme throughout Heidegger's early work is the relationship between the individual and society and how this relationship sets up a tension that the individual, contrary to Nietzsche, never entirely overcomes. For Heidegger and Nietzsche alike, we spend all our lives searching for a feeling of communion only to find our reward is always one more step out of reach. This quest is inconsolable, says Heidegger, because the only way of approximating this feeling (short of falling in love) is by abandoning an essential aspect of what we are about: our personal integrity. Hence, one version of "falling" into inauthenticity describes an aspect of the human condition from which we cannot escape. The other version is manifested when a person *tries* to escape his or her isolation by capitulating to social incentives to conform, a kind of second-order mode of inauthenticity that compounds it even further.

Both Nietzsche and Heidegger recognized the terrible sense of anxiety that lies at the bottom of authenticity, but Heidegger was more adept at characterizing the features of this dread for what it is, the experience of being alive. Instead of trying to flee from our anxieties by suppressing them we can instead choose to listen to what they tell us about ourselves and, hence, respond to our *Angst* authentically. Heidegger observed that because there is no ultimate foundation for our values or our behavior, we can never feel at home in the world. Yet because we are thrown into a world that is not our choosing, it is up to us to determine what meaning our lives will have. The inauthentic individual, like the neurotic, is incapable of accepting the anxiety and hardship that everyday existence entails. Instead, he complains about his lot and the unfairness of the hand that is dealt him. For Heidegger and Laing alike, the ability to accept life on its terms and to suffer the day-to-day blows that are impossible to avoid or escape brings with it a reward that only authenticity can offer: the experience of genuinely being oneself.

Heidegger's and Laing's respective depictions of authenticity have no foundation other than the individual's conscience, for better or worse. In order to *be* one's own, honestly and authentically, one is obliged to suffer the isolation and loneliness that follow when we refuse to compromise our personal values for material or popular gain. For Heidegger, postmodernism is antithetical to a philosophy of authenticity because it embraces inauthenticity as a matter of course. Any perspective that lives on the surface while rejecting a depth to one's deliberations, that celebrates a conception of selfhood which changes as easily as the channels on television, that dismisses traditional values such as conscience, honesty, and goodness just because we lack immutable standards against which such values can be assessed, and whose apparent purpose is to find fault with any aspiration that endeavors to stake a position of one's own, celebrates inauthenticity at every turn. As such, it is a nihilism that feeds on the traditions that preceded it while applauding itself as the latest intellectual fashion.

The primacy of interpretation

If authenticity is the source of divergence between the existential and postmodern traditions, the art of interpretation (or hermeneutics) joins them in common cause. Following Freud, the question of interpretation is of fundamental importance to Laing's conception of psychoanalysis as well as contemporary relational, intersubjective, constructivist, and hermeneutic perspectives. Freud was not alone in his tendency to treat interpretations as pronouncements from the gods, as though he could divine that truth of the matter by virtue of his superior intelligence. Indeed, most psychoanalysts have tended to treat interpretation as *translation* from the patient's utterances into a given theory of underlying reality instead of a means of "opening up" an otherwise closed area of discourse. It is surprising, however, that contemporary hermeneutic and constructivist models would imply that this more skeptical, allegedly postmodern take on the handling of interpretation is something new. Many of the existential analysts from the 1950s and 1960s (who were also critical of Freud in this respect) came to the same conclusion after integrating Heidegger's philosophy into their clinical perspective, evidenced in the publications of Laing ([1960] 1969), Binswanger (1963), Boss (1963, 1979), and a host of European psychoanalysts. Laing noted, for example, that Heidegger's conception of experience *already presupposes* an act of interpretation that, in turn, elicits one's capacity for getting to the heart of the matter. This is a conception of interpretation that has more recently been noted by hermeneutically oriented psychoanalysts such as Donnel Stern (1997), derived from Heidegger's former pupil, Hans Georg Gadamer. According to Laing:

> Our experience of another entails a particular interpretation of his behavior. To feel loved is to perceive and interpret, that is, to experience, the actions of the other as loving. . . . [Hence] in order for the other's behavior to become part of [one's] experience, [one] must perceive it. *The very act of perception [and hence experience] entails interpretation.*
>
> (Laing *et al.* 1966: 10–11, emphasis added)

In other words, everything analytic patients experience is the consequence of interpretations patients have already, instinctively given themselves. This, in turn, influences what a given patient is capable of taking in during the course of analytic work. What the analyst says to a patient is never actually "heard" in the way the analyst necessarily intends it to be, because it is *unconsciously interpreted* and, hence, experienced by the patient according to his or her interpretative schema, a culmination of everything an individual has previously endured and understood by such experiences in the course of a lifetime. In other words, analytic patients experience the world according to a personal bias that is resistant and oftentimes impervious to anything a patient encounters that contradicts it, including the analyst's interpretations. The dogmatic nature of a person's views, held together by a lifetime of neurotic impasse maneuvers, helps explain the difficulty patients experience when invited to question their most basic assumptions.

Since both analyst and patient are always already instinctively interpreting everything each says to the other (but without necessarily realizing they are doing so), what is actually heard by each and in turn experienced is impossible to grasp directly. Every account of a person's experience entails the use of words that, when uttered, are immediately translated by the listener into a schema that the individual, whether analyst or patient, either wants to hear or expects to. This constantly changing interplay of speech, recognition, and misunderstanding helps explain the extraordinary difficulty analysts encounter in their endeavor to converse with their patients and, in turn, understand them, because every attempt at communication is at the mercy of the patient's originary experience, the source of which is notoriously opaque. Because I can never know what a patient's experience is, I can only make a calculated guess as to what it might be, based more or less entirely on what the patient tells me.

Analysts who were influenced by Heidegger's hermeneutic theory of language often focus on the patient's tendency to deflect the analyst's efforts at understanding by resorting to self-deception and even incidents of overt deception. Analysts, in turn, are similarly prone to self-deception and subtle forms of coercion, a point exhaustively chronicled by Laing (Thompson 1998) who cites this as examples of inauthenticity by the analyst (what Freud characterized as therapeutic ambition). More recently, psychoanalysts who are influenced by Gadamer's conception of hermeneutics emphasize the difficulties encountered with virtually all attempts at communication and depict the analytic situation as one of "unraveling" the inherent complexities of speech acts as they occur, a vital feature of Laing's analytic method.

The postmodern rejection of the existentialist conception of self-deception is based on the claim that self-deception is a myth because there is no standard of truth against which one is able to deceive and because there is no "self" to lie to. This criticism is also raised against

Freud's conviction that his patients harbored secrets and that the goal of analysis is to determine what those secrets are by helping patients to disclose them. The fact that neither Laing, Heidegger, Gadamer, or postmodernist thinkers believe that truth is objectively verifiable, however, does not negate the proposition (adopted by both Freud and Laing alike) that human beings are prone to deceive themselves about the nature and content of their experience, no matter how unreliable or objectively inaccurate one's experience may be. What counts is that patients believe in the veracity of what they deceive themselves (and others) about, so the resulting conflict, as Freud point out, is between opposing inclinations "in" oneself, which are in turn derived from a cleavage in the individual's relationship with the world. It seems to me that by rejecting the concept of self-deception postmodernists have taken the terms, self, deception, and truth literally, mistaking the organizing principle of subjectivity for a materialistic notion of the self.

There is an increasing tendency among analysts identified with the relational perspective to characterize the analytic relationship as one between equals, more or less collaborative in spirit, thus minimizing the tension that has traditionally characterized the patient's transference with the analyst. Yet none of these innovations are new, nor are they derived from the postmodern turn in contemporary culture. Matters of technique have been debated since the beginning of psychoanalysis and there is a long history of disagreement between analysts who advocate a more authoritarian posture and those who opt for a user-friendly variety. While some analysts believe that technique should follow theory, others argue that practice is inevitably a creature of experience, a more existential perspective. I remain skeptical that recent so-called innovations in technique are anything new. Psychoanalysis is such a flexible instrument that what finally matters is the person who employs it, not which theory or technical regime the analyst is educated to follow.

The crisis in psychoanalysis

I have tried to show that Laing's relationship with psychoanalysis is both more subtle and complicated than typically appreciated. Many of the so-called innovations of the contemporary relational and postmodern perspectives in psychoanalysis were common coin to Laing and other European psychoanalysts and psychiatrists whose views were then too subversive to be embraced by the conventional psychoanalytic community. Perhaps the North American aversion of philosophy helps to account for why even now there is relatively little knowledge of Laing's contribution to psychoanalysis in the United States or Canada. If this is so, it may also explain why so many psychoanalysts feel it is necessary to incorporate ideas from other disciplines, such as philosophy, linguistics, and religious studies, into psychoanalytic theory and technique. Alternatively, psychoanalysts could employ such ideas as a means of broadening their understanding of the human condition which, in turn, would inform their behavior with patients, but on a more subtle level. To do so would require becoming conversant with other disciplines in order to expand the narrowly conceived boundaries of psychoanalytic theory and its hopelessly narrow technical nomenclature.

Perhaps the day will come when Laing's contribution will finally receive the attention it deserves, when his heretofore extreme ideas will appear less enigmatic than they did a generation ago. There is little dispute that contemporary psychoanalysis, for all its efforts to keep up with the world around it, is in a state of crisis. The culture has turned away from it for a variety of reasons and the reason is difficult to assess, but for all its purported innovation the typical conventional psychoanalyst today is, like the instrument he wields, woefully out of fashion. Laing excited a generation of clinicians and patients alike to use analysis as a vehicle for self-exploration and, ironically, many contemporary analysts attribute their embryonic interest in the field to Laing's influence. It is perhaps ironic that many analysts today fault Laing for having abandoned psychoanalysis when it was they who dismissed his efforts at innovation. Whether recent efforts to address these developments are too late, on the one hand, or whether there is still time to reverse these trends, on the other, we do not know because the future, like the outcome of every treatment experience, is impossible to predict.

References

Atwood, G. and Stolorow, R. (1984) *Structures of Subjectivity: Explorations in Psychoanalytic Phenomenology*. Hillsdale, NJ and London: Analytic Press.

Benjamin, J. (1990) "An outline of intersubjectivity: recognition and destruction," *Psychoanalytic Psychology* 7 (supp.): 33-46.

Binswanger, L. (1963) *Being in the World*, trans. J. Needleman, with critical commentary. New York and London: Basic Books.

Bion, W. R. (1961) *Experiences in Groups*. New York: Basic Books.

—— ([1962] 1983) *Learning from Experience*. New York and London: Jason Aronson.

Boss, M. (1963) *Psychoanalysis and Daseinsanalysis*. New York and London: Basic Books.

Boss, M. (1979) *The Existential Foundations of Medicine and Psychology*, trans. S. Conway and A. Cleaves. New York and London: Jason Aronson.

Burston, D. (1996) *The Wing of Madness: The Life and Work of R. D. Laing*. Cambridge, MA and London: Harvard University Press.

Carman, T. (2000) "Must we be inauthentic?," in M. Wrathall and J. Malpas (eds.) *Heidegger, Authenticity, and Modernity: Essays in Honor of Hubert L. Dreyfus, Volume One*. Cambridge, MA and London: MIT Press.

Elliott, A. and Spezzano, C. (1998) "Psychoanalysis at its limits: navigating the postmodern turn," in O. Renik (ed.) *Knowledge and Authority in the Psychoanalytic Relationship*. Northvale, NJ and London: Jason Aronson.

Friedenberg, E. (1973) *R. D. Laing*. New York: Viking.

Heaton, J. M. (2000) "On R. D. Laing: style, sorcery, alienation," *Psychoanalytic Review* 87: 511–26.

Heidegger, M. (1962) *Being and Time*, trans. J. Macquarrie and E. Robinson. New York: Harper and Row.

——— (1992) *Basic Writings*, revised and expanded edn. San Francisco, CA: HarperCollins.

Jay, M. (1998) "The crisis of experience in a post-subjective age," public lecture, University of California, Berkeley, CA, November 14, 1998.

Kotowicz, Z. (1997) *R. D. Laing and the Paths of Anti-Psychiatry*. London and New York: Routledge.

Laing, R. D. (1960) *The Divided Self*. New York: Pantheon Books.

——— ([1961] 1969) *Self and Others*, 2nd revised edn. New York: Pantheon.

——— (1967) *The Politics of Experience*. New York: Pantheon.

——— (1982) *The Voice of Experience*. New York: Pantheon.

Laing, R. D., Phillipson, H., and Lee, A. R. (1966) *Interpersonal Perception: A Theory and a Method of Research*. New York: Springer.

Leavy, S. (1980) *The Psychoanalytic Dialogue*. New Haven, CT and London: Yale University Press.

——— (1988) *In the Image of God: A Psychoanalyst's View*. New Haven, CT and London: Yale University Press.

Loewald, H. W. (1980) *Papers on Psychoanalysis*. New Haven, CT and London: Yale University Press.

Ogden, T. (1989) *The Primitive Edge of Experience*. Northvale, NJ and London: Jason Aronson.

Schafer, R. (1976) *A New Language for Psychoanalysis*. New Haven, CT and London: Yale University Press.

Stern, D. (1997) *Unformulated Experience: From Dissociation to Imagination in Psychoanalysis*. Hillsdale, NJ and London: Analytic Press.

Stolorow, R. (1997) "Principles of dynamic systems, intersubjectivity, and the obsolete distinction between one-person and two-person psychologies," *Psychoanalytic Dialogues* 7: 859–68.

Stolorow, R. and Atwood, G. (1992) *Contexts of Being*. Hillsdale, NJ: Analytic Press.

Symington, N. (1986) *The Analytic Experience*. New York: St. Martin's Press.

Thompson, M. G. (1994) *The Truth about Freud's Technique: The Encounter with the Real*. New York and London: New York University Press.

—— (1996a) "The rule of neutrality," *Psychoanalysis and Contemporary Thought* 19: 57-84.

—— (1996b) "Deception, mystification, trauma: Laing and Freud," *Psychoanalytic Review* 83: 827–47.

—— (1997) "The fidelity to experience in R. D. Laing's treatment philosophy," *Contemporary Psychoanalysis* 33: 595–614.

—— (1998) "Existential psychoanalysis: a Laingian perspective," in P. Marcus and A. Rosenberg (eds.) *Psychoanalytic Versions of the Human Condition and Clinical Practice*. New York: New York University Press.

—— (2000a) "The crisis of experience in contemporary psychoanalysis," *Contemporary Psychoanalysis* 36: 29–56.

—— (2000b) "The sceptic dimension to psychoanalysis: toward an ethic of experience," *Contemporary Psychoanalysis* 36: 457–81.

—— (2003) "Postmodernism and psychoanalysis: a Heideggerian critique of postmodernist malaise and the question of authenticity," in J. Reppen, M. Schulman and J. Tucker (eds.) *Way beyond Freud: Postmodern Psychoanalysis Evaluated*. London: Open Gate Press.

Chapter 9

The eclipse of the person in psychoanalysis

Jon Frederickson

As is true of all the humanities, psychoanalysis has been much influenced by postmodernism. Classical psychoanalytic theory focused almost entirely on the ways in which the person is determined by internal psychological forces. In contrast, postmodernists have very usefully elucidated how the person is influenced and determined by such forces as language and society, which exist outside of awareness. Postmodern theories have served as a useful corrective to a purely internal focus as a means of understanding the person. Rather than take self-experience as self-evident, postmodern theorists have helped us see how socially constructed concepts shape our experience. Rather than take our identity as simple and consistent, they have helped us look at the multiplicity of our experience, raising questions about simple unitary models of identity.

As a result of the postmodern turn, however, the question "who are you?" has rarely been so puzzling. Contemporary clinicians are struggling with a variety of postmodern theories that deny the existence of an autonomous human subject. The self, person, and psyche are all viewed as constructs of the language, culture, and society in which we exist. Seen from a postmodern perspective, it would seem that we now have an intersubjective psychoanalysis without a subject, an interpersonal psychoanalysis without a person, and even a psychotherapy without a psyche. In the process, postmodern theorists have substituted new forms of determinism for the psychic determinism of classical psychoanalysis that they so fundamentally reject. Indeed, postmodernism has called into question the entire project of self-knowledge. Yet if there is no subject, no person and no psyche, who are clinicians supposed to be analyzing?

This chapter will examine and critique some of the weaknesses of postmodern theories in contemporary psychoanalysis and propose a way to think about the problem of agency. The chapter begins by elaborating the problems posed by postmodern theories in psychoanalysis. After describing postmodern notions of the self, an alternative view of person-hood and agency will be developed by drawing on the work of the Russian personalist philosophers. In particular, the ways in which post-modern theories view the self as determined by contexts will be contrasted with the personalist view of the person as both free and determined.

The postmodern self

Postmodernists generally hold that the world around us is a construct. They contend that we do not discover reality, but invent it (Watzlawick 1976, 1984, 1990). We cannot know the world directly or objectively, but only through language and concepts which we have invented. We are not able to compare our thoughts with any objective reality, because we are unable to transcend the limits of our concepts and language. Hence, all our knowledge of the world is determined by constructs. From this perspective, our thoughts can be compared only with other thoughts, because the concept of reality can not be known directly. It is impossible for us to achieve even an indirect undistorted view of the world. Concepts such as objective reality are deconstructed and from a political perspec-tive are seen as legitimizing a power structure that must be dismantled.

Postmodernism has shown us that we exist within language, culture, and society, which are our organs for knowing and relating to the world. Postmodern proponents in psychotherapy and psychoanalysis claim that the person is merely relative to the forces of language, culture, and society. In so far as these symbols are held to be primary, the person is essentially replaced by a system of signs. This is where we see most clearly the eclipse of the person and the personal: the denial that we exist as existential centers, with purposes, intents, and values as agents.

What are the implications of these theories for psychotherapy and psychoanalysis? From the perspective of constructivism, you and I are human constructs. In other words: "There are . . . no depressions. There is only *talk* . . . about depressions. There are no . . . psyches: just talk about . . . psyches" (de Shazer 1993: 89; quoted in Held 1995). We are not able to know each other in any direct way that transcends language and con-cepts. There is no real you that exists outside language.

You, the subject who takes action and interprets, is replaced in con-structivist thought with "subjectivity," the result of your thinking, feel-ing, and imagining. You and I learn about each other only indirectly through our respective worldviews. This is what some psychoanalysts (Orange *et al.* 1997; Orange 2001) call an intersection of subjectivities. As a therapist I will never know you directly since all of my knowledge is determined by my theories and constructs. Taken to its logical end, I do not think; constructs think through me. Theory brings into being the reality of you that I find. Or as Rosenau puts it: "Subjects are actually contingent effects of language . . . in a particular context" (Rosenau 1992: 47, quoted in Held 1995).

If we are just contingent effects, if we are not directly knowable, who or what does the therapist analyze? The therapist no longer analyzes a unitary self, since it does not exist in this perspective. The therapist might view each experience you have as evidence of a new self, so the analysis involves greater awareness of multiple selves (Bromberg 1998; Stern 1997). As a result, the object of analysis is no longer the human subject, but how the subject thinks about the world. When you speak about something in your life as real, the analyst might think that you have created a fantasy about reality (subjective reality) which you are treating as if it is the same as objective reality. "Attributions of objective reality . . . are concretizations of subjective truth" (Stolorow and Atwood 1992: 92).

From a postmodern, constructivist perspective, therapists do not concern themselves with an "objective" world. They view the task as looking at how your way of constructing the world intersects with their way (Orange *et al.* 1997; Stolorow and Atwood 1992) in order to help you participate optimally in the construction of meaning (Moore 1999). The problem, however, is that if there is no objective reality, neither is there any ground from which to establish what is optimal. The task of therapy might also be to help you construct a meaning for your life that fits traditional artistic criteria of form (Spence 1982).

The traditional psychoanalytic goal of relating more lovingly and realistically to an objective world, has thus given way to the task of creating and recreating a subjective world view. As a result, there is no self left to analyze, only a way of constructing the world. From a political perspective, constructivists seek to expose and deconstruct objective reality as legitimizing the power of the psychoanalyst by suggesting the analyst has a better grasp on reality than the patient. Psychoanalysis, on this view, is no longer a search for the truth. Why? Because truth is viewed as a construction relative to a context. Each context determines what we will know; we can not know any reality independent of the context in which we find ourselves.

Ironically, this approach that is so sensitive to power actually renders the person powerless because it subverts the notion of agency. Like other constructs, agency is seen as illusory (Bromberg 1998; Mitchell 1993). We can have only a sense of agency (Stolorow *et al.* 2001). But, if I have no agency, there is no personal meaning or intent unique to me that guides my actions. The impersonal world of contexts is the source of all intent; our personal intents and purpose have become exteriorized. We can attain a limited freedom to reflect on how we construct meaning and how we are embedded (Levenson 1972). But this is a freedom without content: we can know something but can do nothing about it. We can not act but only reflect on the futility of ever being agents.

In my view there are a number of intractable problems with the constructivist philosophy. Constructivists hold that there is no such thing as an objective truth. However, this is itself a truth claim. Hence, the claim is self-contradictory, suffering from the "Liar's Paradox" (Scruton 2000). Social constructivists who argue that all knowledge is relative to social contexts run into the same problem. If all knowledge is relative to social contexts, then this statement is not true since it is simply the result of a socially negotiated agreement to believe this myth (Haack 1998: 93). Although our narratives are partly determined by the world we live in, we can still study them in order to learn about ourselves and the social realities in which we have lived (Freeman 1993: 202). This points to the problem of determinism. If we were completely determined by contexts in which we exist, we could not be surprised (Haack 1998: 161–2). For instance, my perceptions of you depend on my thinking and interpretation. But what testifies that I am in contact with you, someone real, independent of my interpretations, is the potential for surprise. You can surprise me by doing something I did not expect. Suddenly, I perceive you in a new way, outside my previous context. And even if the context was all my previous knowledge of you, your creativity can reveal something entirely new to me. I can begin to recognize that you are larger than any previous understanding I had about you.

Postmodernism, to be sure, provides many important insights. The difficulty lies not so much with the insights achieved by postmodern proponents, but rather, with their tendency to maximalize them. For instance, we are immersed in language and come to know ourselves, in large part, through language. But that does not mean that language is the only way we come to know ourselves. Postmodernists have made tremendous contributions to our understanding of powerful forces that can determine our behavior, thoughts, and feelings. Yet by viewing the human being as the place where these forces of language, culture, and society intersect, they deny our capacity for freedom.

By emphasizing the relativity of all knowledge, postmodernists absolutize language, culture, and society as the determinants of human experience, giving them a false sacredness. In the process, they subvert the human subject. The existence of these influences does not mean that *all* sense of conscious control is illusory or trivial, "as if language lived itself in man and the reverse were not at all true" (Sass 1992: 48). Their existence only defines the limits of our freedom and agency. Constructivists claim that we are embedded in context. But when we are truly embedded, we do not know it. As soon as we see that we are embedded in a context, we have adopted a point of view outside that context. In so far as we see the situation in which we have been embedded, we have changed that situation and ourselves.

Constructivist psychoanalysis is often thought of as a relational theory because of its emphasis on the relationship between patient and analyst. However, the points above reveal that it is nonrelational in key respects. Why? According to constructivists, you and I can not know or relate to each other directly. Only our worldviews can intersect; there is no subject in traditional terms to relate to. Worldviews can be brought together (note the passive voice) but they can not reach out, connect, and relate actively. Subjectivities do not relate, persons do. The intersection of worldviews is merely the interaction of ideas, not the dynamic relation of persons. Only I can relate to you as a person and encounter your purposes and agency that are different from mine. You, as a person, are more than your worldview. Your worldview, no matter how poetic, can only point to the concrete living experience of being with you.

Constructivism substitutes thoughts and ideas for the concrete person you are. "If we say . . . identity is not what matters, it is still someone who says this" (Rudman 1997: 217). And whoever says this is saying it to someone else, an Other. As the philosopher Paul Ricoeur points out: "[T]o whom does identity no longer matter? Who is called on to be deprived of self-assertion if not the self that has been put in parenthesis in the name of impersonal methodology?" (Ricoeur 1991:193). Even the postmodernist claiming we do not exist as concrete persons is addressing some concrete person who has the choice to agree or disagree. Ironically, we see here the return of the repressed within constructivist thinking: out of the shadows the person emerges. Constructivist thought reduces you, as a person, to a contingent effect of context. Yet somehow you are still endowed with the power to think these thoughts.

According to constructivists, either we have no being or our being is not directly knowable. Constructivism (Orange *et al.* 1997: Moore 1999: Orange 2001), which is fundamentally social, concerns itself not with ontology, with *being*, but with the *relationship* between worldviews. The person as subjectivity does not have any ontological content. Contexts, not the person, have laid claim to the ontological content of human existence (see Zizioulas 1985: 35). It is as if what is personal about us (our agency as existential centers with purposes, intents, and values) has been relocated in an impersonal world. You are not the one who determines your existence through your choice and agency; you are the one who is determined.

One reason this has occurred is that constructivists fail to distinguish between you (the subject) who interpret the world, and your interpretation (subjectivity). "My knowledge and my consciousness belong to me, but I myself do not belong to them; they are my 'properties', my instruments, my functions, and I myself am far from being exhaustively defined by them" (Vysheslavtsev 1999: 161–2). Or as the psychoanalyst William Meissner (1984) has put it, I do not belong to my unconscious, my unconscious belongs to me. When constructivists view you as determined by contexts such as language and culture, you are described as if you are a point without content. You are an empty knower filled by contexts that determine what you will know. In contrast, I suggest that you are also a subject as agent, a sphere with content. You are an active doer filled by your purposes, intents, and values. You are both a self-conscious epistemological subject and an ontological agent, "a bi-unity" of "two different levels or layers in the human spirit'" (Copleston 1988: 67–8).

In so far as constructivists view us as determined by contexts, they regard the idea of a person as agent as a Cartesian fallacy. That is, if we think of ourselves as independent agents, we must be ignoring the ways we are embedded within relationships. Hence, they see us as multiple selves, each self arising in the context of each relationship (Sullivan 1950). On this view, we are not individual agents and persons within relationships, but selves determined by relationships.

Another example of deterministic thinking involves the narrative therapy movement (de Shazer 1993; Watzlawick 1976, 1984, 1990; White and Epston 1990). Postmodern narrative therapists claim that real experiences do not cause problems, the stories you tell about yourself do. Drawing from linguistic philosophy and literary theories, they claim that the language, theory, or story you tell about yourself creates, constitutes, or determines your experience. They rely on three assumptions: you can not independently know what is reality; your language and story alters the nature of any reality to be known; therefore, your story creates your experience.

Narrative therapists would appear to analyze persons as if they are books. However illuminating this metaphor is, it is dangerous to over-extend the notion of the person as a text. A book is a thing, not an agent. A book has a fixed content. It can be read many ways and many meanings can be found within it. A person, however, does not have a fixed content.

Speaking metaphorically, we have not yet been written. We are larger than our pasts. We keep growing and creating ourselves in unpredictable ways. We communicate to others not just through words but actions, our embodiment in life. Our meanings grow because of our self-creation through agency.

From the narrative perspective, however, agency is just another construct, an illusion. McNamee and Gergen (1992: 4) claim: "[O]ne cannot describe the history of a country or oneself on the basis of what actually happened; rather, one has available a repertoire of story-telling devices or narrative forms and these devices are imposed on the past." From this perspective, therapists seek to help their patients tell better stories about their lives. The narrative of the problem is what needs therapy and the solution lies in addressing the problematic discourse. If there is no reality or knowable reality outside of language, however, what is a better story? Patients can tell different and more stories about their life. The patient is liberated from the previous confining story she told about her life. But freedom *from* something restrictive is not the same as freedom *to* (Fromm 1941) or freedom *for* (Meissner 1984). This is freedom without any content.

The postmodern perspective has created a crisis of values because the value of an individual is regarded as merely a social construction. The self has been replaced by "subjectivity," a term that attempts to convey the inevitable sense of individual perspective and individual need and desire, but avoid the essentializing and metaphysical implications of the self. "In the term subjectivity, however, the old self may be latent and that possibility needs to be explored" (Levine 1992: 3). Indeed, postmodern therapies are very concerned with the unique experience of the patient. They undermine this concern, however, with their belief that this unique experience is determined by contexts. If our experience is determined, it is common, not uniquely shaped by agency. Yet in so far as constructivist psychoanalysts (Stolorow; *et al.* 1987; Stolorow and Atwood 1992; Orange *et al.* 1997) are acutely sensitive to the role of empathy with the patient's experience, they recognize the value of the patient's experience, and it is regarded as something that really exists with which the analyst can empathize. But this is merely the shadow of the person as it lurks behind the fragments postmodernists are interested in.

Psychoanalytic challenges to the postmodernist self

Within psychoanalytic thinking, a number of writers have begun to question the postmodern premise that we have no agency. Schafer (1976) and

Leites (1971) decried the way that abstract terms concealed agency in psychoanalysis. A patient is said to have defenses which operate, rather than the patient *chose to avoid* a feeling. This "is psychoanalytic theory in search of the author" (Rubenfeld 2001: 9). From a personal point of view, the patient makes choices. From an impersonal point of view, impersonal things such as invariant thought patterns, states, structures, and energy determine our actions. But when we talk about human behavior in terms of states, structure, and energy, we have "action without an agent" (MacMurray 1961: 83). In the stimulus–response model the patient is not viewed as an agent who has purposes, but as an object whose behaviors are determined by stimuli. From a deterministic point of view, events within the self have causes, just as we see in inanimate objects.

Psychoanalysts have also questioned the postmodern premise that all our knowledge of the world is indirect, mediated by language. Developmental research (Stern 1985) has shown that as infants we possess nonverbal intentionality and knowledge before we can use language to organize our experience. Hence, agency and knowledge exist temporally prior to language. Frie (1999) has shown that prereflective bodily experience precedes thinking. Our tacit nonverbal awareness is larger than what we can state in words. "We remain ever unable to say all that we know" (Polanyi 1958a). We possess a great deal of implicit knowledge based on our actions that is never articulated (Reber 1993). Bucci (1997) has shown that embodied, nonverbal procedural knowledge influences all of our knowledge of relationships. We know the world directly, bodily, in nonverbal forms, some of which are never articulated in language. This nonlinguistic, procedural processing of experience coexists with language throughout the life span. Conscious linguistic knowledge is merely the tip of the iceberg of unconscious nonlinguistic processes of knowing (Westen 1996).

From the perspective of neuroscience, Damasio (1999: 26) has shown that we process information and react to it emotionally first. We then have the feeling of knowing, feel it viscerally, and finally put that experience into language (Damasio 1999: 33–81). His research reveals that linguistic knowledge arises out of nonlinguistic, affective experience. We have "a non-language concept of self before we ever say 'I' " (Damasio 1999: 186). Damasio's research challenges the primacy of language because it shows that feelings alert us to problems that we have already begun to solve nonconsciously and nonlinguistically. In fact, language occurs when we become aware of nonverbal thinking that was already going on in unconscious processing systems (LeDoux 1998: 19). Research into emotions reveals that subjective emotional states and the language we use to describe them are the *end* result of unconscious nonverbal information processing (LeDoux 1998: 37).

We can also see that conscious nonverbal modes of direct knowledge coexist with language throughout our lives.

> It has been said that language is the prelude to the coming of man. That may be, but even before language comes *thinking in terms of tools*, i.e., the realization of mechanical connections and the invention of mechanical means for mechanical ends.
>
> (Buhler quoted in Wilson 1998: 194, emphasis in original)

Language is only *one* of the intellectual tools we use to know the world, and it is not the first. We come to know the world in nonverbal physical ways through the physical tools we use to make and fix things.

> When we become literate we do not cease to be oral-language users, so when we become oral-language users we do not cease to be prelinguistic sense makers. . . . [We] make sense of the world in a distinctly human way that is not linguistic.
>
> (Wilson 1998: 285)

We know the world in many ways other than through language. Through tools we come to know the world directly through touch, not indirectly through language. We often learn a craft by watching and imitating a master, doing what he or she did, touching how the master touched. When my father taught me the craft of blacksmithing he could not tell me all he knew. I had to watch him, imitate him, and learn from the feel and experience of working metal on the anvil.

Psychoanalysts have also begun to critique the emphasis on language as the primary way to know the world and each other because it ignores the other senses. For instance, we communicate and know one another not merely through language but through our bodies and actions (Ekman and Davidson 1994). Without being aware of it, "*human beings are constantly engaged in adjustments to the presence and activities of other human beings. As sensitive organisms, they utilize their full sensory equipment in this adjustment*" (Birdwhistell 1970: 48, emphasis in original). This is obvious in musical performance. As a chamber musician, I and my friends know one another, move together, make music together without words. Musical time is an intersubjective experience, a shared time of growing old together (Schutz 1951).

We communicate and know one another through our bodies, our

gestures and movements. A sentence will have a completely different meaning depending on the bodily movements accompanying it. Gestures, postures, and spacing behaviors frame and punctuate our verbal transactions (Scheflen 1972). Nonverbal forms of communication and response coexist with language. Hall's (1976: 71) cross-cultural research has shown that people in interactions move together in a dance. When we do not move together in the same tempo and rhythm, we feel out of synch. We know and respond to one another through an undercurrent of synchronized bodily movement. As the Sufis say, "You can't send a kiss by messenger." There are some ways of knowing not possible through language that can be accomplished only through touch, and only by you.

Research has shown that we can know ourselves directly through bodily feelings, gestures, and movements. Direct bodily experience and unconscious nonlinguistic modes of knowing are the ground out of which indirect linguistic knowledge arises. Even when we know the world through language, we continue to know it through such other modes as: nonverbal unconscious processing, nonverbal conscious processing, movement, gesture, rhythm, music, and tools.

As we have seen, psychoanalysts have critiqued the postmodern premises that all our knowledge is mediated by language, that we cannot know ourselves directly, and that there is no agency. This last point is perhaps the most urgent for psychotherapy and psychoanalysis. For, without agency, the patient's capacity to exercise freedom and will, no psychotherapy can succeed. Without agency, the therapist and patient can reflect on how they are embedded and determined, but can do nothing about it.

Agency in clinical work

What is the impact of agency on psychotherapy? Let us consider some clinical examples. A patient of mine described the ways he had been self-destructive, concluding, "Masochism is a powerful force." I replied to him: "Yes, you are." Startled, he paused, then said: "Oh. *I* do this to myself." This patient began to realize just how powerful he must be, given how powerfully he had been attacking himself. By owning his agency, he realized how different his life could be if he redirected his powers.

Another patient, when discussing her anger at a boss, became anxious and said she may have to go to the hospital. Given her history of numerous hospitalizations, a therapist might focus on her genetic propensity to bipolar mood disorder or the lowered level of antipsychotic medication in her bloodstream. Alternatively, a therapist could focus on the collapse of the self, the upsurge of the aggressive drive, or the failure of internal structures to regulate her anxiety. Notice that agency does not figure in any of these formulations. Instead, I wondered with the patient if she was tempted to pretend to be crazy as a way to deal with her anger at her boss. She said this was how she had handled anger before. Then we looked at the price she paid for pretending to be crazy rather than face and experience her anger. This patient most likely did have a biological vulnerability. Yet she is still responsible for how she handles and faces that vulnerability.

This same patient in a later session reported an incident in which her sister had insulted her. For the following week the patient had been depressed and was functioning less well. It turned out that after her sister had insulted her, the patient had repeated the sister's words to herself, insulting herself and doubting her abilities the remainder of the week. She said in reference to her sister: "She really flattened me." Here she attributes the power over her life to her sister. I replied, "Well, it's true she flattened you that day and we don't have a lot of control over that. But what worries me is the way you dealt with your anger with her, which was to insult yourself the rest of the week and make yourself depressed. She flattened you once. But you flattened yourself hundreds of times this past week. Can you see that?" The patient replied: "Yes. I guess I just turned it on myself instead of just feeling angry with her." In situations like this, the patient will often focus on the wrong done by a family member. "I feel bad because of what ____ did." However, we often find that the situation is more complex. This portrayal of oneself as a victim often obscures how the patient, as agent, made her suffering worse, by punishing herself or by refusing to stand up for herself. Even when the patient was a victim at a given moment, our concern rises if the patient perpetuates her victimhood, thereby denying her agency.

This is not to deny the powerful impact of trauma. For instance, a patient with a particularly painful history, including a murder attempt on his life, regarded himself as a helpless victim. He described how his psychotic, drug-abusing ex-wife was neglecting his son. I wondered with him about getting custody of the child. He claimed there was nothing he could do. I replied, "You know. This is what your mother [a drug abuser] said when she was lying in bed, strung out on drugs. 'Oh Terry, there's nothing I can do.' Now, was that true?" "No," he replied, "she was just too damned lazy to do anything for me." I continued: "Right. So, you know it's bad enough that you were neglected. That you were beaten and she just watched. That you were abandoned by your father and stepfather. That no one looked out for you. There wasn't a thing you could do about that. But you see, if you take that same helpless stance now with your son that your mother took with you, what's going to happen?" "The same thing," he said, while nodding sadly. I concluded, "Can you really afford to do that? Haven't you punished yourself enough? Isn't it time you let yourself have the chance to be the father you never had? We can see how destructive your ex-wife is. When is someone going to stand up and stop this cycle of destruction?" He suddenly remembered that he had a friend who was a lawyer who specialized in custody law. In the following weeks he found out what he needed to do to get custody of his son and to report his wife's neglect to the authorities. And he got a new, better paying job so that he would be able to afford a better apartment when his son moved in with him. A case like this illustrates how the real powerlessness we experienced in the past can get enlisted to prevent us from exploring what powers we could exercise today.

From a psychoanalytic point of view, it is noteworthy that I did not interpret unconscious fantasies. What the patients were unaware of was their agency. In so far as psychotherapy is based on a model of the subject as thinker, too much emphasis in treatment is often placed upon the interpretation of unconscious fantasies to the exclusion of agency. Yet awareness of content often does not lead to change unless the patient becomes aware of his or her disavowed agency.

This is why the emphasis on the patient's past in terms of what was done to us brings out the impersonal. Instead, when taking a history we need to pay special attention to the ways that patients were *not* determined by their past. How are they larger than their history? How did they transcend their past, their family, their traumas? How do they want to determine their future? Perhaps the essential truth to narrative models of therapy is that we are not merely the author of our narrative: we were and are the subject of a play that we can direct.

Often it is not just the past, but the loss of a sense of agency that is the core of the illness. A foreign refugee speaking to her therapist reported symptoms associated with horrible beatings and torture that she experienced in her homeland. He asked her if she ever revealed any names when she was tortured. She did not. "Even after days of torture you revealed no names?" She did not. The therapist recited all the horrific tortures she received. Then he asked, "And still you revealed no names?" She did not. "Do you know what we call such a person?" "What?" she asked. "Courageous." She doubted this but the therapist kept focusing on the extraordinary courage she had shown. By the end of the session the patient's face was gleaming, no longer depressed, although certainly grief-stricken by her past. The therapist had reminded her of her agency, something she had forgotten in the midst of the overwhelming pain and suffering.

Retrieving the person: the antinomy of freedom and necessity

Postmodernists have revealed the powerful impact that contexts such as language, culture, and society have on our lives. Yet they often ignore agency or treat it as an illusion. Postmodernists have revealed the importance of determinism and necessity in our lives. Yet they often treat the determining effects of contexts as an absolute truth, as though we have no freedom. In fact, these contexts need to be understood as the conditions of our freedom (Ricoeur 1966). Necessity does not negate the existence of freedom and agency in our lives, it merely reveals its limits. Our freedom is limited by the context of its occurrences. In our freedom we either reject necessity that shapes us, or consent to it "as the bond of freedom, but it is only on the basis of consent that freedom can be incarnate totally. For by consenting, one is acknowledging the nature that constitutes the very limit and bond of freedom" (Rasmussen 1971: 67).

Deterministic theories ignore the relationship between necessity and freedom, how we are both free and determined. The problem is "how to understand this unity of freedom and necessity, I-hood and non-I-hood" (Bulgakov 2000: 211). We need to recognize the difference between objective knowledge of the human being as a determined object, and personal knowledge of the human being as a determining person. Both forms of knowledge are true, but objective knowledge of the human being as an object is impersonal and, hence, relative to the personal knowledge of the human being as agent.

A group of Russian thinkers known as the "personalist" philosophers (Bakhtin 1993; Berdiaev 1937, 1944, 1952, 1962; Bulgakov 2000; Florensky [1914] 1997; Solovyov 1995; Vysheslavtsev 1999) has focused specifically on these questions. Since most of their work was untranslated until recently, it has remained largely unknown to the English-speaking readers. The personalist philosophers were critical of neo-Kantian philosophy, which reduced the concrete human person to a conscious, knowing self. For personalists, the neo-Kantians reduced the problem of being to one of how we know the world: the method of knowing. Beginning in the late nineteenth and continuing into the twentieth centuries, personalist philosophers developed a theory of person that emphasized both our agency as individuals and our emergence within relationships. From the personalist perspective the human being has an ontological status. Let us review for a moment a series of perspectives that illustrate how personalist philosophers view the person.

Subject versus subjectivity

Personalist philosophers distinguish the person as subject from his or her subjectivity, the thoughts, symbols, and reflections that individuals create about themselves and their world. "Nothing in Being, apart from myself, is an *I* for me. In all of Being I experience only myself my unique self as an *I*" (Bakhtin 1993: 41). The person has ontological precedence over the thoughts, symbols, and reflections she creates. For these reasons, as persons we are unknowable, non-rational, always surpassing the concepts and symbols that point toward us but can never completely grasp us.

Agency

Whereas Freud regarded thought as trial action, personalists regard action as the ground for thought. In fact, "[k]*nowledge itself is action*, and only its products later acquire the frozen features of objectness" (Bulgakov 2000: 193). We experience and then attempt to make sense of it in words. We experience our agency through action and creation. From this perspective, the subject has ontological precedence. Instead of I think, therefore I am; I love, therefore I am (Bulgakov 2000). Experience is not something that just "happens." We experience because we focus, engage, and relate to the world. Experience is the result of love, our directed relating to the world around us. Experience as grounded in the materialist understandings of neural networks is accurate as far as it goes, but it is an impersonal understanding. The personal meaning of experience is grounded in agency and love.

Freedom and necessity

Personalist philosophers hold that we are free and determined. Necessity and freedom exist as an antinomy. We are influenced very powerfully by many forces in the world (necessity). And we have the capacity to exercise our agency (freedom). Yet neither necessity nor freedom should be absolutized. Although contextually embedded, we have the capacity to recognize this and gain more freedom from whatever limiting forces we deal with. Necessity does not deny the existence of freedom it simply highlights the limits of freedom we are able to exercise.

Berdiaev (1944: 21–2) approached this problem of freedom and necessity by noting that we are both persons who determine and individuals who are determined. He distinguished between the human being as individual, embedded in necessity, whose existence is subjected to determinism, and the human being as personality, a subject who determines his existence through freedom as an existential center. To the extent that we are determined by impersonal forces, our personality is concealed (Berdiaev 1944: 25). "Everything defined from without, everything determined, everything that is based upon the power of the object world . . . is the impersonal in man."

Berdiaev uses the concept of necessity in two ways. The first refers to the real and powerful forces that unavoidably determine our lives. The second and more important one involves the ways we relinquish our freedom. When we attribute our powers and responsibility to others, we essentially become slaves. For instance, the patient who says "I can't help it. This is the way I was raised." [I am determined by my past.] Or, "There's nothing I can do. My wife will not change." [My wife has the power over my life.] Or, "It's not my fault. He started it." [He has the power over my life.] In all these ways we hand the power over our lives to others. Without agency or creativity, determined by others, our "being is exhausted by its psychic content" (Florensky 1997: 175).

When we blame our woes on the past, on our spouses, parents, bosses, chemistry, genes, and culture, we forsake our agency and personhood, instead of the real world and real people, "we find only reflected, secondary, symbolized reality." People and the world now symbolize our externalized power. Thus we create our own determinism. We feel determined by others. Yet, actually, we fall under the power of these symbols of our own disavowed agency and responsibility (Berdiaev 1944: 116). We then respond by trying to leave or rebel against this seemingly violent attack on our lives. We treat ourselves as objects determined by other objects in a mechanistic interaction of stimulus–response.

To regard ourselves as social in this sense, is to make ourselves slaves of others. As individuals, we are not able to use the world to create because we depend on the world to determine our lives. This can take the psychological forms I just described or it can take philosophical forms as well, as we see in materialism, constructivism and other forms of postmodernism. We treat ourselves and others in an impersonal way, denying what is most personal about us: our agency and capacity to be an existential center. In that sense, the individual is a category of naturalism, biology, and sociology because our relationship to others and ourselves is impersonal and mechanical. According to Berdiaev, this type of determinism, which is treated as ontological by some postmodernists, is actually a form of pathology. Exteriorizing our agency into the world, whether linguistic, material, or societal, is a form of slavery to symbols. And if all my actions are determined by language, culture, or society, you cannot hold me responsible. The wish to believe in this kind of deterministic mechanism is itself a wish to be rid of personal responsibility (Fromm 1941; MacMurray 1961: 153; Polanyi 1958b).

In contrast, "personality . . . bears witness to the fact that man is the point of intersection of two worlds, that in him there takes place the conflict . . . between freedom and necessity, independence and dependence" (Berdiaev 1944: 36). The person is neither completely free nor completely determined (Berdiaev 1944: 114). As persons we "oppose determination from without," and determine our future "from within" (Berdiaev 1944: 26–7). Or as Zizioulas states: "[T]he nature does not determine the person; the person enables the nature to exist; freedom is identified with the being of man" (Zizioulas 1985: 57).

Although the past is determined, through our acts we can determine the future. What is important from a personal view is not so much the past circumstances into which we were thrown, but the new creative actions we brought to those circumstances. It is not your past I want to know about, it is what you did with it. Although we depend on the world, we also bring something new to the world. We are able to create something that has never existed which was not given to us. "Freedom is the capacity to act, and to determine the future. This freedom has two dimensions: the capacity to move, and the capacity to know; both of which have reference to the Other" (MacMurray 1961: 166).

By person or personality, Berdiaev refers to the human being as an existential center; person as creative agent (Berdiaev 1944: 24). We create our personalities and by doing so, express them. We exist in our identity not only as that which we are, but as that which we *will become*. My identity, my becoming, is a creative act. This is implicit in psychoanalysis as well. Lear (1990: 168) reads Freud's famous quote "*Wo Es war, soll Ich werden*" as "*where ideal-I was, there I shall become.*" Each of us is becoming ourselves by owning our previously disavowed agency. When Oedipus accepts responsibility for his acts he "constitutes himself as an agent, a locus of activity. *Where it was, there I am*" (Lear 1990: 171). By overcoming this false determinism of the individual, we become persons.

And since the person is a creative agent, personality is unique. The individual is dissolved in the world around him. But the "personal in man is just that in him which he does not have in common with others" (Berdiaev 1944: 21–2), his agency as an existential center, his freedom through creative acts to come into being. As we realize and create ourselves, we do not simply put together parts of people we admire to make ourselves. This personality, this uniqueness that is you is entirely new, is not brought out of anything and not put together from anything. This uniqueness, or precisely what is "youey" about you (Frederickson 2000), is present in everything you do. Just think of someone you love and how their glance or walk says everything at once. Their unique unrepeatable form as a person is present even in that glance (Berdiaev 1944: 22–3).

As an existential center, as someone with freedom, you as a person are creating yourself. As a result, your identity is dynamic, unfolding, "unfinalizable" (Bakhtin 1984). "I-ness is freedom" (Bulgakov 2000: 200; Florensky 1997). You are not a finished, immutable thing as an individual, but a person who is incessantly growing, developing, living, and transcending yourself. This changing relationship of me and you, your unfolding "is life . . . growth, movement and dynamics rather than statics" (Bulgakov 2000: 113). Hence, our identity as persons is not static but "has its roots in the future and is perpetually inspired, or rather maintained and nourished by the future. *The truth and the ontology of the person belong to the future, are images of the future*" (Zizioulas 1985: 62). Rationalism believes that reality consists only of that which is rationally determined, the basis of our conceptual knowledge. Personalism holds that this is only part of reality. Through freedom, we have the capacity to grow, to change, to become what we are not. You are both who you are and who you have not yet become. This is one reason a person is unknowable. In this sense, our identity is not rooted in the symbols we create about ourselves and their logical connection (e.g. our narrative). Our identity is relational, rooted in agency: our directedness, our relationship to the future, and to others.

Conclusion

When psychoanalysts uncritically adopt postmodern theories of self, the result is an interpersonal theory without a concept of the person, an intersubjective theory without a subject, and a psychoanalysis without a psyche. As we have seen, many postmodernists believe that "you" as a concrete person and your agency do not exist. Person and agency are simply constructs. This reduction of the person to the impersonal devalues the personal. The negation of the person and agency is not value-neutral because it ultimately gives way to moral relativism. In contrast, I have argued that the person and agency are primordial, the self and constructions of constructivism are contingent. We are not only individuals determined by contexts. We are also persons who determine and yet are constituted by relationships.

As persons we are unknowable and unfinalizable. Nothing I say will ever exhaust or fully express your life experience or my experience of you. My words "float as it were on a sea of experience they can never wholly capture or reflect or express" (White 2001: 2). Despite the claims of some postmodernists,

> we never become fully defined by our language, or by our languages; there is always something before, or beyond, the words, something they do not and cannot fit. . . . We use words to point or gesture, but compared to the intensity and vividness of the experience, what we say is pallid or obscure.
>
> (White 2001: 5)

Yet precisely because you exist as a concrete person and are unknowable through words, I am compelled to use words, shift perspectives, ask questions, listen, watch you, pointing towards this experience of you. And in this pointing towards my experience of you, I seek to understand you more fully, to apprehend you, having faith that you are a bearer of meaning. When we meet, we do so as if you *incarnate a real presence of significant being*. Your presence is irreducible to any deconstruction or paraphrase. You always have some surplus of meaning that transcends any words and theories used to describe you.

References

Bakhtin, M. (1984) *Problems of Dostoevsky's Poetics*, trans. C. Emerson and W. Booth. Minneapolis, MN: University of Minnesota Press.
—— (1993) *Toward a Philosophy of the Act*, trans. V. Liapunov, ed.V. Liapunov and M. Holquist. Austin, TX: University of Texas Press.
Berdiaev, N. (1937) *The Destiny of Man*. New York: Charles Scribner's Sons.
—— (1944) *Slavery and Freedom*. New York: Charles Scribner's Sons.
—— (1952) *The Beginning and the End*. New York: Harper and Brothers.
—— (1962) *The Meaning of the Creative Act*. New York: Collier.
Birdwhistell, R. (1970) *Kinesics and Context: Essays on Body Motion Communication*. Philadelphia, PA: University of Pennsylvania Press.
Bromberg, P. (1998) *Standing in the Spaces: Essays on Clinical Process, Trauma, and Dissociation*. Hillsdale, NJ: Analytic Press.
Bucci, W. (1997) *Psychoanalysis and Cognitive Science: A Multiple Code Theory*. New York: Guilford.
Buhler, K. (1930) *The Mental Development of the Child*. New York: Harcourt Brace.
Bulgakov, S. (2000) *Philosophy of Economy: The World as Household*, trans. C. Evtuhov. New Haven, CT: Yale University Press. (At times I have used

translation corrections offered by Olga Meerson, Professor of Slavic Studies at Georgetown University.)

Copleston, F. (1988) *Russian Religious Philosophy*. Notre Dame: Search Press.

Damasio, A. (1999) *The Feeling of What Happens: Body and Emotion in the Making of Consciousness*. New York: Harcourt, Brace.

de Shazer, S. (1993) "Creative misunderstanding: there is no escape from language," in S. Gilligan and R. Price (eds.) *Therapeutic Conversations*. New York: W. W. Norton.

Ekman, P. and Davidson, R. (1994) *The Nature of Emotion: Fundamental Questions*. New York: Oxford University Press.

Florensky, P. ([1914] 1997) *The Pillar and Ground of the Truth*, trans. B. Jakim. Princeton, NJ: Princeton University Press.

Frederickson, J. (2000) "There's something 'youey' about you," *Contemporary Psychoanalysis* 36(4): 587–617.

Freeman, M. (1993) *Rewriting the Self: History, Memory, Narrative*. London: Routledge.

Frie, R. (1999) "Psychoanalysis and the linguistic turn," *Contemporary Psychoanalysis* 35: 673–97.

Fromm, E. ([1941] 1965) *Escape from Freedom*. New York: Avon.

Haack, S. (1998) *Manifesto of a Passionate Moderate*. Chicago: University of Chicago Press.

Hall, E. (1976) *Beyond Culture*. Garden City, NY: Anchor.

Held, B. (1995) *Back to Reality*. New York: W. W. Norton.

Kirkpatrick, F. (1991) Introduction, in J. MacMurray ([1961] 1991) *Persons in Relation*. New York: Humanity Books.

Lear, J. (1990) *Love and its Place in Nature: A Philosophical Interpretation of Freudian Psychoanalysis*. New Haven, CT: Yale University Press.

LeDoux, J. (1998) *The Emotional Brain: The Mysterious Underpinnings of Emotional Life*. London: Weidenfeld and Nicolson.

Leites, N. (1971) *The New Ego: Pitfalls in Current Thinking about Psychoanalysis*. New York: Science Press.

Levenson, E. (1972) *The Fallacy of Understanding*. New York: Basic Books.

Levine, G. (ed.) (1992) *Constructions of the Self*. New Brunswick, NJ: Rutgers University Press.

MacMurray, J. ([1957] 1991) *The Self as Agent*. New York: Humanity Books.

—— (1961) *Persons in Relation*. New York: Humanity Books.

McNamee, S. and Gergen, K. (1992) Introduction, in S. McNamee and K. Gergen (eds.) *Therapy as Social Construcion*. Newbury Park, CA: Sage.

Meissner, W. (1984) *Psychoanalysis and Religion*. New Haven, CT: Yale University Press.

Mitchell, S. (1993) *Hope and Dread in Psychoanalysis*. New York: Basic Books.

—— (2000) *Relationality: From Attachment to Intersubjectivity*. Hillsdale, NJ: Analytic Press.

Moore, R. (1999) *The Creation of Reality in Psychoanalysis*. Hillsdale, NJ: Analytic Press.

Orange, D. (2001) "From Cartesian minds to experiential worlds in psycho-analysis," *Psychoanalytic Psychology* 18: 287–302.

Orange, D., Atwood, G. and Stolorow, R. (1997) *Working Intersubjectively: Contextualism in Psychoanalytic Practice*. Hillsdale, NJ: Analytic Press.

Polanyi, M. (1958a) *Personal Knowledge: Towards a Post-Critical Philosophy*. Chicago: University of Chicago Press.

—— (1958b) *The Study of Man*. Chicago: University of Chicago Press.

Rasmussen (1971) *Mythic-Symbolic Language and Philosophical Anthropology; a Constructive Interpretation of the Thought of Paul Ricoeur*. The Hague: Martinus Nijhoff.

Reber, A. (1993) *Implicit Learning and Tacit Knowledge: An Essay on the Cognitive Unconscious*. Oxford: Oxford University Press.

Ricoeur, P. (1966) *Freedom and Nature: The Voluntary and the Involuntary*, trans. E. Kohak. Evanston, IL: Northwestern University Press.

—— (1991) *Narrative Identity*, in D. Wood (ed.) *On Paul Ricoeur*. London: Routledge.

—— (1992) *Oneself as Another*, trans. K. Blamey. Chicago: University of Chicago Press.

Rosenau, P. (1992) *Post-modernism and the Social Sciences: Insights, Inroads, and Intrusions*. Princeton: Princeton University Press. Cited in Held (1995).

Rubenfeld, S. (2001) "Personal agency versus self: purpose in the embodied mind," unpublished paper.

Rudman, S. (1997) *Concepts of Person and Christian Ethics*. Cambridge: Cambridge University Press.

Sass, L. (1992) "The self and its vicissitudes in the psychoanalytic avant-garde," in G. Levine (ed.) *Constructions of the Self*. New Brunswick, NJ: Rutgers University Press.

Schafer, R. (1976) *A New Language for Psychoanalysis*. New Haven, CT: Yale University Press.

Scheflen, A. (1972) *Body Language and Social Order: Communication as Behavioral Control*. Englewood Cliffs, NJ: Prentice Hall.

Schutz, A. (1951) "Making music together. a study in social relationship," in *Collected Papers*, vol. 2. The Hague: Martinus Nijhoff.

Scruton, R. (2000) *The Intelligent Person's Guide to Modern Culture*. South Bend, IN: St. Augustine's Press.

Solovyov, V. (1995) *Lectures on Divine Humanity*, trans. P. Zouboff. Hudson, NY: Lindisfarne Press.

Spence, D. (1982) *Narrative Truth and Historical Truth: Meaning and Interpretation in Psychoanalysis*. New York: W. W. Norton.

Stern, D. (1985) *The Interpersonal World of the Infant*. New York: Basic Books.

—— (1997) *Unformulated Experience: From Dissociation to Imagination in Psychoanalysis*. Hillsdale, NJ: Analytic Press.

Stolorow, R. and Atwood, G. (1992) *Contexts of Being: The Intersubjective Foundations of Psychological Life*. Hillsdale, NJ: Analytic Press.

Stolorow, R., Brandchaft, B. and Atwood, G. (1987) *Psychoanalytic Treatment: An Intersubjective Approach*. Hillsdale, NJ: Analytic Press.

Stolorow, R., Orange, D. and Atwood, G. (2001) "Cartesian and post-cartesian trends in relational psychoanalysis," *Psychoanalytic Psychology*, 18(3): 468–84.

Sullivan, H. S. ([1950] 1971) "The illusion of personal individuality," in *The Fusion of Psychiatry and the Social Sciences*. New York: W. W. Norton.

Vysheslavtsev, B. P. (1999) *The Eternal in Russian Philosophy*, trans. P. Burt. Grand Rapids, MI: Eerdmans Press.

Watzlawick, P. (1976) *How Real is Real?* New York: Random House.

—— (1984) *The Invented Reality: How Do We Know What We Know? Contributions to Constructivism*. New York: W. W. Norton.

—— (1990) *Munchhausen's Pigtail or Psychotherapy and "Reality."* New York: W. W. Norton.

Westen, D. (1996) "The Scientific Status of Unconscious Processes: Is Freud Really Dead?," unpublished paper.

White, J. (2001) *The Edge of Meaning*. Chicago: University of Chicago Press.

White, M. and Epston, P. (1990) *Narrative Means to Therapeutic Ends*. New York: W. W. Norton.

Wilson, F. (1998) *The Hand: How its Use Shapes the Brain, Language, and Human Culture*. New York: Random House.

Zizioulas, I. (1985) *Being as Communion*. Crestwood, NY: St. Vladimir's Press.

Index